CQ GUIDE TO

CURRENT AMERICAN GOVERNMENT

Spring 2000

CQ GUIDE TO

CURRENT AMERICAN GOVERNMENT

Spring 2000

CQ PRESS

A Division of Congressional Quarterly Inc.

Washington, D.C.

Congressional Quarterly Inc.

Congressional Quarterly Inc., an editorial research service and publishing company, serves clients in the fields of news, education, business, and government. It combines the specific coverage of Congress, government, and politics contained in *CQ Weekly* with the more general subject range of an affiliated service, the *CQ Researcher*.

Under the CQ Press imprint, Congressional Quarterly also publishes a variety of books, including college political science textbooks and public affairs paperbacks on developing issues and events, information directories and reference books on the federal government, national elections, and politics, including the *Guide to the Presidency*, the *Guide to Congress*, the *Guide to the U.S. Supreme Court*, the *Guide to U.S. Elections*, and *Politics in America*. CQ's *A-Z Collection* is a four-volume reference series providing essential information about American government and the electoral process. The *CQ Almanac*, a compendium of legislation for one session of Congress, is published each year. *Congress and the Nation*, a record of government for a presidential term, is published every four years.

CQ publishes the *Daily Monitor*, a report on the current and future activities of congressional committees. An online information system, cq.com, provides immediate access to CQ's databases of legislative action, votes, schedules, profiles, and analyses.

CQ Press
A Division of Congressional Quarterly Inc.
1414 22nd St. N.W.
Washington, DC 20037
(202) 822-1475; (800) 638-1710

www.cqpress.com

Printed in the United States of America

03 02 01 00   5 4 3 2 1

Cover photo by R. Michael Jenkins

ISSN 0196-612X
ISBN 1-56802-105-4

Contents

Contents

Politics and Public Policy

Appendix

Introduction

Congressional Quarterly's *Guide to Current American Government* contains articles selected from the *CQ Weekly* and related CQ publications. The articles have been chosen to complement existing texts with up-to-date examinations of current issues and controversies. The *Guide* is divided into four sections—foundations of American government, political participation, government institutions, and politics and public policy—that correspond with the framework of standard introductory American government textbooks.

Foundations of American Government. This section treats current issues that have implications for interpretation of the U.S. Constitution or the broad workings the federal government. The first article examines the 1978 independent counsel law, which expired on June 30, 1999, and analyzes its influence on how power was divided among the three government branches. The second article argues that recent Supreme Court decisions refusing to hold states to federal laws are part of a larger trend toward federalism, or devolving power from the federal government to the states. These precedents, if followed, could overturn or render unenforceable many of the nation's civil rights laws.

Political Participation. This section, on current issues in electoral politics, includes a series of articles from CQ's *OnPolitics* newsletter previewing the 2000 elections. Articles from *CQ Weekly* show how Republican and Democratic congressional leaders are staking out positions on issues such as Social Security, the budget, and managed care reforms. The section concludes with a discussion of the debate over campaign finance reform and details the politics behind the defeat of the McCain-Feingold bill at the end of the 106th Congress's first session.

Government Institutions. The articles in this section look at the inner workings of the major institutions of American government. The first article discusses proposed changes in the House budget process. The second tracks appropriations bills through various stages and illustrates political pressures on congressional leaders who were anticipating a possible veto by the president. The Senate recently rejected the nomination of a black Missouri judge to a seat on the U.S. District Court. CQ editors examine the likely effect the rejection will have on the nomination process; as vacancies mount the courts struggle under their workload.

Politics and Public Policy. This section provides in-depth coverage of major social policy issues, including articles on the Senate's rejection of the nuclear test ban treaty, the budget, the managed care debate, Congress's plans to regulate the Internet, gun control, and the recent financial services overhaul.

By reprinting articles as they appeared originally in the *CQ Weekly*, the *Guide*'s editors provide a handy source of information about contemporary political issues. The date of original publication is noted with each article to give readers a time frame for the events that are described. Although new developments have occurred subsequently, updates of articles are provided only when they are essential to an understanding of the basic operations of American government. Page number references to related and background articles in the *CQ Weekly* and the *CQ Almanac* are provided to facilitate additional research on topical events. Both are available at many school and public libraries.

Foundations of American Government

One of the pillars of the U.S. Constitution is the division of power among the executive, legislative, and judicial branches of government. Another is federalism, or the sharing of power between the federal government and the states. Both concepts have been subject to reinterpretation throughout the nation's history. The two articles in this section examine recent issues—the 1978 independent counsel law and the federal government's attempts to force states to adhere to fair labor standards—affecting the practical application of each of these concepts.

On June 30, 1999, Congress allowed the independent counsel law to lapse. Opposition to reauthorizing the measure was almost universal, and no similar measure was expected to take its place. The first article in this section discusses charges made by the law's many critics, who generally cite the political nature of recent inquiries and raise questions about whether it is constitutional. By shifting responsibility for policing the chief executive to an independent agency, the law in effect skirted the system of separation of power instituted by the Framers of the Constitution. The 1978 law called for independent counsels to be appointed by a panel of federal judges and thereafter divorced from any of the three branches, more or less free to investigate where they saw fit. This was the law's most controversial aspect—that the prosecutor was chosen by federal judges and free from almost all oversight. Most proposals for replacing it called for substantial checks on the prosecutor's authority.

The article discusses the implications of the alternatives that have been proposed, most of which involve returning to something like the special prosecutor system in place before 1978. Under the special prosecutor system, prosecutorial power was held by the executive branch, and executive branch officials—usually kept in line through congressional oversight, judicial rulings, and public opinion—could be subject to investigation by special prosecutors hired from outside the Justice Department and given objectives by the attorney general. This system was challenged when President Richard M. Nixon fired the prosecutor in charge of investigating his own administration during the Watergate scandal. Lawmakers are now faced with the conundrum of how to police the executive branch without creating what Kenneth Starr, the independent counsel who investigated President Bill Clinton and who is an unlikely critic of the law, argued was in effect a fourth branch of government.

The second article in this section examines another recurring constitutional issue, the distribution of power between the federal government and the states. In a series of Supreme Court decisions holding that citizens may not use federal laws to sue states, the Court has acted to curb the power of the federal government in deference to the rights and prerogatives of the states. The trend to devolve power from the federal government to the states—known as federalism, although the term *federalism* referred to the opposite trend when the Constitution was drafted—has so far affected limited groups, who have labor grievances and who believe that their grievances are not sufficiently addressed by the laws of their home state. But the rulings have set precedents that, if followed, could be used to overturn, or at least render unenforceable, a broad range of civil rights laws.

Members seek ways to root out misconduct without criminalizing policy differences

Who Polices Politicians After Counsel Law Expires?

In December 1992, Theodore B. Olson, who had been an assistant attorney general in the Reagan administration, threw a party to celebrate the demise of the independent counsel law. But unfortunately for Olson, who was one of the earliest officials targeted under the law and remains one if its most vociferous critics, the festivities proved premature; the law was revised and reinstated a year-and-a-half later.

Now Olson has reason for another fete. The 1994 version of the independent counsel law (PL 103-270) lapses on June 30. "And this time," Olson says with considerable satisfaction, "I think it will stick."

Olson appears justified in his optimism, even in light of his previous disappointment. Unlike the last time — when reauthorization was quietly blocked by Senate Republicans just before Republican President George Bush stood for re-election — this time the opposition appears to be as bipartisan as it is vocal and widespread. Sentiment against the law has been fueled by the low standing in public opinion polls of the most famous independent counsel ever, Kenneth W. Starr; by the public's opposition to the impeachment of President Clinton that grew from Starr's inquiry;

and by the roster of exonerations, acquittals and mistrials that dominates the legal scorecard of cases brought during the 20 independent counsel investigations made public in the past 21 years. (*List, this page*)

This time, too, the law's expiration appears to be part of a broader trend in Washington away from hewing to inflexible mechanisms for policing the conduct of public officials. Two years ago, the House rewrote its ethics procedures in an attempt to streamline them and make them more bipartisan. Two months ago, the Supreme Court narrowed the grounds for alleging corruption of federal officials.

Some lawmakers and congressional experts see the demise of the independent counsel law as heralding a more civil era of political battle. Republicans and Democrats are not about to call a truce, they say, but may be signaling a willingness to unilaterally disarm themselves of a powerful weapon for settling their differences.

"It isn't that partisanship is going to be any less," said Rep. Howard L. Berman of Califor-

The Most Famous Case

Independent counsel: **Kenneth W. Starr**

Target: **Whitewater, Monica Lewinsky**

Starr's place in history was secured on Sept. 9, 1998, when he delivered to the House a report required of any independent counsel who finds "substantial and credible information . . . that may constitute grounds for an impeachment." It had nothing to do with Clinton's Arkansas land deals while governor, the original target of a Starr inquiry that has so far produced 12 guilty pleas, three convictions and three acquittals.

The First Case

Independent counsel: **Arthur H. Christy**

Target: **Hamilton Jordan**

The first independent counsel was appointed 13 months after President Jimmy Carter signed the law creating the job. After spending six months and $182,000 investigating allegations that Jordan, the White House chief of staff, used cocaine in a New York nightclub, Christy announced in May 1980 that there was insufficient evidence for an indictment. Four months later, the second independent counsel was named, to investigate alleged cocaine use by Carter campaign manager Timothy Kraft. No charges were brought in that case, either, the last involving a Democratic administration until Starr's work began.

nia, the ranking Democrat on the ethics committee and a member of the Judiciary Committee that turned Starr's findings on Clinton into four articles of impeachment last year. "It's just that we are trying to fence off certain areas."

"I think that we have asked more than we should have from our criminal justice system," Chairman Fred Thompson, R-Tenn., of the Senate Governmental Affairs Committee said June 21. "You know, a lot of things you just can't cure until the next election."

Thompson has unveiled his own proposal for replacing the independent counsel law. Other options have been put forward by the independent citizens' lobbying group Common Cause and by a bipartisan commission convened by the Brookings Institution and the American Enterprise Institute (AEI). All three call for a return to something like the special prosecutor system in place before the first counsel law (PL 95-521) was enacted. (*1978 Almanac, p. 835*)

Only a proposal emerging from a bipartisan group of four on Thompson's committee — Joseph I. Lieberman, D-Conn.; Carl Levin, D-Mich.; Arlen Specter, R-Pa.; and Susan Collins, R-Maine — would retain the law's most controversial aspect, that independent counsels are chosen by federal judges and are thereafter insulated from almost all Justice Department oversight. That makes their plan the least likely to succeed, a wide variety of lawmakers say. (*Current law, 1994 Almanac, p. 295*)

"I think that the idea of an independent counsel, appointed by a three-judge panel, is done," said Rep. Asa Hutchinson, R-Ark. "I think we're looking in another direction."

"I don't see anything like the current statute ever being reauthorized," said Rep. Bill Delahunt, D-Mass., like Hutchinson a member of the Judiciary Committee.

'Decriminalizing' Politics

Allowing the law to expire would help in the "decriminalization" of the political process, many of its opponents say, because under the statute many inquiries became political weapons even when they had mixed results in policing corruption.

"We have been so intent on writing detailed rules about political ethics, we have lost sight of what it means to actually have ethics," said Norman Ornstein, resident scholar at AEI. "Now the system, I think, is finally adjusting, and trying to strike a better balance."

Even some lawmakers who want to revive the law say politics has become too much of a blood sport. "It seems like we have criminalized politics," Lieberman said in an interview June 11. "And criminal investigations have become politics by another name. I just wish we didn't have to let the statute lapse to realize this."

Members of the public have been in front of lawmakers on the issue of independent counsels, registering their opposition in polls and a series of verdicts. A Washington Post poll of 1,010 people in February, just after Clinton's impeachment trial acquittal, found 59 percent with an "unfavorable" view of Starr to 27 percent "favorable."

Federal juries in the last three trials prosecuted by independent counsels all declined to convict. Former Agriculture Secretary Mike Espy was acquitted Dec. 2 of taking illegal gratuities; former Clinton business partner Susan McDougal was acquitted April 12 of obstruction of justice, while the jury deadlocked on other counts; and a mistrial was declared May 7 in the obstruction of justice trial of Julie Hiatt Steele, who questioned the validity of assertions that Clinton groped former White House volunteer Kathleen Willey.

The public mood, the spate of recent verdicts and a halt to new independent counsel inquiries will help Washington tone down its attack politics, predicted Stanley M. Brand, who specializes in defending federal officials charged with ethical lapses or public corruption.

"We're certainly scaling back to what I think is a more reasonable regime," said Brand. "We've over-criminalized a lot of conduct. There is some sense in the country that this is contrary to good government."

Brand suggested this trend would be supported by the unanimous Supreme Court ruling of April 27 in *U.S. v. Sun-Diamond Growers of California* rejecting the expansive interpretation of the illegal gratuities law (PL 87-849) that Independent Counsel Donald C. Smaltz had used to prosecute an agricultural cooperative that had given gifts to Espy.

One group that does not think these developments constitute a healthy trend is the Congressional Accountability Project, a non-profit group focused on making sure federal officials obey campaign finance and ethics laws. The group is concerned about letting the independent counsel statute lapse but is even more troubled by a change two years ago in House ethics rules, which now bar nonmembers from filing complaints with the ethics committee. The Government Accountability Project had used the old rules to force several inquiries by the Committee on Standards of Official Conduct. (*1997 Almanac, p. 1-32*)

The group's executive director, Gary

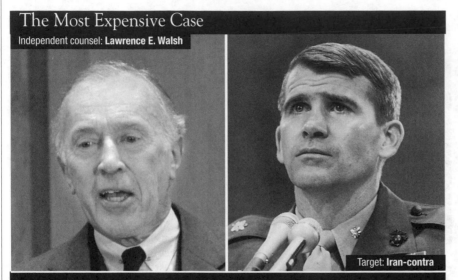

The Most Expensive Case

Independent counsel: **Lawrence E. Walsh**

Target: **Iran-contra**

At $47.9 million, Walsh's investigation is the most costly by an independent counsel, although the five still under way could go higher. Fourteen indictments resulted from his inquiry into whether Reagan administration officials broke laws in selling arms to Iran and diverting profits to the Nicaraguan contras. One was dismissed, seven defendants pleaded guilty and four were convicted. Two — Oliver L. North, at right, and John M. Poindexter — won their appeals. A month before he left office, President George Bush pardoned four who had been convicted and two who were under indictment, including Defense Secretary Casper W. Weinberger.

Ruskin, also criticizes Speaker J. Dennis Hastert, R-Ill., for naming as that panel's chairman Lamar Smith, R-Texas, who cast the only vote on the panel in 1997 against the punishment the House ultimately levied against Speaker Newt Gingrich, R-Ga. (1979-99.) "He is the icon of liberal permissiveness in the ethics process," Ruskin said of Smith.

So far this year, the committee has opened just one new inquiry, into allegations against Rep. Corrine Brown, D-Fla. (*1999 CQ Weekly, p. 1387*)

"The bottom line for all of this," Ruskin said in an interview June 7, referring both to ethics changes and the lapse of the counsel law, "is that it will lead to a climate where public corruption is increasingly possible."

Few Convictions

Independent counsels were major distractions for Presidents Bush and Ronald Reagan. And the Clinton presidency has been forever altered by Starr's probe.

But for all the prosecutorial power granted to independent counsels in the past two decades, their efforts have resulted in few lasting convictions of senior executive branch officials — even though the law was designed to enhance the scrutiny of those officials. Most of the lasting convictions have been of people who were subordinate or peripheral to — and whose malfeasance

was tangential to — the stated targets of the independent counsels' efforts.

In 11 of the 15 investigations that have been formally concluded, no charges were filed at all. In three of those cases, the names of the onetime targets have been kept sealed. In another, Independent Counsel Joseph E. diGenova wrote a letter apologizing to the people he was called on to investigate.

At the same time, critics of the law say, dozens of secondary players have been prosecuted — and hundreds of innocent people have seen their lives turned upside down and their bank accounts emptied out — only because they had the misfortune of having some tangential connection to a line of inquiry being pursued by an independent counsel with officially unfettered curiosity. (*Representative inquiries, 1999 CQ Weekly, pp. 1523-26*)

Former Associate Attorney General Webster L. Hubbell and former Gov. Jim Guy Tucker, D-Ark., are the highest-ranking officials to be convicted by independent counsels, and both were on the margins of Starr's probe of the Arkansas real estate investments of Bill and Hillary Rodham Clinton. Tucker's case is still on appeal. Michael K. Deaver, who was Reagan's deputy chief of staff, is the highest White House official who stands convicted under an independent counsel inquiry, because

the convictions of two top presidential aides connected to the sales of arms to Iran that generated funds for the anti-communist contra rebels in Nicaragua, Rear Adm. John M. Poindexter and Marine Lt. Col. Oliver L. North, were overturned on appeal.

The work of Starr and four other independent counsels investigating alleged wrongdoing by Clinton administration figures — including five Cabinet secretaries — may continue under a grandfather clause written into the 1994 law. (*1999 CQ Weekly, p. 473*)

One case, David M. Barrett's prosecution of Henry G. Cisneros for allegedly lying to the FBI to ease his Senate confirmation as Housing and Urban Development secretary, is scheduled to go to trial this fall. Starr's latest case against Hubbell is set for trial in August, although he suggested to the Senate this spring his work is otherwise nearing an end. He also joined those labeling the independent counsel law not worthy of renewal. (*1999 CQ Weekly, p. 884*)

Return to Past System

Before there was an independent counsel law, executive branch scandals generally were addressed by special prosecutors hired from outside the Justice Department and given objectives by the attorney general. This system will be revived when the counsel law lapses, and Attorney General Janet Reno said June 24 that the Justice Department is working on guidelines — in consultation with Congress — for how she will appoint special prosecutors and oversee their work.

Until Watergate, the belief was that public pressure — exerted by Congress or through the media — guaranteed fairness. That belief dissipated quickly after the "Saturday Night Massacre," during which President Richard M. Nixon ordered the firing of Archibald Cox, the special prosecutor who was investigating the Watergate scandal. (*1973 Almanac, p. 1007*)

That Nixon gained no lasting peace from that action — public outrage prompted him to pick Leon Jaworski to complete the job — was not seen by Congress as evidence that the system of reliance on public pressure had worked, but that it almost failed. "It pays to remember how thin a thread our justice system hung on from the time between Cox's firing and Jaworski's hiring," Lieberman said.

The Precedent-Setting Case

Independent counsel: **Donald C. Smaltz**

Target: **Mike Espy**

Smaltz's inquiry into allegations that Agriculture Secretary Mike Espy took illegal gratuities netted eight guilty pleas, six trial convictions and two civil suit settlements. But five people, including the central figure, have been acquitted — an outcome that critics say illustrates how the broad jurisdiction of independent counsels too often leads them to pursue peripheral figures when prosecutions of their targets prove difficult. In addition, the Supreme Court unanimously rejected Smaltz's argument that federal law should be interpreted to outlaw almost all gift-giving to officials by those doing business with them.

The 1978 law, and the three reauthorizations since, all were premised on the belief that an administration could not be trusted to investigate itself. So, to minimize Justice Department discretion, each law set a mechanism under which appointment of counsels was automatic under certain circumstances.

The initial version of the law was used just twice, and the initial reauthorization (PL 97-409) occurred with minimal fanfare. (*1982 Almanac, p. 386*)

It was in the Reagan administration that the law began to attract serious opposition, as a string of officials — including three Cabinet secretaries — became targets with the help of vigorous public pressure applied by congressional Democrats. Reagan was pressed by Olson — ultimately cleared in 1989 after a three-year, $2.1 million probe of whether he had lied to a House subcommittee — to veto the reauthorization. But, at a time when the Iran-contra scandal was in full bloom, Reagan signed the legislation (PL 100-191).

Five years later, Republican resolve against the measure was strong enough to kill it. Had a reauthorization come to a vote, sponsors asserted, it would have passed. But Bob Dole, R-Kan. (1969-96), then the Senate minority leader, bottled the measure up in the waning days of the 102nd Congress. (*1992 Almanac, p. 315*)

"We may rue the day that we presided over the final rites of this legislation should there be a Democratic president," said Sen. William S. Cohen, R-Maine (1979-97), now the Defense secretary, and when Clinton was elected the next month, Republican opposition soon began to fade.

What distinguishes the mood of 1999 from that of 1992 is that, by now, both Democrats and Republicans have been bloodied by independent counsels. Until Clinton's election, the statute had been written mostly by Democratic Congresses and used mostly against Republican administrations, in a type of a political corollary to Mark Twain's adage that "nothing so needs reforming as other people's habits."

But during the Clinton administration the Democrats' handiwork was turned against them, culminating in a presidential impeachment that grew out of Starr's scrutiny of a sexual affair that had not even begun when he was named to investigate a completely different matter. (*1998 Almanac, p. 12-3*)

"Democrats got a good object lesson in reality versus theory," said Berman. "We were all very imbued with the attractiveness of independent counsels. A lot of that came from Richard Nixon, and a lot of it came from 12 years of Republican rule. There was a theoretical attractiveness to the statute. But it met our partisan interests as well."

New Proposals

Lieberman says his group's plan — still being drafted the week of June 21 — would maintain the procedure for three judges appointing a counsel independent of the Justice Department. But their proposal would place a number of limits. Only the president, the vice president, Cabinet secretaries and maybe a few others would be subject to such a probe, although the attorney general could seek appointment of a counsel in other cases. The proposal would eliminate the requirement that an independent counsel file a final report. It would also attempt to limit a counsel's role in spawning an impeachment and make it more difficult to expand the scope of an investigation.

Thompson's proposal is more in line with the sentiment on the rest of his committee. He would clarify that the attorney general has the power to appoint a special prosecutor, and he would have the Justice Department's rules on when to appoint one subjected to congressional approval. Thompson said he will likely submit his plan as an amendment to the fiscal 2000 appropriations bill (S 1217) for the departments of Justice, Commerce and State.

In the House, a minimalist approach is expected this year. Lawmakers feel little motivation to act and doubt whether they could have a constructive debate any time soon, given that the Judiciary Committee is still reeling with bad feelings. "I think we're all so burned out by impeachment that nothing will happen any time soon," said Lindsey Graham, R-S.C. "But hopefully we will find a way to get back into this."

Common Cause recommends handing allegations of executive branch malfeasance to the Justice Department's criminal division. The group would try to insulate the assistant attorney general in charge by making it more difficult for senior officials to overrule his or her decisions.

The commission assembled by AEI and Brookings recommends an almost complete reversion to the old system. Decisions on whom to investigate and how to do so would be left to the attorney general under departmental guidelines on when a special prosecutor should be appointed. If a special prosecutor were appointed, the attorney general would be able to terminate the probe at the end of two years, or annually subsequent to that. At other times the prosecutor could be fired for good cause. ◆

In three cases, justices narrowly rule that citizens may not use federal laws to sue states

Latest Supreme Court Rulings Reinforce the Federalist Trend

Arguably the most significant impact of the Supreme Court headed by Chief Justice William H. Rehnquist is its steadfast determination to rein in the powers of Congress and to bolster those of the states. Dramatic evidence to support this contention was furnished by the court June 23, the final day of its 1998-99 term, when it issued three more in a series of rulings that reconfigure the parameters of federalism.

The three cases — the most notable of which was *Alden v. Maine*, a case limiting the reach of a federal labor law that has been on the books for 61 years — all centered on the question of whether a federal law may be used by a private citizen to sue a state in state courts. With the court sharply but identically divided 5-4 in each, it said no.

In *Seminole Tribe of Florida v. Florida* three years ago, the same five-justice majority blocked similar suits from the federal courts. The cumulative effect of the 1996 and 1999 rulings is to severely restrict citizens who want to invoke a federal law to seek damages from any state in any court.

More broadly, the *Alden* ruling highlights the question of how far the court will take its crusade for federalism — the term now used in legal circles to describe devolving power away from the national government and to the states, not the other way around as it was when the Constitution was drafted.

In a series of sweeping rulings since 1992, the court has cut back congressional powers in the name of states' rights and state sovereignty. Perhaps as early as the next term, the court could signal whether it intends to curtail congressional power for its own sake, outside the context of enhancing state prerogatives. (*Recent cases, this page*)

In the long term, some constitutional experts see the potential for a host of federal civil rights laws to be struck down. That would undercut one of the main

Reining In Congress

Since 1992, a Supreme Court with a majority of justices nominated by Presidents Ronald Reagan and George Bush has curbed the power of Congress, ruling in these key cases that lawmakers have exceeded the powers given them by the Constitution.

- *New York v. United States* **1992**
  By 6-3, struck down a portion of a federal law (PL 99-240) making the states liable for nuclear waste created by commercial reactors. (*1992 Almanac, p. 329*)

- *United States v. Lopez* **1995**
  By 5-4, said Constitution's "commerce clause" was exceeded in part of a crime law (PL 101-647) that created gun-free zones within 1,000 feet of schools. (*1995 Almanac, p. 6-40*)

- *Seminole Tribe of Florida v. Florida* **1996**
  By 5-4, cited the 11th Amendment in blocking a law (PL 100-497) that allowed tribes to file federal suits when states failed to negotiate gambling compacts. (*1996 Almanac, p. 5-51*)

- *City of Boerne v. Flores* **1997**
  By 6-3, said Congress exceeded its 14th Amendment powers with a law (PL 103-141) barring states from enacting laws interfering with citizens' First Amendment rights of religious expression, unless states had a "compelling interest." (*1997 Almanac, p. 5-23*)

- *Printz v. United States, and Mack v. United States* **1997**
  By 5-4, struck down that portion of the Brady Act (PL 103-159) ordering local sheriffs to check the backgrounds of gun buyers. (*1997 Almanac, p. 5-21*)

reasons why Congress has expanded the reach of federal legislation in the past four decades: to countermand states when they insisted on their right to carry out their own views of civil rights.

On its face the *Alden* case affects a relatively small group of people — those citizens, generally state employees, who have labor gripes with a state government and do not think that their home state laws sufficiently address their grievances. But the decision's impact on both current and future federal laws cannot be overestimated.

Already, legal experts say, the decision could throw into question the enforceability of a bill designed to enhance religious liberties (HR 1691) that the House Judiciary Committee approved the same day as the Supreme Court ruling. Ironically, that measure is an attempt to salvage some federal enforcement of First Amendment rights of religious expression in the wake of a

Supreme Court ruling two years ago that struck down a previous religious liberties law as having exceeded congressional authority. (*Religious liberties, 1999 CQ Weekly, p. 1555*)

The *Alden* ruling also raises questions about future enforcement of several other laws. The court is expected to accept for arguments in the next term a federalism challenge to a portion of the 1994 anti-crime (PL 103-322) designed to combat violence against women. And it has already agreed to decide federalism challenges to the Equal Pay Act (PL 88-38), the False Claims Act (PL 97-258) and the Americans With Disabilities Act (PL 101-336), the scope of which was limited by the Supreme Court on June 22. (*Crime law, 1994 Almanac, p. 273; disabilities law, 1999 CQ Weekly, p. 1556*)

In these instances, the laws may not be declared unconstitutional. But if the justices hold to their recent trend, all the statutes could be largely neutralized by greatly limiting citizens' rights to force the laws' application.

Already, the *Alden* case has spawned an expression among legal scholars for what they think the Supreme Court is saying that Congress may confer on its constituents: "Rights without remedies."

The case not only cuts away at congressional power, but it also seems to preclude any possibility that Congress could find a clever legislative route around these new limitations, said Jonathan R. Siegel, a law professor at George Washington University.

"What the Supreme Court said to Congress is: 'No, no, no, we're not interested in your schemes. We really mean it. The states have immunity,' " he said.

For the Republicans who control Congress, the precedent presents something of a double-edged sword. While many conservative lawmakers advocate a devolution of federal power to the states, they still have come to expect that whatever legislation they do promote could be used by their constituents to redress grievances in the courts.

11th Amendment

The majority in *Alden* — Rehnquist, Anthony M. Kennedy, Antonin Scalia, Sandra Day O'Connor and Clarence Thomas — based their decision on an expansive reading of the 11th Amendment, which prohibits the federal courts from adjudicating cases brought against a state by citizens of another state or another country. From this amendment, as well as from various arguments said to be implicit in the structure of the Constitution, Kennedy wrote an opinion that constructed a doctrine of "sovereign immunity" from lawsuits.

Writing for the majority, Kennedy cited the established principle in English law at the time of the writing of the Constitution that the sovereign could not be sued. He also turned to various writings of the Founding Fathers. And he placed great weight on the deference given to states in the Constitution — particularly by the 10th Amendment, which limits federal powers.

"The generation that designed and adopted our federal system considered immunity from private suits central to sovereign dignity," said Kennedy.

In an impassioned dissent, Justice David H. Souter dismissed that notion. "There is no evidence that the 10th Amendment constitutionalized a concept of sovereign immunity as inherent in the notion of statehood," he said.

In a statement delivered from the bench, Justice John Paul Stevens went even further. He said that in *Alden* and other recent rulings the court was heading back to the period from 1781 until the ratification of the Constitution in 1789, when the nation was little more than a loose affiliation of states under the Articles of Confederation.

The *Alden* case involved a group of state probation officers and juvenile caseworkers who sued in Maine's state courts to be paid overtime under the Fair Labor Standards Act (PL 75-718), enacted in 1938 and extended in 1974 (PL 93-259) to explicitly cover state workers — a law upheld by the Supreme Court 14 years ago. (*1974 Almanac, p. 293; 1985 Almanac, p. 16-A*)

The other cases decided June 23, *Florida v. College Savings Bank* and *College Savings Bank v. Florida*, invalidated twin laws (PL 102-560, PL 102-542) that permitted lawsuits against state agencies alleging violations of federal patent and trademark laws. (*1992 Almanac, p. 303*)

These rulings are particularly dramatic in the context of those on federalism in the past seven years. "When you put these together, what you do is substantially limit the power of the federal government, and expand the power of states to escape the federal system," said Elliott Mincberg of People for the American Way, a liberal public advocacy group.

Such liberal legal experts say the court is engaging in a new type of judicial activism, and in doing so curbing the powers of the legislative branch in the name of a brand of federalism not explicitly cited in the Constitution.

Conservative groups, such as the Pacific Legal Foundation in Sacramento, Calif., welcomed the latest advancement in that direction.

"I'm pleased. I honestly didn't think the court would make such a strong statement on federalism and the original intent of the Founding Fathers," Anne M. Hughes, an attorney with the foundation who drafted a friend of the court brief in the *Alden* case, said in an interview June 25.

Congress' Powers

From the New Deal until the 1990s, the Supreme Court has generally upheld broad federal laws and policies even in light of 10th Amendment admonition to the federal government to stick to the enumerated powers granted it by the Constitution.

Congress has generally used three avenues for broadening its reach. The first is the power to regulate interstate commerce granted in Article I of the Constitution, perhaps the broadest and most vaguely enumerated power. So inclusive had the court's interpretation of this power been that in *Wickard v. Filburn*, in 1942, it upheld a law regulating crops grown for home consumption. If someone raises his own crops, the court reasoned, he affects overall demand, and by extension interstate commerce. Huge sections of the U.S. Code are built on this concept, including the Fair Labor Standards Act.

The second is Section 5 of the 14th Amendment, ratified after the Civil War to explicitly give Congress the right to enact legislation to protect citizens. This serves as the basis for numerous civil rights laws.

The third is to make federal funding to the states conditional on their taking certain actions. Until it was repealed in 1995, a national motorcycle helmet requirement was not a federal law but a precondition on states receiving highway funding. (*1995 Almanac, p. 3-60*)

In its recent rulings, the Supreme Court has narrowed the scope of the interstate commerce clause and the 14th Amendment. It has not gotten into the federal funding question. More important, it has not had much to say about Congress' use of the commerce clause and the 14th Amendment in instances that do not directly involve state prerogatives.

That may be about to change. On March 5 the 4th U.S. Circuit Court of Appeals, based in Richmond, Va., ruled unconstitutional the Violence Against Women Act, which gives victims of sexual assault the right to sue in federal court. That court's rationale, which relied heavily on the Supreme Court's 1995 decision in *U.S. v. Lopez*, is likely to be reviewed by the Supreme Court in the next year. That illustrates the snowballing effect of court rulings: The more they chip away at congressional power, the more new challenges are brought to federal laws — and the more cases come back to the Supreme Court. ◆

Political Participation

The articles in this section examine some of the key players in American politics: candidates and their election campaigns, political parties, and interest groups.

The national elections of 2000, the most important in decades, were in full swing by the fall of 1999. Presidential candidates were preparing for the array of primaries from coast to coast, and congressional candidates began planning their campaigns. On the outside, third-party candidates were seeking ways to be players in the election sweepstakes. To preview the coming elections, the editors have chosen four analytical articles written by Ronald D. Elving for CQ's *OnPolitics* newsletter, discussing, in turn, the presidential campaign, the Republican Party's southern base, the Senate elections, and the future of the Reform Party. The final article about the 2000 campaigns, from *CQ Weekly*, details the fundraising strategies of one presidential candidate, Texas governor George W. Bush, particularly his success in raising money from donors new to the political process.

As the first session of the 106th Congress drew to a close, Republicans and Democrats were positioning themselves for the election showdown. Articles on the GOP-proposed tax cut and the budget process illustrate the strategy of the two parties, as leaders sought to maintain solidarity and emphasize their differences from the opposition. In the case of the proposed tax cut, leaders of both parties even showed a willingness to sacrifice possible legislative achievement in order to take stands likely to appeal to voters. A central campaign issue will be managed care reform, and House Republican leaders suffered a defeat when a coalition of Democrats and moderate Republicans passed a bipartisan managed care reform bill. One article from *CQ Weekly* examines the contents of the bill, and another shows how Republicans lost the support of a formerly loyal constituency, doctors.

The debate over managed care reform is being carried out by two competing interest groups, the insurance industry and the health care industry. The first article in the interest group section describes the lobbying efforts of the two groups. Another interest group with a stake in managed care reform is senior citizens, a traditionally Democratic voting bloc who have lately shifted in part to the Republican Party. Both parties are actively courting seniors, with Democrats working for a Medicare prescription drug benefit plan and Republicans promising to protect the Social Security surplus from being spent on other programs. Following an article about both parties' general strategies for appealing to seniors is one about proposed legislation that would have overhauled the nation's pension laws. Another interest group discussed is the education lobby, which is threatened by cutbacks in many programs as Congress rewrites federal education law.

Our section on interest groups is concluded by a discussion of recent attempts to reform the campaign finance system. An article in question-and-answer format provides an overview of the debate, while another one, written shortly after Congress defeated the latest proposal by Sens. John McCain (R-Ariz.) and Russell D. Feingold (D-Wis.), emphasizes the political challenges faced by the measure and offers speculation about the bill's prospects in future sessions.

Eighty-Eight to Double-Aught: The 2000 Election Recalls Precursor from a Dozen Years in the Past

The fall of 1999 has a few elections of its own, including three gover-nornorships and a handfulof major mayoral races. But what's really raising the political animal's blood is the scent of 2000. The big cycle looms so close and looks so crucial that it seems already upon us.

Today, at his boyhood home in Missouri, former New Jersey Sen. Bill Bradley holds a campaign kickoff rally as he bids for the Democratic presidential nomination. Bradley has been buoyed by a recent poll showing him even with Vice President Al Gore, the putative Democratic front-runner, in New Hampshire — where the 2000 Republican front-runner, Texas Gov. George W. Bush, happens to be touring this week in a campaign bus.

Congress is back today, too, with members returning from their summer recess as fraught with campaign hyper-awareness as they would be in an even-numbered year. Watch for lots of talk about Waco and Russian money-laundering and other issues that can be tied like so many cans to Gore's tail.

No one can deny the 2000 election's importance for the future. Nor can we hope to escape hearing endless invocations of that future — the dawning millennium — in the months to come.

The future, however, stubbornly refuses to let us peek. So we are thrown back on the past, ready as ever with its contradictory lessons and prospective parallels.

It's hard to resist the analogy between Gore's bid for the presidency and that of George Bush — the elder, that is — in 1988.

Like Gore, who has been President Clinton's understudy, Bush was running for president in 1988 as the two-term vice president (in his case under Presi-

Originally published in the CQ Newsletter OnPolitics, September 8, 1999

Democratic presidential candidates Al Gore and Bill Bradley face off in the first debate of the 2000 primary season, at Dartmouth College in Hanover, New Hampshire

den: Ronald Reagan). Both settled in for their tenures as the number-two man after unsuccessful first tries for president (Bush in 1980, Gore in 1988).

And Bush, like Gore after him, humbled himself as vice president, subordinated his views and stood by his boss through good times and bad.

Bush had no choice, as vice presidents never do. But in 1988, it was not obvious that being Reagan's heir was a ticket to anything. Late in his presidency, Reagan remained personally popular, but his policies had lost momentum. Poll respondents in 1988 were about evenly split between staying the course and trying something new.

There was also a residue of contro-

versy and even scandal in the administration that Reagan's reputation could not entirely overcome. There had been more independent counsels appointed than in any previous administration. The sale of arms to Iran in an attempt to free American hostages in the Middle East and raise money for U.S.-backed forces in Central America had disillusioned many. Democrats liked to talk about the "sleaze factor" in the Reagan administration.

Election results were also trending Democratic. The Senate, Republican since the 1980 elections, had reverted to Democratic control in 1986. House Democrats had regained their footing as well.

Besides all that, Bush was far from a consensus nominee. The party's right wing, especially social conservatives, found the Connecticut Yankee—turned-Texan suspect. Commentators noted that the previous vice president elected to succeed his boss had been Martin Van Buren — in 1836.

And Bush, while bearing contumely such as a Newsweek cover story headlined "The Wimp Factor," had to watch a crop of challengers emerge, including Senate Republican leader Bob Dole of Kansas, Rep. Jack F. Kemp of New York, and religious broadcaster Pat Robertson, who soon would establish the Christian Coalition.

Gore's road may not look quite so steep, but it's been getting more treacherous of late.

After falling well short in 1988, Gore decided to sit out the 1992 contest and build his reputation as a youthful senator primarily focused on high-tech issues and the environment. But when Clinton held out the vice presidential brass ring that year, Gore grabbed it.

The result was success at the polls but a long haul of soldiering on through serial crises. Gore did it well enough to be renominated without challenge in 1996. But like Bush in 1988, he has his share of doubters in the party.

Organized labor is lukewarm because of his free-trade stance. Many blacks remember his arm's length attitude toward them in 1988. Women voters tell pollsters they find him uninspiring. And who in the Democratic Party matters more than labor, blacks and women?

And if there was a "sleaze factor" in Reagan's White House, it has long since been eclipsed by the incessant scandal in Clinton's. In fact, the "Clinton fatigue" factor has become a burden for Gore, not just among Republicans but among independents and Democrats as well.

In the end, though, the most telling commonality between Gore and Bush may be their failure to match their bosses' performing skills. Neither Bush nor Gore is a natural speaker, yet both must endure comparison with the best communicators of their eras. Bush appeared unheroic next to Reagan, Gore comes off as stiff alongside Clinton.

Texas Governor George W. Bush rallies supporters in preparation for the Republican Party's straw poll on August 14, 1999, in Ames, Iowa.

Not many of these Gore-Bush parallels are flattering. But the Gore campaign is glad to recall how Bush 1988 turned into a success story.

It started badly. Bush ran third in the Iowa precinct caucuses. Even after coming off the ropes to win his nomination, Bush was down in polls by as much as 15 percentage points to the Democratic nominee, Massachusetts Gov. Michael S. Dukakis.

Bush was also battling the two-term thing. Consciously or not, Americans seemed to like alternating Republicans and Democrats in the White House at intervals of eight years.

Harry S Truman, a Democrat, served nearly eight years (1945–53) before giving over to Republican Dwight D. Eisenhower. Ike's eight years were followed by eight for Democrats John F. Kennedy and Lyndon B. Johnson, who in turn yielded to Republicans Richard M. Nixon and Gerald R. Ford for eight more.

In 1976, right on schedule, Democrat Jimmy Carter won the presidency. But Carter was a weak president, poorly staffed and clueless about Congress. Double-digit inflation and interest rates, plus the year-long Iran hostage crisis, left him at the brink. Yet it took a stronger-than-expected campaign by Reagan to wrest the presidency away in 1980 when the next Republican was not "due" until 1984.

Thus, in 1988, the Democrats had reason to believe their turn had come. But Bush rode a strong economy and a flawed performance by his opponent to victory in November.

Economic factors were important then, as they ought to be for Gore in 2000. Growth was back, a robust recovery after the deep recession of the early 1980s, and inflation and interest rates were down.

In the end, however, Bush also got a boost from the wonkish Dukakis, who insisted that the election was about competence, not ideology. Bush ran aggressive, negative ads; Dukakis' replies were late and lackluster. Bush came across better in debates.

But having broken the eight-year rhythm in 1988, Bush fell victim to another exception himself four years later. The economy had soured, and Bush seemed distant from domestic concerns.

It was Clinton who re-established the eight-year standard in 1996, benefiting from an improved economy and an opponent in Bob Dole who never seemed to get on track.

Unfortunately for Gore, the eight-year interval — if it holds — would make it the Republicans' turn again in 2000. ◆

South-centered GOP Will Go On Playing Dixie, But Must Keep Other Regions from Tuning Out

Something happened to the Republicans on their way to being America's majority party: They became the South's majority party. The question now is whether Southern hegemony is a natural step in national ascendancy — or a dead end that will keep the party from reaching its ultimate goal.

Surely the Republicanizing of the South is the most remarkable regional shift in the history of American politics. The Republican Party scarcely existed in the region for nearly a century after the Civil War.

The very letters GOP, for Grand Old Party, date from the Reconstruction era and echo the name of the Grand Army of the Republic. For decades, Republicans won elections in the North by waving what was called "the bloody shirt" and telling men to "vote as you shot."

As recently as the Eisenhower era, when the Republicans last controlled both chambers of Congress (1953-54), Democrats outnumbered Republicans 25 to 1 among Southern senators and 111 to 9 among Southern members of the House.

Yet today, the South is the Republican Party's new homeland. Exit polls show Republican candidates now receive a higher percentage of the vote in the South (long defined by CQ as the 11 states of the Confederacy plus their voting-profile cousins Kentucky and Oklahoma) than in the Northeast, Midwest or West.

Most of the region's governors are Republicans, as are three-fifths of its representatives in Congress and two-thirds of its U.S. senators. Not bad for a party mired in minority status in all three categories for 120 years before the breakthrough election of 1994.

The big shift really began decades earlier. This July marks the 35th anniversary of the Civil Rights Act of 1964, which outlawed racial discrimination in public accommodations. The Southern Democrats who had battled such legislation in both chambers for generations felt betrayed and cast out.

In that same month, the Republican Party nominated Sen. Barry Goldwater of Arizona for president. Goldwater had opposed the Civil Rights Act, and his rough-and-ready definition of conservatism had appeal in the South.

That August, an effort by a group of black civil rights activists from Mississippi to be seated at the 1964 Democratic convention, though largely unsuccessful, spurred a boycott by most of that state's regular, all-white delegation. And in September, Sen. Strom Thurmond of South Carolina announced he was switching from the Democratic Party to the Republicans to stump for Goldwater.

In November, Goldwater carried his home state, Thurmond's home state and the Deep South quartet of Georgia, Alabama, Mississippi and Louisiana. President Lyndon B. Johnson carried the other 44 states but told friends he feared his party had lost the South for a generation. The only question about that now is whether he underestimated the time frame.

Sons of Dixie

The impact of the Republicans' new base in the South on presidential contests can scarcely be overstated. The region has historically tended to vote as a bloc, and laying

Republican Strom Thurmond of South Carolina, the Senate pro tempore and longest serving senator ever.

CQ PHOTO / DOUGLAS GRAHAM

Originally published in the CQ Newsletter OnPolitics, September 15, 1999

claim to it enabled Republican candidates to win Electoral College landslides in 1972, 1980, 1984 and 1988. It was even the best region for the party in the losing campaigns of 1992 and 1996.

Let us assume for the moment that the nominees in 2000 are Democrat Al Gore of Tennessee and George W. Bush of Texas. Bush could plausibly carry every Southern state save Gore's own. That would mean a trove of 152 electoral votes for Bush, well over half the 270 needed for election.

Already the nation's most populous region, the South still is growing faster than the nation as a whole. It will have well over 140 seats in the House after the next census. The Northeast, which now has 100 seats, and perhaps the Midwest (now 105 seats), will fall into the 90s, where they will be matched or exceeded by the growing states of the West (now 93).

But the Republican Party's Southern triumph has come at a price. As its center of gravity relocates below the Mason-Dixon line, the party of Lincoln confronts the identity crisis that often accompanies success. Can the party that lives in the suburbs of Atlanta and Dallas co-exist with the party still rooted in the land and legacy of Lincoln?

As the South has risen, the Republicans have become heavily reliant on it. The region now sends 27 more Republicans to the House than Democrats. That more than accounts for the overall GOP majority of 223-211 (with one independent). In the Senate, the 18-8 bulge Republicans enjoy among the Southern delegations produces the chamber's 10-seat GOP majority.

Small wonder that the leaders in both chambers are sons of Dixie. In the Senate, there are Majority Leader Trent Lott of Mississippi; the phenomenal Thurmond, the Senate president pro tempore and both the

oldest and longest-serving senator ever; and Don Nickles of Oklahoma, who is Lott's assistant majority leader. The GOP's Senate campaign committee chairman, Mitch McConnell, is from Kentucky.

On the House side, the top leadership jobs last year were all held by members from Georgia and Texas. And when Newt Gingrich resigned as Speaker following the 1998 elections, the first man up to replace him was Robert L. Livingston of Louisiana.

When Livingston resigned to escape scandal, the Speaker's gavel went to J. Dennis Hastert from Illinois. But anyone thinking that this represented a Northern restoration in the Republican Party had only to watch the first few months of the 106th Congress to know better.

Too Reliant on the South?

The new Southern stamp on the GOP goes well beyond the names on office doors. The South is not only its bastion but its beacon.

Whether the issue is taxes, religion, schools, crime, guns, gays or defense spending, the view from the South is the view of Congress' majority party.

Nowhere has this been clearer than on the House response to the proposed new gun restrictions approved by the Senate. After making sure no such provisions would appear in the House bill, Majority Whip Tom DeLay of Texas backed a provision to allow the Ten Commandments to be posted in schoolrooms. The motion was offered by Robert B. Aderholt, a two-term Republican from Alabama.

The party's national future — particularly in congressional elections — now depends on dominating the Southern vote without paying too much of a price for it elsewhere. That was why the 1998 congressional vote was such a double disappointment for many Republicans.

In last November's tally, the GOP was less dominating in the South than in 1994 or 1996. They lost the governorships in Alabama and South Carolina and saw House seats recaptured by old-fashioned conservative Democrats in Kentucky and Mississippi.

But even more ominous were the portents for the party elsewhere in the country. The Republicans now have 40 seats fewer in the Midwest — and 42 fewer in the Northeast — than they had when Ike was first elected. Their numbers in the Senate have dropped by one-third in the Midwest and by nearly half in the Northeast.

No wonder Republicans elsewhere ask how much stronger they can afford to have their party become in the new solid South. ◆

A powerful leader in the House, Majority Whip Tom DeLay hails from Texas.

Republican Majorities: Then and Now

The following are geographical breakdowns of the numbers of House and Senate seats held by Republicans when they were in the majority in the 1950s and currently.

The figures illustrate the sharp growth of the South as a Republican power base, and its decline in the Northeast and Midwest regions that were the traditional heartland of the "party of Lincoln."

House

	1953-54	Now
South	9	82
Midwest	94	54
Northeast	80	38
West	38	49
Total	221	223

Senate

	1953-54	Now
South	1	18
Midwest	19	12
Northeast	17	9
West	11	16
Total	48*	55

* The party lineup in 1953–54 was 48 Republicans, 47 Democrats and 1 independent. There were 96 total seats, as Alaska and Hawaii had not yet become states.

Shifting Seasons, Changing Line-Ups Let Democrats Reclaim Momentum in the 2000 Senate Campaign

Not so long ago, Republicans expected to reach 60 seats in the Senate on Election Day 2000. Today, that prospect has receded to the vanishing point. Indeed, the Democrats bid fair to gain ground in the chamber for the first time since 1990.

The momentum shift is not yet powerful enough to jeopardize the Republican majority, won in 1994. But if it holds, it could cripple the Senate Republican leadership, just as adverse election results brought down Speaker Newt Gingrich and other members of the House Republican leadership last November.

It is hard to overstate the significance and allure of 60 seats. Far from being just another symbolic number, 60 confers the power to cut off debate: It is the threshold for true control under Senate rules.

As recently as last fall, 60 Senate Republicans in the 107th Congress seemed entirely plausible. But that expectation was based on a GOP net pickup of two or three seats in 1998. That didn't happen, though: Republicans did take away three seats that had been held by Democrats, but they also lost three of their own and wound up stuck at 55.

So far in 1999, campaign developments have that 55 looking more like a limit than a launching pad.

Neither party should look to a banner year on the order of the Republican takeovers in 1994 and 1980, or the Democrats' recapture of control in 1986. The problem is simple math: relatively few seats among the 33 on the ballot are truly in play.

Republicans have an excellent chance at takeaways in Nevada and Virginia and a shot at two more in New Jersey and New York. But even if 2000 were to turn into a better Republican year than expected, where do they go for the fifth seat to get to 60? The other

Originally published in the CQ Newsletter OnPolitics, June 30, 1999

10 Democrats facing re-election are all running in the clear.

And it now appears that the 2000 elections have downside potential for Republicans as well as up. The greater probability is that they will lose more than they gain, winding up at least a little weaker - and perhaps a lot.

Actually, a modest majority for one party or the other may be the Senate's natural state of equilibrium, especially in good economic times. But the rapid rise of the current Republican cohort, especially the all-GOP freshman class of 11 elected in 1994, spurred more ambitious thinking.

The GOP has captured 17 Democratic seats in the Senate and lost just five since President Clinton was inaugurated in 1993. Such numbers suggested a broad realignment. The magic of 60 seemed only a cycle or two away.

Yet much of the dramatic gain in 1994 had come in the South and the Mountain West, the strongholds of the contemporary Republican Party. Those gains have proven hard to extend, in part because the GOP has little of this territory left to conquer.

In the eight states of the Mountain West, Republicans now hold 12 of the 16 seats. They hope to add one more in Nevada next year, but that may be it for a while. Republicans also have 18 of the 26 seats in the South; but here too their long march has reached a plateau.

For a decade after Democrat John B. Breaux was elected to succeed Russell Long in Louisiana in 1986, every Southern Democratic senator who retired was replaced by a Republican. But in the past two cycles, three retiring Democrats have had Democratic successors. Even more notable was the 1998 upset scored by first-time Democratic candidate John Edwards of North Carolina, a wealthy trial lawyer, over Republican incumbent Lauch Faircloth.

Possible GOP Gains

Only a handful of Southern senators are on the ballot in 2000. Among them only Democrat Charles S. Robb of Vir-

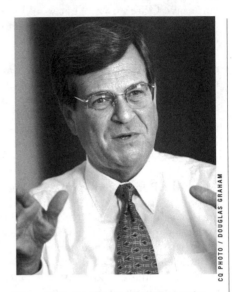

It is unlikely that Senate Majority Leader Trett Lott will see a filibuster-proof GOP Senate in 2001.

ginia is in trouble. In fact, Robb is the only Democratic incumbent anywhere who looks shaky. He has kept quietly busy since holding off his 1994 Republican challenger, Iran-contra figure Oliver North. But in 2000, he must face a far more formidable GOP opponent in former Gov. George F. Allen, who leads in polls.

The Democrats' greater concerns lie with their three vacancies. In Nevada, they so far have no candidate to succeed Richard H. Bryan - while the Republicans almost certainly will nominate former Rep. John Ensign, who came within an eyelash of winning the state's other seat in 1998. Democrats were looking to state Attorney General Frankie Sue Del Papa, but she dropped out of the race last week.

In New Jersey, the stunning reversal by Republican Gov. Christine Todd Whitman, who last week backed out on plans to seek retiring Democrat Frank R. Lautenberg's seat, has Democrats ecstatic. But they still need to choose between former Gov. Jim Florio, who lost to Whitman in 1993, and a New York investment banker, Jon Corzine.

The other Democratic problem is Daniel Patrick Moynihan's long-held seat in New York. Democrat Hillary Rodham Clinton, seemingly certain to make an unprecedented Senate bid as first lady, has had a difficult September. First, she highlighted her carpetbagger status with her purchase of a posh suburban home. Then she advertised her lack of candidate savvy on the issue of clemency for Puerto Rican nationalists.

Yet Clinton remains almost dead even in the polls with New York Mayor Rudolph Giuliani. That is surprising in part because Giuliani, a moderate on social issues and an irritant to his rivals for GOP power in New York, has benefited from his party's efforts to rally themselves and their Clinton-hating conservative brethren on his behalf.

Few Targets for Democrats

If Bryan, Lautenberg and Moynihan were all running again, the Democrats could dream. They might even see visions of 1986, when they stormed back from a six-year stint in the Senate minority with a net gain of eight seats.

But 1986 was a target-rich cycle.

The 16 Senate Republicans who had first won with Ronald Reagan in 1980 had a soft center: Seven were gone after their first term (although one of them, Slade Gorton of Washington, later made a comeback).

The 2000 cycle presents no such wealth of opportunity, although the Republicans are showing more vulnerability than they had expected. The Senate GOP's fundraising machinery has actually raised slightly less money so far in the cycle than it had two years earlier. That has allowed the Democrats to approach at least temporary parity.

Only two incumbent Republicans are retiring: Connie Mack of Florida, John H. Chafee of Rhode Island. But both seats are in states Clinton carried in 1996, and quality Democratic candidates are on hand in both.

Four other states that Clinton carried (Michigan, Minnesota, Missouri and Pennsylvania) will be asked in 2000 to re-elect the Republican freshmen they first sent to the Senate in 1994. Missouri's John Ashcroft's opponent will be popular two-term Democ-

ratic Gov. Mel Carnahan. Michigan's Spencer Abraham cannot count on an easy time against two-term Democratic Rep. Debbie Stabenow. Abraham, a longtime party activist, had perfect timing when he ran in 1994 but has made little dent since on the state's political consciousness.

Republicans in the other two states could benefit from crowded fields of would-be Democratic challengers. But Minnesota's Rod Grams, a conservative stalwart in a state often associated with Democrats, just fired his top staff. And Pennsylvania's Rick Santorum, a brash overachiever elected to the Senate at 36, has only begun to moderate his politics to fit the diversity of his state.

The Democrats would need to come up with every rebound and loose ball to come close to 50 seats. But they can breathe easier about the trends of the mid-90s. There is no longer much chance the GOP will even add seats in 2000, let alone find the Holy Grail of 60. And that is true even if a Republican wins the White House and the GOP holds the House. ◆

A Brief History of a Short-Lived Phenomenon: Is It Time to Say Goodbye to the Reform Party?

The rise and fall of Ross Perot and his third-party movement proves once again that democracy obeys the law of supply and demand.

Perot was a fresh breeze in June 1992, when more than 60 percent of Americans told pollsters they wanted an alternative for president to Republican incumbent George Bush and his Democratic challenger Bill Clinton. The force of that moment was enough to fuel two Perot presidential bids and beget a new political organization, United We Stand, which became the Reform Party.

But seven years later, the political scene has been altered beyond recognition. The nation's remarkable economic recovery and comparative strength abroad have instilled a new optimism.

Only about one-third of Americans now tell pollsters they are dissatisfied with a prospective choice in 2000 between Bush's

Originally published in the CQ Newsletter OnPolitics, September 8, 1999

son, Texas Gov. George W. Bush, and Clinton's vice president, Al Gore.

As if on cue, Perot and his party have imploded.

The denouement was on display last month at the annual Reform Party convention in Dearborn, Mich. Nearly 600 delegates were eligible to attend, but only about 350 registered. And at this crucial moment in the movement's nascent history, the party's two leading figures, Perot and Minnesota Gov. Jesse Ventura, both failed to take the helm.

Perot showed up, but only to deliver a reprise of his old stump speech. He made no mention whatsoever of Ventura, the party's one major officeholder. Waving goodbye to the faithful, the founder fled the scene without so much as shaking hands with those on stage.

Goodbye, Ross, thanks for the memories.

For his part, Ventura was grounded by thunderstorms back home and did not appear. He did address the delegates via telephone, wowing the crowd but then deflating the mood by ruling himself out of the 2000 presidential race. Jesse fans now believe he has his eye on 2004.

For the moment, let us allow The Body to be true to his code. He has promised Minnesotans four years of his time and they deserve no less. But we can also expect growing pressure on him to revisit his vow, because without him it is hard to see the Reform Party amounting to anything next year on the national level.

A decent showing in the popular vote matters because anything less than 5 percent of that vote will cost the party its claim to federal funds. And the pot of $12.6 million in public money for which the party qualified in 1996 now appears to be all that is holding the fledgling party together.

The existence of a national party with automatic ballot status in 19 states and ready cash might be expected to draw a crowd. But to date, the party's past with Perot and its present identification with Ventura have made it difficult, if not impossible, for others to step up.

Who would want to enter this pit after watching what Perot did last time around to Dick Lamm, the former Democratic governor of Colorado? To give the Reform nomination

Ross Perot, shown on a video screen, addresses the Reform Party national convention on July 24, 1999, in Dearborn, Michigan.

a semblance of competition in 1996, Perot lured Lamm into the fray. Expecting at least the respect due a sparring partner, Lamm found himself treated more like bait in a cage.

For that matter, who would want to climb through the ropes with the party's latest symbol? Some party people have talked about Oklahoma's David L. Boren, a Democratic former governor and senator who is now president of the University of Oklahoma. But would the bright but bland Boren fit a party still pining

Minnesota governor Jesse Ventura may hold the key for future Reform Party success.

for a former pro wrestler who used to wear feather boas in his act? Would this subliminal competition appeal to another independent-minded Democrat, the highly proper Sam Nunn, longtime senator from Georgia?

Ventura himself has urged the honor on Lowell P. Weicker Jr., a former Republican senator who served a turbulent term as a third-party governor of Connecticut. In one recent poll, only a small fraction of Connecticut voters warmed to the idea of Weicker in the White House.

There will always be happy talk about drafting Colin Powell, but the former chairman of the Joint Chiefs of Staff steadfastly refuses to be considered. Enthusiasts also hope to recruit from the ranks of the major parties' primaries. Top mentionees are Sen. John McCain, R-Ariz., and former Sen. Bill Bradley,

D-N.J. But both disavowed any interest immediately after the Reform convention.

Anyone who attended the Dearborn do, or tuned in on C-SPAN, has an inkling as to why. The party has become a stage for performance art by an impossibly mixed bag of madcaps and malcontents. "We've got people to the right of Pat Buchanan and people to the left of Jesse Jackson," said Tom McLaughlin, a Pennsylvania delegate.

Indeed, the party now exists as the free-form alternative to whatever and whomever. Its common denominator is a grand faith in "the people." But in the tradition of American populism, its true lodestar is antipathy toward elites. This enables various elements of the party to fire freely at the right (big banks, wicked Wall Street financiers, do-gooders and bluenoses) and at the left (government bureaucrats, union bosses, bleeding hearts and ivory tower academics). The target often shifts in mid-rant.

Perhaps the best symbol of the new party is its new chairman, Jack Gargan, 68, a retired life insurance salesman. Gargan was an often-frustrated candidate for local offices in Tampa before he retired in 1990. Since then, he has won renown as an anti-deficit, anti-government, anti-incumbent Jeremiah traveling the highways and byways in a van. His organization, THRO, for Throw the Hypocritical Rascals Out, bought full-page ads in hundreds of newspapers in 1992 urging the defeat of all incumbents regardless of party or philosophy.

In those days, Gargan was selling the deficit as the apocalypse and Perot as the nation's savior. Today he peddles the Y2K computer problem and Ventura.

If the current "economic bubble" is burst by computer disruptions at year's end, Gargan says, the ensuing depression will turn the populace against the two major parties. That's one reason Gargan intends to move the Reform headquarters from Dallas to his home, Cedar Key, Fla. The island can only be reached by a narrow road he says can be "easily defended" in the parlous times he sees ahead.

Survivalism is not exactly the direction that all third-party fans had in mind for the post-Perot period. ◆

CQ PHOTO / DOUGLAS GRAHAM

Reform Party Blues: By The Numbers

States in which Reform Party already has ballot status for 2000: 19

States in which Republican and Democratic parties have ballot status: 50

Percentage of Time/CNN poll respondents saying they could vote for Minnesota Reform Gov. Jesse Ventura for president: 17

Percentage of Pew poll respondents dissatisfied with Bill Clinton/George Bush choice in 1992: 61

Percentage of Pew poll respondents dissatisfied with possible Al Gore/George W. Bush choice in 2000: 35

Personal funds spent by Ross Perot as independent presidential candidate in 1992: $66 million

Federal funds available to Reform Party nominee in 2000: $12.6 million

Federal funds available for Republican/Democratic nominees in 2000: $66 million each

Federal funds available for Reform Party convention in 2000: $3 million

Federal funds available for Republican/Democratic conventions in 2000: $12.3 million each

Buchanan Tries Reform Party Route

Patrick J. Buchanan, the 60-year-old *enfant terrible* of the Republican right, finally left home this week to start a new life in the Reform Party.

Will he establish a new empire in the uncharted territory beyond or wander in a wilderness he finds ever more bewildering? Right now, the latter looks the likelier scenario.

The initial news coverage was adulterated with references to Donald Trump, the New York real-estate and Atlantic City resort tycoon who had also announced his own switch to the Reform Party and his own presidential notions.

Buchanan's bolting got comparatively short shrift on CNN, the cable network that had sustained his career as a conservative commentator after his boss, Ronald Reagan, left the White House more than a decade ago.

How galling this must have been to Buchanan. He has lived out his life in politics, in journalism and in suits and ties dull even by Washington standards. How could he be lumped with Trump, a smirking casino operator known for his financial hi-jinks and flamboyant lifestyle.

Buchanan has every reason to resent this. He has been deeply engaged in the political wars of four decades and a presidential candidate in his own right through three cycles, including the current one. The last time New Hampshire had a Republican primary, in 1996, Buchanan won it.

To be sure, the latest Buchanan bid had been wobbly and woebegone from the start. He could not compete in the "invisible primary" conducted among fundraisers and party regulars. His speech at the Iowa straw poll in August (where he finished fifth with 7 percent of the attendees' votes) sounded a lot like a valedictory.

But none of that matters if Buchanan, born again as a Reform Party champion, can get on the ballot in all 50 states (the Reform Party is on automatically in fewer than half the states, based on its 1996 performance).

Then, if he could garner the mail-in vote which will in part determine the Reform nomination and then hold on at the party's convention, he would get his hands on the $12.6 million in federal matching funds that the party has coming.

More important, this would get him on a debate stage with the major party nominees next fall. And that would give him a chance to do what he does best: Put the establishment candidates on the spot with his pungent, populist rhetoric. Buchanan believes that a bravura performance in such debates could make him more than a spoiler. He points to some polls that show, in a contest between himself, Bush and Gore, his share would be in the mid-teens (though other polls show him in the low single digits).

Buchanan sees himself as the champion of a new party on par with the old ones. But by stepping outside the confines of his lifetime party, he is also taking a risk. He has abandoned much of his old support system and cannot assume the Reform Party will provide him with a new one. Buchanan will continue to command attention, if only because his bellicose style and high-profile apostasy make him newsworthy. But when sheer notoriety has run its course, what then?

Buchanan has caught waves of sudden fortune before only to be dragged under. In 1992, after scaring President George Bush with 37 percent of the vote in New Hampshire, Buchanan never did as well again (his final tally for all primaries was less than 23 percent). Four years later, he again found the glare of success blinding: After winning New Hampshire, he went to Arizona and finished an ignominious third in the state's primary. By the time South Carolina voted in early March, Buchanan was finished.

What will Buchanan do now to upstage the major parties and expand his appeal? The Reform calendar has no primaries. That means no chance to win events, compel media coverage, and build momentum.

The Reform Party itself remains more an attitude than an organization, and as such it is subject to whim. That is why even an entrant as seemingly ephemeral as Trump cannot be dismissed out of hand.

Trump has the backing of Minnesota Gov. Jesse Ventura, the party's one major officeholder. He shares Ventura's philosophic mix of economic and social laissez-faire.

Trump has a less noticed affinity with Reform's founding father, Texas billionaire and two-time presidential candidate Ross Perot. Like Ross the Boss, The Donald (Trump's trademarked nickname) proposes to take "a business approach" to the presidency, telegraphing his contempt for government even as he asks to be part of it. Foreign policy? Trump refers to his deal-making experience and says he would "negotiate terrific treaties."

Trump may be a Manhattan peacock to Perot's Texarkana rooster, but both rely on the same thing to overcome their political innocence — hundreds of millions in ready cash. This is the kind of asset that lowers hurdles such as ballot qualification.

What happens if Buchanan does not sweep to the fore of Reform as he plans? If he needs to make deals with Lenora Fulani, a new Reform Party factor late of the socialist New Alliance Party, can he still claim the conservative crusader's sheen?

Much of the country has lost faith in the major parties. These facts lend the Reform Party a reason to exist, at least in the abstract. It's the transition to the real that's the problem. Celebrity alone does not achieve that transition, and Reform has yet to attract candidates who might offer real solutions.

When will there be a third party that works and wins? When a third party arises that has a coherent view of the issues and a slate of candidates who attract not just media attention but citizen interest and commitment.

That was what happened in the 1850s, when an upstart known as the Republican Party arose, challenged the Democrats and the Whigs and reordered America's two-party system. But it has not happened since.

Candidate's filings illustrate his success in attracting money from first-time donors

Bush's Fundraising Net Hauls In Newcomers

Whatever the result of Iowa's straw poll, the real early momentum behind George W. Bush's quest for the Republican presidential nomination remains the unprecedented amount of money he has already collected for the campaign — and the fact that his coffer was filled by hundreds of newcomers to the experience of bankrolling a national campaign.

In yet another sign of the Texas governor's fundraising prowess — which went on prominent display Aug. 14 in Ames, Iowa, where the campaign was prepared to spend $750,000 to woo participants in the non-binding straw poll with barbecue, Tejano and country music, and celebrity appearances — Bush's finance reports show that many of his early benefactors were making a large contribution to a presidential candidate for the first time in more than two decades, since the Federal Election Commission (FEC) began keeping computerized records in 1978.

An examination of the filings by Congressional Quarterly found that contributors in this category made up almost half the donor lists from the four states — other than the candidate's own — that have so far been the most generous to the Bush campaign. The review included nearly 1,000 contributors from Michigan, Florida, California and New York who each gave $1,000 to the Bush campaign during the first three months of 1999. Texas was excluded from the analysis in the belief that the governor, relying on his own contributor network, would have found an especially large group of new presidential givers there.

These donations are part of the gargantuan $37 million the campaign had taken in by June 30. Bush is so far ahead of all his rivals in raising money — he also leads all GOP and Democratic candidates in public opinion polls — that he has decided to eschew federal matching funds, and thereby the spending limitations that come with them.

Donations from individuals accounted for all but $809,000 of Bush's take for the first six months of the year, a staggering total considering that each donor may contribute no more than $1,000 for the primary election and another $1,000 toward the campaign for the Nov. 7, 2000, general election. (Political action committees may give $5,000.)

To put up such figures, Bush needed to expand his contributor network beyond typical Republican Party donors. He began by organizing the Pioneers, well-connected allies who each agreed to raise at least $100,000 for the campaign. Last month, the Bush campaign made public the names of 119 of these volunteers, omitting those who had not yet met their fundraising target and not specifying how much beyond the threshold each successful Pioneer had brought in.

"He has as his chief fundraisers people who are not the usual party hacks, who are themselves contributors, and they have reached out to potential new supporters," said Ellen S. Miller, executive director of Public Campaign. That nonprofit group has endorsed the campaign finance overhaul legislation (HR 417, S 26) the House and Senate will take up this fall but would prefer a system of voluntary spending limits in return for public financing of all campaigns for federal office.

While Bush's donor roster may be larded with newcomers, it "still represents an extraordinarily small percentage of the American people," Miller said.

"It's highly unusual to have such a well-developed, extensive fundraising machine at such an early stage," said Fred Wertheimer, the president of Democracy 21, another nonprofit group pressing to change campaign finance law. "The role of the Pioneers, both at this stage and potentially in a much greater role in raising soft money if Bush is nominated, will be the campaign finance story of the 2000 election."

Array of Givers

Of the 976 Bush contributors whose history of political giving was reviewed by CQ, 454, or 47 percent, were making their first contributions to a presidential candidate of at least $200, the threshold for having a donor's name added to the FEC database. And 195 of them, or 20 percent, were making their first large contribution to any candidate for federal office since the FEC started keeping computerized records.

The list of new donors included ordinary people and celebrities, young high-tech workers taking their first political stand and longtime Republicans who have never before gone to their checkbooks to express their loyalties. Among them are Walker Stapleton, a

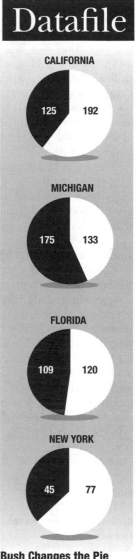

Datafile

CALIFORNIA

125 192

MICHIGAN

175 133

FLORIDA

109 120

NEW YORK

45 77

Bush Changes the Pie
Above are the total number of $1,000 donors to George W. Bush's presidential campaign during the first quarter of 1999 from the four states — other than his home state of Texas — that have given the most to his campaign. Shaded areas represent those donors who were giving to a presidential candidate for the first time since 1978.

SOURCE: Federal Election Commission

25-year old cousin of the candidate living in San Francisco, and Florida State University football coach Bobby Bowden. In many cases, they were drawn by friends of friends, or by direct appeals from the campaign.

"This has been a very easy sell," said Richard Hug, Bush's Maryland finance chairman.

Hug said he has raised more than $1.1 million for Bush since March 1, including $500,000 at a $1,000 per person reception that Bush attended July 14 in Baltimore. Hug, who led the $6.4 million fundraising effort for the 1998 campaign of Maryland GOP gubernatorial candidate Ellen R. Sauerbrey, said he knew of no other single Maryland fundraising event where so much had been collected.

Money is being raised for Bush in Maryland by about 100 volunteers, two-thirds of whom were Sauerbrey contributors and the rest relative political newcomers, Hug added.

Indicator of Strength?

Campaign finance watchers attribute the rush of new contributors to several factors, including Bush's widely acknowledged status as the presumptive nominee, the "Clinton fatigue" accentuated by the president's yearlong struggle against impeachment, and an economic boom that has generated new wealth and spread much of it to a new group of potential donors.

"After seven years in the wilderness, you really want to get behind a winner," said Craig Richardson of Washington Strategies, a GOP consulting firm. "It's a great indicator of how strong a candidate he is."

In California, especially, employees and executives of technology companies have responded to the call for contributions. Former Netscape Communications Corp. executive James L. Barksdale is one of Bush's main contacts and has helped deliver thousands from the booming industry. Gregory W. Slayton, president and CEO of MySoftware Co., who made his first-ever significant contribution to a presidential candidate this year, said that the Silicon Valley network he co-chairs expanded from his personal circle of friends and business associates to include hundreds of people this year.

"There are people calling me up out of the blue and saying, I want to get involved," he said, citing Bush's knowledge of technology issues and an "any-body but Clinton" sentiment.

Presidential campaigns usually draw more participation, but it is too soon to tell how much that trend will grow before more election statistics are studied, said Larry Makinson of the Center for Responsive Politics, which analyzes campaign finance records.

James Antrim, president of Antex Electronics Corp. in Gardena, Calif., and a self-described "dyed-in-the-wool Republican," gave a small amount to publisher Steve Forbes' first bid for the

One in three of Bush's volunteer Maryland fundraisers is a relative newcomer to politics, said the governor's state finance chairman. Many came to this July 14 fundraiser in Baltimore.

GOP presidential nomination, in 1996, but this year he contributed the maximum $1,000 to Bush. Antrim said a letter from a longtime business associate soliciting contributions for Bush was a factor that influenced his decision.

Bush also is reactivating donors who sat out the 1996 presidential election, when Bob Dole (House 1961-69, Senate 1969-96) resigned while he was Senate majority leader to become the GOP nominee. Several of Bush's early donors made their last contributions in 1987 and 1988, when his father, George Bush, was running to succeed Ronald Reagan as president. A few contributors date back even further, to the presidential campaigns of Reagan in 1984 and former Texas Gov. John B. Connally in 1980.

A Shallow Pool for Opponents

The reach of Bush's network is bad news for his GOP opponents, who largely have been confined to the same donor pool and are losing some of their previous supporters to the Bush campaign. On the four-state list of donors who gave $1,000 to Bush, for example, are 86 people who four years ago contributed to former Education Secretary Lamar Alexander.

Bush's roster may also be disheartening for Vice President Al Gore and his only current rival for the Democratic presidential nomination, former New Jersey Sen. Bill Bradley (1979-97). Several on Bush's contribution lists are previous generous donors to Democrats. Past donations by Andrea E. Bernstein of Riverdale, N.Y., depict her as a loyal Democrat: She gave to the 1996 Clinton-Gore re-election campaign, Democratic Sen. Charles E. Schumer's 1996 House re-election campaign and 1998 Senate bid, and the Democratic National Committee. But on March 23, she wrote a $1,000 check to Bush, joining 28 other Bush contributors who had given to Clinton's 1992 or 1996 campaigns. Hollywood film director James Burrows and his wife, Debbie, both contributed to the 1998 re-election campaign of Sen. Barbara Boxer, D-Calif. James Burrows was a Clinton donor in 1996. But both contributed to Bush in 1999.

For Bradley, the CQ study offers one consolation: Seventeen individuals in New York and California have given the maximum to both him and Bush, compared with the seven who have supported both Bush and Gore. ◆

Strategy for regaining House majority is to emphasize differences between parties

Democrats Hope To Win By Staying Unified in Defeat

The tally on the electronic scoreboards in the House chamber July 22 gave Republicans a cherished victory: passage of what would be the largest tax cut since the Reagan era. But Democrats also were smiling.

Of the 209 House Democrats who cast ballots on the legislation, 97 percent voted "no" — a degree of unity that made the minority leadership gleeful. By persuading their troops to stand firm against the crown jewel of the GOP legislative strategy for holding on to control of the House, the Democratic leadership had simultaneously solidified a cornerstone of *their* strategy: Create a record for the 106th Congress that puts the differences between the two parties in stark contrast, and the voters will choose to switch control of the House back to the Democrats in November 2000.

Another Democratic rationale for turning out the GOP is that the current razor-thin and frequently fractured majority has proved incapable of governing effectively. House Democrats were able to seize a key piece of evidence to bolster that point July 21, when the scheduled markup of the biggest domestic appropri-

ations measure for fiscal 2000 — covering the departments of Labor, Health and Human Services, and Education — was called off because of the continuing internecine GOP battle over whether to devote the surplus more to spending than tax cuts. (*Appropriations, 1999 CQ Weekly, p. 1770*)

But the House Democrats' symbolic highlight of the week — if not the year — had come July 17, when iconoclastic Rep. Michael P. Forbes of New York suddenly bolted the Republican Party and announced he was joining the Democratic Caucus. The reason, he said, was that he could no longer belong to a party run by conservative "extremists." (*Forbes, 1999 CQ Weekly, p. 1778*)

"This was a great week!" grinned Robert Menendez of New Jersey, vice chairman of the House Democratic Caucus.

Forbes' defection gives the Democrats 211 seats, the same number they had until George E. Brown Jr. of California died July

CQ Weekly July 24, 1999

Still just six seats away from claiming a working majority in the House, Democrats are taking comfort in their solidarity — even when they lose legislative skirmishes. In standing aside, Democrats say GOP leaders are too "extremist" to reach out for bipartisan compromise. Republican leaders say the true motive of the minority is to be "obstructionist." Each side hopes its catchword for the other will resonate more with the voters of 2000.

CQ PHOTO / SCOTT J. FERRELL

"What I will do, if we get the opportunity, is try to move legislation in a bipartisan way," Gephardt told reporters July 15. For now, he is taking comfort in the frequent unity of his troops against GOP legislation.

Forbes' Independent Streak Persists During His Debut as a Democrat

Forbes, right, confers July 22 with acting chief of staff Kris Kolluri, on loan from the Democratic leader's office. The previous staff quit en masse after Forbes quit the GOP.

Emerging from his first meeting with the House Democratic Caucus on July 21, Republican-turned-Democrat Michael P. Forbes dodged the first two questions posed by reporters trying to gauge his loyalty to his new party: Would he now oppose the Republican tax bill? Would he now support Hillary Rodham Clinton?

"Those kinds of political decisions will have to wait for another day," Forbes said about his pick for the Senate in New York. He was even more equivocal about the tax bill. In the end he joined all but six members of his new party in voting against the measure (HR 2488). Before then, however, he had voted against the

majority of Democrats on seven of the first 19 votes that were called after he announced his surprise switch of parties on July 17.

That only added to the bipartisan perplexity created by one of the most difficult-to-explain such switches in recent congressional history — and the first from Republican to Democratic since Rep. Donald W. Riegle Jr. of Michigan in 1973. (Riegle later won three terms in the Senate.) Forbes' move also set the stage for a political battle in New York's 1st District, which GOP leaders had thought was a seat they did not have to worry about while trying to hold on to their House majority next year.

Forbes told his constituents that he was quitting a GOP that "has become an angry, narrow-minded, intolerant and uncaring majority, incapable of governing at all — much less from the center — and tone-deaf to the concerns of a vast majority of Americans."

Republicans bid good riddance and vowed to end Forbes' congressional career next fall. "I thought it was probably one of the most unique

15. Because they can normally count on the vote of independent Bernard Sanders of Vermont, the minority's total potential strength is 212 votes — just six fewer than the number needed to guarantee legislative victory.

To claim political victory, however, they have concluded that what they need to do is to stay as unified as possible in defeat, and the week of July 19 was the latest in a recent period in which they have had considerable success in achieving that aim.

While Democratic leaders were holding all but six votes against the tax bill (HR 2488), they watched as GOP leaders worked feverishly to alter the legislation enough to assuage both a dozen doubtful party moderates and a cadre of conservatives — either of which could have sunk the bill altogether.

But it was Forbes' announcement

that served as the exclamation point to the Democrats' chief debating point: That Republicans are not interested in bipartisan compromises on issues that are on the minds of the electorate, from education to health insurance to campaign finance.

"Forbes is the best argument and validates what we have been saying," Minority Leader Richard A. Gephardt, D-Mo., said in an interview July 21.

"Does the Speaker want to work with those in the middle and, frankly, help the Republican Party, or does he want to go to the right?" Gephardt asked, referring to J. Dennis Hastert, R-Ill., who took office this year with the pledge that he would be a better listener — and a more collegial leader — than his predecessor, Newt Gingrich, R-Ga. (1979-99).

Predictably, Gephardt's question is

dismissed by Republicans, who view the minority leader as the person in the House least interested in compromise. Instead, they charge, Gephardt hopes to become Speaker by leveraging Democratic opposition into a "do-nothing" record for the 106th Congress. (*1999 CQ Weekly, p. 1696*)

"The do-nothing Democrats have become the have-nothing party," Majority Leader Dick Armey, R-Texas, said in a floor speech July 20 that repeated this Republican theme. "They have no ideas; they have no solutions. They only have partisan, risky, political schemes."

"That's why they are still in the minority, and they will stay in the minority," added Majority Whip Tom DeLay, R-Texas, as the votes were cast on the Republican tax package. "They just don't get it."

retirement announcements I have observed in a long time," quipped House Majority Leader Dick Armey, R-Texas. At least six senior GOP officials at the eastern end of Long Island now are considering a run.

Even Minority Leader Richard A. Gephardt, D-Mo., said he was dumbfounded in June when he first started discussions with Forbes. Gephardt called the defection a validation of the longstanding Democratic argument that "the Republican Party has been hijacked by the extreme right wing."

Nonetheless, the transition was troublesome for Democrats, too. Gephardt made about 50 telephone calls to New York Democrats to dissuade them from backing a primary challenge to Forbes by Tony Bullock, chief of staff to retiring Sen. Daniel Patrick Moynihan, D-N.Y. Democrats had to arrange overnight to assemble at least a temporary team of aides for Forbes, whose GOP staff resigned en masse July 19. And aides said it may take several weeks for Gephardt to finalize an unusual arrangement under which several other Democrats would take a series of short, temporary leaves in order to allow Forbes to stay on the Appropriations Committee.

GOP leaders, meanwhile, arranged to temporarily fill the GOP vacancy on the panel with Chief Deputy Majority Whip Roy Blunt of Missouri until they could decide among at least a half-dozen applicants for the unanticipated opening.

A Self-Confident Iconoclast

Having defeated a four-term Democrat as part of the 1994 GOP sweep, Forbes was rewarded with an Appropriations seat as a freshman and backed the "Contract With America" before beginning to stake out a reputation as a showy and self-confident iconoclast — siding with Democrats on several high-profile issues and opposing a second term as Speaker for Newt Gingrich, R-Ga. (1979-99).

Still, Forbes is a firm foe of abortion, backed repealing the ban on certain assault weapons, generally supported GOP leaders on fiscal policy and voted for President Clinton's impeachment. This year, he endorsed Gov. George W. Bush, R-Texas, for president and — weeks before going to the Oval Office to discuss his possible switch — asked Speaker J. Dennis Hastert, R-Ill., to sign a fundraising letter in his behalf.

"Most people go through their midlife crises in private. Mike is going through it in a very public manner," said Rep. Thomas M. Davis III, R-Va., chairman of the National Republican Congressional Committee.

"If this was about politics, this would not have happened," Forbes, who turned 47 a day before his announcement, said in an interview July 20. The decision, which he is "greatly at peace with," was based only on policy differences. He cited his recent annoyance with the GOP for arranging debates on resolutions — one calling for a day of prayer and fasting, the other condemning sex between adults and children — instead of legislation on patients' rights, environmental protection and campaign finance.

Because Forbes risked so much, his motives should not be questioned, Democrats said. John P. Murtha, D-Pa., who has often bucked his leadership, predicted that the party will be tolerant of Forbes' conservative views. "All I told him was to stick to his principles," Murtha said after a talk with Forbes.

Republicans maintained that the decision was driven by ego and frustration at being back outside the GOP inner circle. Forbes' stock inside the GOP Conference, which plummeted after his open opposition to Gingrich, had soared in the few weeks when his chief patron, Robert L. Livingston, R-La. (1977-99), became the presumed Speaker and tapped Forbes as one of his top lieutenants.

"I think he made a mistake," said GOP moderate Peter T. King of Long Island. "To me, there's plenty of room in the Republican Party for us to fight over what we believe in."

The Recent Pattern

What the Democratic leadership has gotten in recent months is rare party unity, which jelled after last November — the first time since 1934 that the party in control of the White House gained seats in the House in a midterm election.

Guided by President Clinton's popular agenda — topped with shoring up Social Security and Medicare, regulating health maintenance organizations and boosting aid to education — House Democrats have settled into a pattern in which they call for legislation that they know Republicans will oppose, voting against the top-priority GOP measures virtually en masse, then standing back and watching the Republican hierarchy struggle with their working six-seat majority to pass bills that can navigate the crosscurrents of Republican conservatives and moderates.

With this pattern in place, each side has framed its case with a single word: Democrats say Republicans are "extremist" while Republicans call Democrats "obstructionist."

Members on both sides acknowledge that this hardening of partisan position has not only made compromise on important legislation less likely, but also has fueled public cynicism about Congress.

Even in the rare instances of bipartisan accord, mistrust runs high. Fearful of a last-second double-cross, before taking the Africa trade bill (HR 434) to the floor July 16, Republicans insisted on receiving from the other side's leadership a written list of Democrats who were committed to the legislation. (CQ *Weekly*, p. 1742)

Republicans and Democrats may talk about wanting to work together, but they privately acknowledge that factions in each party believe ideological splits will motivate their voter base in 2000.

At this point, it is impossible to predict who will control the House after the next election, although some veteran congressional watchers suggest that at the moment the rhetorical and policy advantage goes to the Democrats.

"The president has demonstrated a remarkable ability to shape the agenda and has done so in ways that allow Democrats to talk about issues that are comfortable to them, while forcing Republicans to divide, rather than unify. And Republicans have responded by putting off some of those issues," Thomas E. Mann, a Brookings Institution senior fellow, said July 14 at a meeting of the Republican Main Street Partnership, which promotes moderate GOP views.

By declaring a desire to dedicate so much of the hard-sought surplus on tax cuts, he said, Republicans have given Democrats an opening to seize a mantle that has traditionally been held by the GOP: chief advocates of paying down the $3.6 trillion national debt.

"I don't have any confidence now in forecasting which party will emerge politically victorious from this particular engagement. I do think the Republicans are running a very risky strategy in embracing a very ambitious tax cut proposal, given the nature of public opinion and the ordering of priorities that they have demonstrated," Mann concluded.

While public opinion polls rank tax cuts below education, Social Security and Medicare on the list of voters' priorities, a recent bipartisan survey suggested that Democrats should not get too comfortable. In February, after Clinton was acquitted in his impeachment trial, Democrats held about a 10 percentage point lead when pollsters asked, generically, which party should be elected to Congress. That lead has statistically disappeared, according to the "Battleground 2000" survey released in June by Republican strategist Ed Goeas and Democrat strategist Celinda Lake.

Those polled, however, preferred the Democrats' strategy to shore up Social Security and Medicare over the GOP plan to put the Social Security trust fund in a "lockbox" while cutting taxes. Health care continues to work in Democrats' favor, the survey concluded, but Republicans have cut in half what was once a 30-point lead for Democrats when those polled were asked which party is a better steward on education.

"Democrats need to have visible and aggressive fights with the Republicans on investing in education and safe schools, a patient bill of rights and strengthening Medicare" in order to be successful, Lake suggested.

Charges of Obstructionism

Democrats fought over a GOP education bill July 20 — but the disagreement was within their own ranks, as 24 Democrats bucked the party line and supported a teacher training measure (HR 1995). The outcome gave the GOP a "do-nothing Democrats" debating point, but it also gave Democratic leaders some small consolation in that they held together enough votes to suggest they could sustain a promised Clinton veto. (*Teacher training, 1999 CQ Weekly, p. 1787*)

To bolster their "obstructionist" charge, Republicans point to the fi-

nancial services bill (HR 10), which Democrats originally moved to block because Republicans dropped language that Democrats maintained would have prevented discrimination in lending. (*1999 CQ Weekly, p. 1675*)

In enacting the law (HR 775 — PL 106-37) to limit the liability of companies that fail to fix Year 2000 computer glitches, Republicans say, they had to overcome early Democratic objections. But even then the measure — which pitted trial lawyers against high-tech companies and small businesses — did not move until Clinton stepped in to cut a deal. (*Y2K provisions, 1999 CQ Weekly, p. 1815*)

GOP leaders also carry their Democratic obstructionists charge to the debate over gun control.

"We had a bill on the floor that had four of the five points that the Democrats wanted, and they voted it down, thus exhibiting their longstanding lack of understanding that the perfect is the enemy of the good," Armey told reporters June 22.

The argument infuriates Democratic leaders, who argue that it was a team of pivotal Republicans who gutted the gun control bill (HR 2122) in order to ensure its defeat on June 18. Still, conferees may be appointed to a related juvenile crime bill (HR 1501) the week of July 26.

The Democrats' list goes on.

"Who is holding up campaign finance reform? Who has watered down patients' bill of rights?" asked Rosa DeLauro, D-Conn., in discussing why her party has launched a series of discharge petitions that would force action on legislation over GOP leaders' objections. In the absence of unexpected GOP signatures, however, none are expected to succeed.

On managed care regulation, Republican infighting has kept legislation bottled up in committee. Several Republicans are threatening to vote with Democrats on various amendments to improve patient protections.

Now, the Commerce Committee is drafting language, opposed by GOP leaders but backed by Democrats, that would let patients sue their health insurers for damages. Chairman Thomas J. Bliley Jr., R-Va., is working with John D. Dingell, D-Mich., a partnership supported at this stage by Gephardt. (*Managed care, 1999 CQ Weekly, p. 1789*)

"We want a bill," Gephardt said, so if Dingell "can work out a bill, we're for it."

Separately, a small group of Democrats, including moderate Cal Dooley of California, are working with Ways and Means Health Subcommittee Chairman Bill Thomas, R-Calif., on a broad Medicare overhaul that goes beyond the current narrow debate over how to add a prescription drug benefit to the program this year.

"I think that Democrats do best politically when they are advancing good policies, whether or not it's a bipartisan or a partisan approach," Dooley said.

Rhetoric vs. Reality

There is talk of bipartisanship on both sides, but only up to a point.

"We have a six-vote lead. You cannot just put the blame here. People expect us to work with parties to get things done. Dennis Hastert knows that; Dick Gephardt knows that," said Thomas M. Davis III, R-Va., chairman of the National Republican Congressional Committee. Still, he said, Democratic "rhetoric does not match the reality."

A similar charge is returned by Joseph M. Hoeffel, D-Pa., a freshman in a marginal district whose defeat is a top Republican priority.

"They hate Clinton so much they cannot seem to see straight or walk straight," Hoeffel said of the GOP. "Whatever Clinton is for the Republican majority is against."

Part of the GOP frustration is with Clinton's ability to shape public debate, even during the nadir of impeachment. Given that, even the man in charge of House GOP communications strategy is not overly confident his side can win the public relations war.

"One reason, I think, the president is good at communicating is he knows how to tap into people's values, whether they agree with him or not," Republican J.C. Watts Jr. of Oklahoma said July 21.

If the result is a Democratic House in 2001, Gephardt told reporters July 15, he will run the House differently than the GOP has since 1995.

"What I will do, if we get the opportunity, is try to move legislation in a bipartisan way. Look, when you've got a small majority you have no choice but to try to reach over to the other side of the aisle and get a lot of Republicans and a lot of Democrats to support sound, moderate legislation."

Is there middle ground on some of this year's big issues? "I guess I think the middle is a little bit different than some people do," Gephardt replied. ◆

Leaders dig in as some put odds for a deal at 'no way under any condition'

Parties' Plan on Spending, Taxes: Do Nothing Rather Than Yield

Clinton speaks to Democrats at a rally on Capitol Hill on Aug. 5 . He has promised to veto Republicans' $792 billion tax cut package. Behind Clinton is House Minority Leader Richard A. Gephardt, D-Mo.

The question for Congress is not when but whether partisanship on the budget and taxes will ever yield to dealmaking and legislation.

Earlier this year, many lawmakers would have said yes. Over the past several weeks, however, battle lines have hardened, and it appears increasingly likely that budget gridlock will grip the Capitol after President Clinton carries out his promise to veto the GOP's $792 billion tax bill (HR 2488).

In the wake of impeachment and with presidential and congressional elections little more than a year away, the atmosphere in the Capitol has rarely been so partisan. Relations between the congressional majority and a president from the other party have not featured so much distrust and disdain since Watergate.

After passing their massive tax cut, many Republicans are not eager to compromise with Clinton — even if it means they get no tax cut at all. Instead, said Senate Majority Whip Don Nickles, R-Okla., "We might wait 18 months and have a new president and get a good tax bill." Added Majority Leader Trent Lott, R-Miss.: "Sometimes inaction is better than the wrong action."

If the size of the surplus — $161 billion in 2000 alone — were the only consideration, one could easily envision a deal. The 1997

budget deal, which did not project a surplus until 2002, contained a tax cut of only $89 billion over five years. (*1997 Almanac, p. 2-3*)

But Senate Republicans are increasingly cool to the idea of making a deal. And while House GOP leaders are more receptive, they are hobbled by a four-vote majority and a Democratic minority dead set against the idea.

Furthermore, Clinton has set an almost impossible threshold for agreement on taxes: revamping Medicare. Administration officials vow that Clinton will veto any tax bill not preceded by a Medicare bill.

That will prove enormously difficult.

"Everybody keeps talking about how we're going to do a Medicare bill this year. We're not. It's not going to happen," said Sen. John D. Rockefeller IV, D-W.Va. Rockefeller is just as dubious on taxes: "If Clinton holds firm on vetoing any [tax cut] over $300 billion, there's no way the Republicans are going to settle for that. There's no way under any condition. . . . I think he will [hold firm] and therefore there's no resolution possible."

Added Sen. Connie Mack, R-Fla.: "I'm not very optimistic at all. I just don't see anything on their side that indicates they're serious about getting legislation through."

On the House side, Republicans appear more eager to reach a deal with Clinton. "Let's say there's a $350 billion tax bill. I think that's a win," said Rep. Robert L. Ehrlich Jr., R-Md., a confidant of House Speaker J. Dennis Hastert, R-Ill. "Anything in positive [tax cut] numbers is a win."

Added a senior House GOP aide: "Sooner or later, Republicans are going to sit down with the White House and work stuff out. It's going to happen. It always does."

After a July 12 meeting at the White House, there was a boomlet of optimism for a potential agreement. But it began to fizzle a few weeks later after White House officials promised that Clinton would veto a tax bill of $500 billion over 10 years. Such a measure, backed by moderate Senate Democrats and Republicans, would roughly split the difference between Clinton's proposals and the GOP-passed bill.

Buying Down Debt

Even as they touted their tax bill, Republicans began to signal that devoting the surplus to buying down the national debt would be preferable to a deal on Clinton's terms.

The message: Failure is an option. If there is no deal on taxes, there is that much more of the budget surplus available to reduce the national debt — an outcome that both liberal and conservative economists agree would be the single best use of the surplus, and one favored by many lawmakers.

"There's a strong possibility that nothing would be done . . . and all of that money would go to buy down the debt," said Sen. Larry E. Craig, R-Idaho.

The White House position is that paying down debt is preferable to cutting taxes. It will occur automatically if Clinton vetoes all tax bills and Congress avoids too much new spending.

"It would be better to do nothing and pay down . . . our national debt than to sign a large and irresponsible tax cut that would send a signal to the world that the era of fiscal discipline in the United States is over," National Economic Council Chairman Gene Sperling said Aug. 1 on NBC's "Meet the Press."

Still another factor invites deadlock: bipartisan vows not to use Social Security revenues to finance tax cuts or new spending. Clinton rocked Republicans on their heels in his 1998 State of the Union speech with the warning to "save Social Security first." That scuttled any chance last year for a tax cut from the newfound surplus. This year, Republicans vowed not to "spend" any portion of the surplus generated from Social Security revenues. But ever more promis-

ing budget estimates project non-Social Security surpluses that Republicans can claim for tax cuts.

This "on-budget" surplus (projected at $14 billion in 2000 and $38 billion in 2001) is likely to be consumed entirely by increases in appropriations, however, especially over the next few years. That would leave little money available for a tax cut unless lawmakers chose to retreat from their pledge to put Social Security surpluses in a "lockbox."

Different in 1997

This is the fifth budget cycle in which majority Republicans have squared off against Clinton. Only once, in 1997, have they agreed on taxes. But the 1997 budget deal (PL 105-33, PL 105-34) was crafted in an environment much different from this one. Both Republicans and Clinton viewed the split-decision 1996 election as a mandate from the public to work together. Much of the deal built on earlier GOP budget frameworks and Clinton's submission of a balanced budget. Clinton pushed hard for a deal, and months of secret talks preceded the handshake.

Today's landscape is not the same. Leaving the surplus alone is an acceptable option. There has been none of the spadework that led to the 1997 agreement. Republicans say Clinton killed the most significant work, a Medicare plan devised by Sen. John B. Breaux, D-La., co-chairman of the National Bipartisan Commission on the Future of Medicare. (*1999 CQ Weekly, p. 703*)

"It just doesn't seem at this point that it's as likely to come together as before," said Martin C. Corry, top lobbyist for the AARP, which represents senior citizens. "There was a caucus that believed there was potential for a deal. . . . Right now it looks like that caucus could fit in a phone booth in the Longworth Office Building."

Instead of following the bipartisan model of 1997, Republicans appear to be following the approach that worked when they passed the 1996 welfare overhaul. "It could be that the Republicans are looking at the model of welfare reform, where you go through vetoes and eventually you bring the president to sign the bill that you want him to sign," said Arne Christensen, former chief of staff to Speaker Newt Gingrich, R-Ga. (1979-99), now a lobbyist for home mortgage giant Fannie Mae.

But Republicans sent the welfare

overhaul (PL 104-193) to Clinton months before his 1996 re-election. The political pressure on Clinton, who had vowed during the 1992 campaign to "end welfare as we know it," was considerably more intense than he feels now on taxes. (*1996 Almanac, p. 6-3*)

Clinton and Democrats feel no pressure on tax cuts, which voters typically rank below Social Security, Medicare and education in public opinion polls. "This tax bill, after it passed . . . had absolutely no traction," said Rep. Robert T. Matsui, D-Calif.

Also, the 1997 agreement was massaged by senior White House officials such as former Chief of Staff Erskine Bowles and Office of Management and Budget (OMB) Director Franklin D. Raines, both of whom were trusted by Republicans. That cannot be said of current OMB Director Jack Lew or Chief of Staff John D. Podesta. "There is no trust," said a senior Senate GOP aide. "The people at the White House are not Erskine Bowles. . . . There is just no sense of an ability to work with them."

At the same time, Republicans are split between those who want an agreement on taxes, even if it is only $300 billion, and those who would not accept so little. Senate Budget Committee Chairman Pete V. Domenici, R-N.M., floated the idea of keeping open the tax reconciliation bill (HR 2488) — the only Senate vehicle not subject to a filibuster — to retain the option of using it after reaching a deal with Clinton in the fall. The idea was summarily rejected by Lott.

Several lawmakers and staff aides said House Republicans are more eager than their Senate counterparts to reach an agreement in the fall. "The House believes emotionally that they must return to their voters in November [2000] with a major accomplishment," said a senior Senate GOP aide. "We tried this little game in 1997 . . . that we'd be able to give ourselves a heaping teaspoon of extra credit come November 1998. It didn't work out that way. Nobody remembered that we passed a tax cut."

At the same time, Clinton is poised to again extract concessions from congressional Republicans in the endgame on appropriations. "I don't see anything in it for the White House to come up with a deal at this point," said Stanley E. Collender, managing director of Fleishman-Hillard's Federal Budget Consulting Group. "Anything on appropriations they're going to get anyway." ◆

House leaders in a weaker position for the coming budget showdown with Clinton

GOP's Fragile Unity Fractures In Managed Care Decision

The thought no doubt has crossed their minds before, but the overwhelming defeat that was suffered by House Republicans on managed care suddenly gives a shockingly real dimension to the words "Speaker Gephardt."

If that's too much to contemplate, picture the imposing John D. Dingell, D-Mich., the former committee baron of the House who has been chafing in the minority for five years, now transfigured into the leader of a moderate swing faction.

The 275-151 vote on Oct. 7 — with 68 GOP defections from the position staked out by Speaker J. Dennis Hastert — was another defeat in a succession for GOP leaders, who time and again have been forced to cede control of the House to a bipartisan band of centrist renegades. As a consequence, the Democratic minority led by Richard A. Gephardt of Missouri has been able to set the floor agenda by craftily exploiting the slim, nine-vote spread dividing the two parties.

The bill (HR 2723) to grant new rights for patients of health insurance plans, including the right to sue insurers for coverage decisions that cause injury or harm, was written by Dingell, long-deposed chairman of the Commerce Committee, and by Charlie Norwood, a Republican dentist from Georgia, who weeks ago gave up trying to draft a bill with members of his own party.

After the dramatic floor votes, Republicans and Democrats who worked on the winning bill shared the podium at a news conference to celebrate their victory, a bipartisan display of enthusiasm rarely seen since Republicans came to power in 1995.

"This bill could not have happened if it hadn't been a bipartisan effort every step of the way," Gephardt said.

Indeed, the House has been repeatedly forced onto moderate turf on such issues as campaign finance reform and gun control. Next, the GOP leadership likely will have to contend with clamor from a similar center-left coalition for a $1 increase in the minimum wage over three years. And although they will likely win some tax breaks for small business as part of a bipartisan deal, there is

little doubt that the issue is a bigger winner for Democrats than it is for Republicans.

Squeezed on one side by Democrats, House Republicans are also being battered from the other by the GOP presidential front-runner, Texas Gov. George W. Bush.

Bush on Sept. 30 surprised House leaders by sharply attacking their plan to delay tax credits for the working poor as part of their struggle to find the funds to proceed with the nettlesome appropriations bill that pays for the Labor, Health and Human Services, and Education departments. Bush said congressional Republicans are trying to "balance their budget on the backs of the poor."

Marshall Wittmann, director of Senate relations at the Heritage Foundation, a conservative think tank, said House Republicans "are in the worst of all possible political worlds."

"They are being attacked by their own front-runner for president and seeing defections in their ranks," he said.

Spurning the Speaker's Choice

The same day the House passed the Norwood-Dingell plan, members rejected an alternative backed by Hastert, R-Ill., dismissing the Speaker's entreaties for Republicans to stick together and deny Democrats a victory. In that instance, 29 members of the GOP voted against the Speaker, who took pains to describe the alternative as a common-sense "consensus" bill.

That measure also would have opened the way for lawsuits against managed care companies, which are currently barred in most cases, but it put several obstacles in the way of plaintiffs, including giving an independent auditor the power to block suits.

In coming weeks, the House leadership may be able to shape the legislation more to its liking in negotiations with the Senate. A companion bill (S 1344) passed by the Senate on July 15 has no similar provision granting patients the right to sue, suggesting that the final legislation will have to be an altered version of the House bill. The sheer numbers

Quick Contents

The House-passed managed care bill may have been a product of bipartisanship, but GOP leaders were sidelined. They were caught, as one analyst put it, in the "worst of all possible political worlds."

Managed Care Rebels

In the end, 68 Republicans voted for the bipartisan managed care bill (HR 2723), but some of them had voted for other versions earlier. This chart tracks how the 68 voted on the GOP access plan (vote 485), the Boehner substitute (vote 487), the Goss-Coburn-Shadegg substitute (vote 488) and finally the Norwood-Dingell bill (vote 490). Votes for the entire House are on p. 2408-2410.

Member	485	487	488	490	Member	485	487	488	490	Member	485	487	488	490	Member	485	487	488	490
Bachus	Y	N	N	Y	Davis	Y	N	Y	Y	Jenkins	Y	Y	Y	Y	Saxton	Y	N	N	Y
Barr	Y	N	N	Y	Diaz-Balart	Y	N	Y	Y	Jones, N.C.	Y	Y	Y	Y	Sessions	Y	N	Y	Y
Bateman	Y	N	Y	Y	Duncan	Y	N	Y	Y	Kelly	Y	N	Y	Y	Shaw	Y	N	Y	Y
Bilbray	Y	N	N	Y	Foley	Y	N	N	Y	King	Y	N	N	Y	Shays	Y	N	Y	Y
Bilirakis	Y	Y	Y	Y	Franks	Y	N	N	Y	LaTourette	Y	N	Y	Y	Sherwood	Y	Y	Y	Y
Boehlert	Y	N	N	Y	Frelinghuysen	Y	N	N	Y	Leach	Y	N	N	Y	Smith, N.J.	Y	N	N	Y
Bono	Y	N	Y	Y	Gallegly	Y	N	Y	Y	LoBiondo	Y	N	N	Y	Spence	Y	N	Y	Y
Brady	Y	Y	Y	Y	Ganske	N	N	N	Y	McCollum	Y	N	N	Y	Sweeney	Y	N	Y	Y
Callahan	Y	Y	Y	Y	Gibbons	Y	Y	Y	Y	McHugh	Y	N	Y	Y	Thornberry	Y	N	Y	Y
Canady	Y	N	Y	Y	Gilchrest	Y	N	Y	Y	Moran	Y	N	Y	Y	Vitter	Y	N	Y	Y
Cannon	Y	Y	Y	Y	Gilman	N	N	N	Y	Morella	N	N	N	Y	Walsh	Y	N	Y	Y
Castle	Y	N	Y	Y	Graham	Y	N	Y	Y	Norwood	N	N	N	Y	Wamp	Y	N	Y	Y
Chambliss	Y	Y	Y	Y	Greenwood	Y	N	Y	Y	Porter	Y	N	Y	Y	Weldon, Fla.	Y	Y	Y	Y
Coble	Y	Y	Y	Y	Hefley	Y	Y	Y	Y	Quinn	Y	N	N	Y	Weldon, Pa.	Y	Y	Y	Y
Coburn	Y	N	Y	Y	Horn	Y	N	N	Y	Reynolds	Y	N	Y	Y	Wilson	Y	N	Y	Y
Cook	Y	N	N	Y	Hunter	Y	N	Y	Y	Ros-Lehtinen	Y	N	Y	Y	Wolf	Y	N	Y	Y
Cooksey	Y	N	Y	Y	Hyde	Y	Y	Y	Y	Roukema	Y	N	N	Y	Young, Fla.	Y	N	Y	Y

of House Republicans who crossed over to support it suggests that Senate conservatives could pay a price if they go too far in weakening the House version.

The managed care outcome weakens House leaders considerably as they head into a difficult season of resolving spending issues with Clinton. At the moment, congressional Republicans are having a hard time finishing the 13 must-do appropriations bills for fiscal 2000, and the bills of consequence they have managed to send to the president, he has threatened to veto. It all adds up to a trying budget endgame for Republican House leaders, who since the 1995-96 government shutdown fiasco with Clinton have been perennial whipping boys in any fiscal dealings with the White House.

The problem only worsened with the election in November 1998, which narrowed the GOP hold on the House to just five seats above a majority.

"They have never adjusted to the fact that they are only nominally in control," said Larry J. Sabato, a University of Virginia political scientist. "It will be very difficult for them to negotiate on a united front in the upcoming budget battles."

Added Wittman of the Heritage Foundation: "The bottom line here is: How do you get out of town with your dignity in November?"

A Speaker who made his reputation for an ability to build consensus was oddly frustrated for several weeks by his inability to find one on health care, long one of his pet issues.

When Hastert finally endorsed the GOP consensus bill Oct. 5, just two days before the scheduled vote, it was far too little time to put together the necessary 218 votes for passage, especially considering the serious divisions in GOP ranks over how far-reaching the liability provision should be.

Republicans who worked on the legislation attributed the fatal delay to the reluctance of House leaders, most notably Hastert and Majority Leader Dick Armey, R-Texas, to acknowledge that their preferred position — a bill with no lawsuit provision — was not likely to prevail in the House.

"The Speaker has strongly held views that opening the door to liability is a mistake," said John Shadegg, R-Ariz., who cosponsored the GOP bill. "He had to come to grips with that, and it took a while."

Armey said: "There were people like myself who held out hopes for the right approach."

Hastert fended off a similar attempt to include the right to sue managed care firms in a patients' rights bill he co-authored last year, when he was chief deputy whip under Newt Gingrich, R-Ga. (1979-99), whom he succeeded as Speaker. That bill passed the House narrowly, 216-210, on July 24, 1998, and never saw Senate action.

(*1998 Almanac, p. 14-3*)

James C. Greenwood, R-Pa., a moderate and cosponsor of the GOP leaders' alternative, said the leadership for several weeks seemed to think it could block the liability provision because it succeeded in doing so in the previous Congress.

"The leadership began the debate thinking we could do that again," Greenwood said. "The reality is, they won only [narrowly] in the 105th Congress, and given the fact that we lost seats since then, it stands to reason that their position does not carry the day in the 106th."

Other conservatives were also waking up to the new reality. "There's only so much you can do when 80 percent of the people want HMO reform," said Republican Mark Souder of Indiana. "You end up fighting a battle that is not winnable."

Hastert acknowledged that his effort to find a consensus position for Republicans that included a liability provision had been painstaking and slow. And at the time, the leadership was distracted by several problems with the appropriations bills.

"It took a long time to get people in agreement," Hastert said in an interview, noting the wide range of Republicans who finally coalesced around it, from moderate Greenwood to conservatives like Shadegg and Tom Coburn of Oklahoma. Also sponsoring the leadership alternative were Porter J. Goss of

Florida and Bill Thomas of California, chairman of the Ways and Means Health Subcommittee.

Then, when Hastert finally threw his weight behind what he believed to be the middle-ground approach devised by the authors, it was too late. The Speaker was boxed in by his own deadline to hold a vote. "I wasn't about to postpone the vote," he said. "I told

gage the vaunted arm-twisting operation of Majority Whip Tom DeLay, R-Texas, out of concern that it would only anger already divided Republicans.

Rather, the Speaker deployed an informal whip team, including the authors of the Goss-Coburn-Shadegg bill, committee chairmen and deans of state delegations , who button-holed colleagues and gently pressed them for support.

who were united behind Norwood-Dingell. Moderate Marge Roukema said the Speaker tried to convince them that the leadership alternative "satisfied everybody."

Nevertheless, each of the six Republicans in the delegation, including Roukema, voted against the bill.

Democrats were as united as Republicans were splintered, which compounded the leadership's troubles. Ways and Means ranking member Charles B. Rangel, D-N.Y., said that in caucus meetings preceding the vote, Gephardt stressed the need for Democrats not only to unite behind the Norwood-Dingell bill but also to stick together in opposing the GOP alternative.

That meant that Hastert had nowhere to go other than his own caucus to find votes for the alternative. And he would have to hold just about every Republican, a virtually impossible task given the differences of opinion in the GOP.

Only two Democrats crossed party lines to vote for the Hastert-backed measure, Virgil H. Goode Jr. of Virginia and Ken Lucas of Kentucky.

Yet Hastert, despite his earlier misgivings about granting patients greater access to court remedies, is determined to produce a bill for the president, whether or not Clinton signs it, said spokesman John Feehery.

From left, Coburn, Greenwood and Shadegg listen to Thomas as he discusses the failure of their substitute legislation, which had been endorsed by the House leadership.

members we would have the vote at this time, and I stuck to my word."

Fellow Republicans say the leadership was handicapped by a political "tin ear," as the public's unhappiness with managed care escalated and a core GOP constituency — doctors from the American Medical Association – agitated for Congress to respond.

"We should have been doing this last year," said Mark Foley, R-Fla., who supported the Norwood-Dingell bill. "No one was paying attention to the people back home."

Resigned to Defeat

By the time the day of the vote rolled around, House leaders dejectedly admitted they were probably beaten before the voting began. Hastert declined to en-

"We have a narrow majority, and so you can't on every issue force people into boxes, especially when you have such a divergence of opinion," said a leading House Republican, speaking on condition of anonymity.

"There really was no illusion that there would be a victory on this," said David Dreier, R-Calif., chairman of the Rules Committee. "Sure, there was hope. But realistically, no."

Armey spokeswoman Michele Davis said the job of leadership is "recognizing where the votes are and when you can move things, and when you can't."

Hastert personally appealed for votes in some cases, with mixed results. For instance, at Thomas' urging, he called a meeting the day before the vote with New Jersey Republicans,

If Clinton winds up signing legislation that includes some Republican priorities, like the tax breaks, Republicans could claim at least a partial victory. And, by the time the 2000 election rolls around, they may even get a little credit for the managed care reforms.

William F. Connelly Jr., a political scholar at Washington and Lee University who has studied the congressional Republicans, says the public tends to credit legislative accomplishments to the party in control, long after the fine points of who supported what are forgotten.

"It's not clear that the public is going to make the distinction that it was a Democratic agenda item," Connelly said. "There still is some reasonable hope that they will come out of this OK." ◆

To hear Dr. Dan McCoy tell it, he did not leave the Republican Party, the Republican Party left him.

Doctors and GOP, Longtime Allies, Part Company on Managed Care

AMA President Thomas R. Reardon, center, appeared at a news conference Sept. 23 with Norwood, left, and Dingell, right, to promote their managed care bill.

Like many of his peers, the dermatologist from Corsicana, Texas is looking at the Democratic Party for the first time as a potential political home. Doctors, once solidly loyal to the GOP, are finding that their concerns are more likely to find a voice in the party that traditionally has represented hard hats and blue collars.

"I think the Republican Party has missed the boat on managed care," Mc-Coy said. "There was a time when doctors would have considered it medical malpractice to support the Democratic Party. I think that's changing."

The advent of managed care in the nation's health care delivery system in the past decade has radically changed the medical workplace. Many doctors believe they have lost their independence to insurance companies, which they complain are putting cost considerations ahead of patient care and in-

terfering with the medical judgments of physicians.

"I don't think physicians have ever been so upset and so concerned," said Dr. Thomas R. Reardon, president of the American Medical Association (AMA).

After many years of sharing the GOP's philosophy of less government, physicians are now calling for more government regulation of insurers, a view more often shared by Democrats.

At a gathering of politically active doctors at the Mayflower Hotel Sept. 22-23 in Washington, the AMA arranged for Vice President Al Gore and Sen. Edward M. Kennedy, D-Mass., to speak. Also appearing were Republican Reps. Greg Ganske of Iowa, Charlie Norwood of Georgia and Sen. Peter G. Fitzgerald of Illinois, all of whom have supported the doctors' side in the current debate.

A group of doctors on Sept. 23 sponsored a fundraising event for House Minority Leader Richard A.

Gephardt, D-Mo., raising $100,000 for Gephardt.

"The managed care issue is putting many physicians left of center," said Connie Barron, chief lobbyist for the Texas Medical Association. "They view Democrats as friends for the first time, and it's kind of a shock for some of them."

Issues important to physicians over the next few years may serve to strengthen the bond. Democrats are more apt to be sympathetic to doctors as they seek greater powers to collectively bargain with managed care companies and more protections for the privacy of medical records. (*Collective bargaining,* 1999 CQ *Weekly, p. 877; privacy, p. 1468*)

The question remains whether the partisan shift represents a permanent realignment or an issue by issue drift between the parties.

Physicians continue to contribute more to the GOP than to Democrats. In 1997 and 1998, the AMA's political action committee gave $1.7 million to Republicans running for Congress — about 70 percent of its total — and $704,800 to Democrats. However, during the debate over President Clinton's proposed health care program in 1993-94, the AMA divided its contributions more evenly, 58 percent for Republicans and 42 percent for Democrats.

Some Republicans believe physicians will return to the fold if the health care debate turns to the issue of insuring the millions of uninsured Americans — the crux of the 1993-94 debate over Clinton's proposal.

Most Democratic fixes have called for some form of controls on doctors' payments, which physicians adamantly oppose, as do many Republicans in Congress.

Said Mark Isakowitz, a lobbyist for the managed care industry: "I suspect next time we get into a discussion of universal coverage, [physicians] may well swing to the Republican side." ◆

CQ Weekly Oct. 2, 1999

Home-districts ads, campaign donations among weapons of choice in lobbying blitz

Doctors, Insurers Step Up Lobbying Pressure in HMO Reform Debate

In a national television ad sponsored by the managed care industry, Robert A. Bonifas, a security systems company owner in Aurora, Ill., offers one of those firsthand testimonials about how proposed regulations from Washington are going to hurt the little guy.

"We work hard to give our employees health insurance," Bonifas says earnestly to the camera as he strolls through his office suite past occupied workers. "And now some politicians are bashing HMOs and adding expensive new regulations."

Like most ads of its kind, this one was aimed at a mass audience in an attempt to sway public opinion. But it also targeted a select audience of one: Speaker J. Dennis Hastert, R-Ill.

Bonifas, who is a friend and constituent of the Speaker's, served on Hastert's campaign finance committee. It is not by accident that he wound up on national television in behalf of the managed care industry.

He was recruited by The Direct Impact Co. of Alexandria, Va., a grassroots firm that specializes in identifying opinion leaders for use in lobby campaigns. Direct Impact had been hired by the American Association of Health Plans (AAHP) to find people such as Bonifas who, because of their close ties to lawmakers or stature in their districts, carry more sway than the industry's hired guns on the Hill.

"So here you had a key constituent of Hastert's on national television, saying, 'Don't do this to me,' " said Mark Merritt, AAHP's vice president and chief strategist. "It's high-tech grassroots."

The recruitment of Bonifas demonstrates how far a well-financed industry will go these days in the ever more sophisticated and aggressive business of lobbying Capitol Hill. The ad is part of an intricate, full-bore lobbying blitz leading up to an expected House showdown vote on legislation that would tighten regulations on the managed care industry. (*Health care debate*, 1999 CQ

Bonifas, an Illinois businessman who was chosen to appear in an insurance industry sponsored ad against managed care regulations, is one of Hastert's key constituents.

Directory, p. 2274)

The effort, which industry officials estimate will cost at least $10 million, involves some of the heaviest hitters inside the Beltway: on one side, the health insurance industry, allied with small employers and members of the Fortune 500-studded Business Roundtable; on the other, doctors, the American Medical Association (AMA), the American Association of Trial Lawyers and consumer groups.

In addition to national television ads, special interests have used targeted radio and TV advertising in the districts of key lawmakers as well as full-page print advertisements in the newspapers that members read back home. The health insurance industry also has paid for polls and studies supporting its contention that the legislation will result in cost increases, expose employers who provide insurance to costly lawsuits and ultimately force companies to stop providing insurance for employees. In the most recent statistical volley, the AAHP re-

leased a survey Sept. 29 that showed HMO regulation ranked 21st on the list of issues that people consider most important, far behind Social Security, Medicare and education.

Managed care's critics point to independent polls in recent months that show the majority of Americans believe there are problems in the health care delivery system. For instance, 61 percent of respondents in a CBS News survey in July said that health maintenance organizations have impeded doctors' control over medical decisions.

Both sides have employed grass-roots techniques and increasingly popular "grass-tops" strategies involving local opinion leaders like Bonifas. Washington's revolving door has been spinning, with industry groups retaining former Hill staff-cum-lobbyists who have personal contacts with members on important committees and in the leadership.

Campaign contributions are also part of the mix. The Center for Responsive Politics reported Sept. 13 that during the first six months of this year the members of the Health Benefits Coalition, a leading business group, gave more than $1.3 million in political action committee (PAC) contributions to lawmakers, more than 80 percent of it to Republicans.

For its part, the AMA PAC has given nearly $200,000 to lawmakers this year. In the last election cycle in 1997 and 1998, the doctors' PAC contributed $2.4 million, about 70 percent of that to Republicans. (*AMA politics, 1999 CQ Weekly, p. 2285*)

One of the easiest ways for a member to raise a buck at the moment is to hold a fundraiser and invite people from both sides of the issue. A $1,000-a-head event Sept. 29 for moderate and conservative "Blue Dog" Democrats attracted representatives from the AMA, the insurance industry and hospitals.

"This is a special-interest-driven debate," lamented Rep. Lindsey Graham of South Carolina, one of 21 Republicans who have crossed party lines to support tighter controls on managed care. "If you left it up to the doctors, we do away with managed care. If you left it up to the lawyers, they would have a litigation playground where employers could be sued for just offering health benefits."

Patients' Rights

The so-called patients' rights bills pending in the House aim to give patients more leverage in dealing with managed care firms that now control about 85 percent of the employer-based health insurance market. The most contentious issue is whether patients should be allowed to sue their managed care companies if they feel they have been harmed by insurers' coverage decisions.

The issue has split the old health care coalition of 1993 and 1994, when doctors, hospitals and insurers were united against President Clinton's proposal to impose sweeping regulations on the health care delivery system. This time around, doctors are opposing insurers and have allied with their old arch enemies, the trial lawyers. The doctors, lawyers and patients' groups, such as Families USA, contend that the threat of lawsuits would make health maintenance organizations and other managed care companies accountable to patients. (*1994 Almanac, p. 319*)

The insurers, knowing they are not the most loved interest group in town, are working in the Health Benefits Coalition with employers, who, as job providers, are more apt to have the sympathy of members.

"Congress is more interested in our members than they are in us," said Chip Kahn, president of the Health Insurance Association of America (HIAA), a coalition member.

The coalition includes several politically connected groups: the AAHP, The Business Roundtable (an association of chief executive officers), the U.S. Chamber of Commerce, the National Association of Manufacturers, the National Retail Federation, the National Restaurant Association, the Healthcare Leadership Council and the BlueCross BlueShield Association.

The intensity of the lobbying campaign on both sides may wind up contributing to the death of any legislation.

The managed care lobby probably will not be able to stop a bipartisan House bill (HR 2723), cosponsored by Charlie Norwood, R-Ga., and John D. Dingell, D-Mich., from passing the House. But they have a chance of winning in conference. Even if the House enters the talks in favor of allowing patients to sue their health plans, the Senate bill (S 1344) has no such provision. And any legislation coming out of the negotiations may well have provisions likely to be vetoed by Clinton, such as caps on penalties awarded in medical malpractice lawsuits. (*Senate bill, 1999 CQ Weekly, p. 1715*)

Ronald G. Shaiko, director of The Lobbying Institute at American University in Washington, said the managed care debate demonstrates how difficult it is for Congress to pass "macropolicies" that have consequential real world effects.

"Getting nothing to happen is a winning strategy for most organized interests," Shaiko said.

The question for lawmakers facing re-election in 2000: Is the status quo the best deal for consumers of health care? If not, some Republicans fear that their failure to take action this Congress will hurt them with voters at a time when they are hanging on to the majority by a thread.

Rep. John Cooksey, R-La., who also defied his leadership to support the Norwood-Dingell bill, said: "I'm afraid there is not nearly enough attention being paid to the needs of the patients."

HIAA's Kahn and others on the managed care side have tried to assuage those concerns with arguments that the issue will not be a make-or-break one for candidates in 2000.

"Half the problems with managed care have nothing to do with managed care," Kahn said. "They're problems of people's resentment that they sometimes have to fill out a form if they have a claim. . . . There are no people dying in the streets."

August Immobility

To date, a whole lot of effort has gone into making nothing happen.

During the August recess, lawmakers were peppered with broadcast advertising that in some cases went beyond generic blandishments. Rep. Mark Foley, R-Fla., said that a Business Roundtable radio ad in his district depicted him as a friend of trial lawyers, an idea Foley called "silly."

The trial lawyers' association leans heavily to the left and gives most of its political money to Democrats, making it a useful bugbear against Republicans, who generally view the group as litigation-happy and eager to expand, rather than limit, the use of civil suits.

"You have to do things to get people to think about it," said one top insurance industry lobbyist. "When you have subcommittee chairmen and members of the Republican establishment getting on a bill that's good for trial lawyers, who want to do nothing but put them in the minority, you have to remind people of that."

Another television ad that ran in targeted congressional districts invoked about every lawyer cliché known to the lobbying world. It opens with a scene of lawyers and politicians mixing it up in a noisy smoke-filled room on election night. An announcer says, "American trial lawyers have spent millions to elect their friends to Congress. Now it's payback time."

The ad does not mention the millions of dollars in campaign contributions by managed care companies to support their friends in Congress. It ends with five smirking men with slicked back hair, standing cross-armed in a courtroom.

Carlton Carl, spokesman for the trial lawyers' association, said the group's strategy is not to respond publicly to such attacks but to work behind the scenes to promote the Norwood-Dingell bill.

"People may not like lawyers, but they don't like insurance companies either," Carl said. "Anyone who has ever had to file a claim knows you can get screwed by an insurance company."

The lobby campaign reflects some subtle changes in grass-roots methodology.

The activation of everyday people to call or write letters advocating a point of view has been a lobbying staple since the 1993-94 debate. And it certainly is being employed in the current battle. Most of the broadcast ads used toll-free numbers allowing people to pick up the phone and immediately be patched through to their representative's office in Washington.

But equally important this time is the use of opinion leaders, who either have a pre-existing relationship with a lawmaker or, by dint of their profession or standing in a member's district, have a greater degree of influence than the average constituent.

Members of Congress say lobbying from both sides has generated a moderate level of phone calls and letters to their offices. However, activity at the "grass-tops" level has been brisk. Many lawmakers, especially Republicans who have supported the bill, report getting visits from influential county medical societies or from the business leaders in their districts.

For instance, the Business Roundtable had its president, Samuel L. Maury, pay a call on Rep. Amo Houghton, R-N.Y., a former roundtable member himself and former head of Corning, Inc. And Houghton also heard from several small businesses in his district who are members of the National Federation of Independent Business (NFIB), which is active in the coalition.

The visit had an impact. Houghton said that while he still supports the leading managed care bill, he is worried about employers' possible exposure to lawsuits. "There is a glitch in the Norwood-Dingell bill, and unless we can fix that, it's not a good bill," he said Sept. 22.

On a single day recently, Foley participated in a telephone conference call with several members of the roundtable in his district; Rep. E. Clay Shaw Jr., R-Fla., met with six local chambers of commerce; and Rep. Lincoln Diaz-Balart, R-Fla., met in his office with the head of the Florida Medical Association and its former head lobbyist, Donald "Scotty" Fraser, a

Houghton, shown in his office Sept. 28, is a sponsor of the Norwood-Dingell bill, but says it has one glitch.

friend of Diaz-Balart's from his days as a Florida state legislator.

Rep. Wayne T. Gilchrest, R-Md., said that since the beginning of August, "I've probably met with every doctor in every county."

During the week of Sept. 20, 80 industry chieftains paid visits to members of Congress, while the AMA arranged to have 300 physicians fan out on Capitol Hill to talk to House members.

Doctors have jumped into the lobbying action in a big way. Although politically active doctors have long represented a high-end grass-roots group on their own, they are asking their patients to also get involved.

The tactic has been employed at the state level but is being used for the first time by the powerful doctors' lobby in a national debate, said AMA President Dr. Thomas R. Reardon. "It has taken very little effort to get patients to call," Reardon said. "We want to let members know that patients are going to hold them accountable for these decisions."

Ex-Staff Members Lobby

The managed care debate has also brought a number of former staff members back to Capitol Hill, recruited by special interests hoping to make use of both their policy expertise and their

contacts with members and their top aides. All are lobbyists who once worked the health care issue from the other side.

Kahn, who heads HIAA, is the former staff director to the Ways and Means Health Subcommittee. The AAHP is getting help from Dan Meyer, who was chief of staff to former Speaker Newt Gingrich, R-Ga. (1979-99), and is now a lobbyist with the Duberstein Group Inc.; and Ed Kutler, who was Gingrich's top health policy aide and is now a lobbyist with Clark & Weinstock Inc.

AAHP in July also hired Howard Cohen, former counsel to the Commerce Committee, who has ties to Hastert and worked with the Speaker on a leadership health care task force in the 105th Congress.

Plugged-in former aides give the coalition enviable access to congressional leaders. Before the House vote, for instance, Kahn was scheduled for meetings with Majority Leader Dick Armey, R-Texas, Ways and Means Health Subcommittee Chairman Bill Thomas, R-Calif., and John A. Boehner, R-Ohio, an influential member of the subcommittee.

The coalition, which is headed by Dan Danner, vice president of the National Federation of Independent Business, has a budget of roughly $2.5 million and is run day-to-day by Mark Isakowitz, a former top lobbyist with NFIB, now with the lobby firm Fierce & Isakowitz.

The coalition has taken a hard line against any form of liability legislation, refusing to even consider compromise options. The strategy is a calculated risk, and could backfire with lawmakers if the business groups come to be viewed as too intransigent. But it is designed to keep the pro-liability forces from going even further, especially if a conference eventually agrees to some form of liability legislation.

Rep. Graham said he believes that despite the intensive lobbying, the final bill will go further than the Senate bill, which has no liability provision at all.

"Lobbying inside the Beltway is one thing," he said. "But trying to convince the American people there is no need for HMO reform is another. If we leave this Congress with our only statement being the Senate bill, we are going to get whacked at the polls." ◆

Members boxed in by promises to protect traditional benefits, proposals to create new ones

Parties Tailor Hill Agendas To Win Seniors' Loyalty

Datafile

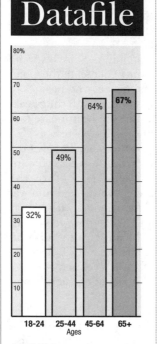

1996 Voters
Senior citizens are more likely than younger people to show up at the polls on Election Day. As the chart above shows, 67 percent of voters 65 and older voted in 1996, double the rate for those age 18-24.

SOURCE: U.S. Census Bureau

So much for the notion that the elderly are set in their ways. Since 1994, senior citizens have been abandoning Democratic congressional candidates at the polls, a shift that helped Republicans win and keep control of the House.

As the 2000 campaign approaches, Democrats are determined to reverse that trend and lure back those age 60 and over, who because of their high turnout rates make up more than a quarter of actual voters. Republicans, with a scant five-seat House majority, are just as determined to hold on to seniors, who supported them by a 10-point margin in 1998.

"Older voters are a group that both parties try to appeal to, no question about it," said Rep. E. Clay Shaw Jr., R-Fla., chairman of the Ways and Means Social Security Subcommittee.

Led by President Clinton, Democrats are trying to court those voters and their Baby Boomer children by demanding a Medicare prescription drug benefit. Republicans have vowed to protect the Social Security trust fund by enacting a legislative "lockbox" that would protect the program's surplus from being spent. There are bipartisan efforts to rewrite the Older Americans Act to aid individuals caring for elderly relatives. And, in an answer to complaints from seniors and health care providers, members of both parties are pushing measures to restore billions of dollars in Medicare funds cut in the 1997 budget law (PL 105-33). (*1997 CQ Almanac, p 2-27, 1999 CQ Weekly, reauthorization, p. 2172*)

As the end of the session approaches, however, lawmakers are seeing the risks inherent in special-interest politics. They have promised themselves into a legislative corner. GOP vows to protect Social Security, by fencing off a needed source of money, might well bring the fiscal 2000 appropriations process to a crashing halt. Republican lawmakers said the White House drive for a Medicare drug benefit could torpedo efforts for a year-end tax and budget deal.

The attention to seniors complicates an already scrambled legislative session. Republicans staked their agenda on a tax bill that did not catch fire. At the same time, the budget surplus and a booming economy have created an expectation — perhaps unrealistic — that Congress has the financial ability to make good on promises to protect Social Security and Medicare.

"The issue that's got the most energy going for it right now is the prescription drug issue," said John Rother, legislative director of the AARP. "With the lockbox, you do get a positive reaction. However, if one result of the lockbox is fairly drastic cuts in health care and services in appropriations, what was an advantage will turn into a negative."

Locked in the Lockbox

Democrats won congressional seats in the 1980s partly by accusing Republicans of trying to cut Social Security. They have tried the same tactics in the 1990s, with less success. The GOP has been winning the senior vote even as Democrats attacked them on Medicare and resurrected Social Security attacks in 1998, challenging the GOP to save the program before enacting a tax cut. (*Taxes, 1999 CQ Weekly, p. 2160*)

In 1990, 52 percent of voters age 60 and older voted for Democratic House candidates and 42 percent backed the GOP. In 1998, 44 percent of voters age 60 and over supported Democrats, 54 percent Republicans, according to exit polling by the Voter News Service. The 1998 race was the first time in recent history a majority of older women backed the GOP.

This year, Republicans, who sent a $792 billion tax cut bill (HR 2488) to Clinton on Sept. 15, have fought back. They now promise to protect the Social Security trust fund — which has been routinely used as a piggybank to pay for other federal programs — in the so-called lockbox.

"We are not going to let one dime of Social Security money be spent," House Majority Leader Dick Armey, R-Texas, said Sept. 9. "Not touching Social Security is the categorical imperative of the moment."

Older voters, an electoral battleground in 2000, are wielding their influence in Congress. At left, a small group of senior citizens demonstrated Aug. 30 outside the Olympia, Wash., office of GOP Sen. Slade Gorton, who is up for re-election next year.

AP PHOTO / LOUIE BALUKOFF

The good news for the GOP is that its slogan has caught on with voters. The bad news is that if Republicans keep their word and stay away from Social Security, they could end up billions of dollars short of cash needed for must-pass spending bills. (*Appropriations, 1999 CQ Weekly, p. 2153*)

To avoid tapping the $147 billion Social Security surplus for fiscal 2000 and comply with spending caps approved in the 1997 budget law, GOP leaders may cut Medicaid and welfare, spread out paying a tax credit for the poor or invent a host of new budget gimmicks.

With House Republicans more than $16 billion short of funds needed to pass just the spending bill for the departments of Labor, Health and Human Services (HHS), and Education, even those tactics may not be enough to keep Social Security off limits.

The lockbox "will create the biggest mess that you could possibly find," said Robert Bixby, policy director of the Concord Coalition, a budget watchdog group. "They've almost locked themselves, instead of the Social Security surplus, in this box."

Clinton, who kicked off the debate with his 1998 State of the Union call to "save Social Security first," has endorsed the concept of the lockbox, and House Democrats voted for it (HR 1259). The White House has tried to steer clear of using the Social Security surplus by seeking higher tobacco taxes and other fees to cover spending.

Minority Leader Tom Daschle, D-S.D., has blocked Republican efforts to vote on the lockbox in the Senate (S 557), complaining that the bill contained too many loopholes.

"Democrats are on the defensive," said Marit Babin, a spokeswoman for the National Republican Congressional Committee. "They are trying to get back this constituency that they can't rely on anymore because Republicans are passing legislation like the lockbox."

Medicare Drugs

Clinton and Democrats have further raised the end-of-year stakes by insisting that Congress use part of the projected federal budget surplus to create a new Medicare prescription drug benefit. White House officials have told congressional Democrats that they would not sign off on any broad tax-and-spending agreement that did not address Medicare. (*Medicare, 1999 CQ Weekly, p. 2149*)

GOP leaders now say they will not give in to new spending demands in order to get Clinton's signature on a radically slimmed-down tax bill. If that is the case, Clinton's bargaining position may be diminished. Still, the pressure for a drug benefit helped scuttle the efforts of a special bipartisan Medicare commission, disbanded in March, that was supposed to make recommendations for ensuring the long-term solvency of the health insurance program for the elderly.

And it is one of the factors complicating efforts by the Senate Finance and House Ways and Means committees to draft narrower Medicare legislation that would constrain costs by introducing more private insurance options into the system, while restoring billions of dollars in cuts made in the 1997 budget law.

Sen. John B. Breaux, D-La., holds out

hope that Congress will pass a Medicare bill that is more than a give-back and giveaway. He adds a caveat.

"Congress has traditionally caved in [to senior citizens]. That's always the possibility as we get close to the election," he said in a recent interview.

Republican lawmakers want to include a drug benefit in their Medicare bills, though it is unlikely to be as generous as the White House wants.

The AFL-CIO on Sept. 15 started running radio and television ads targeting vulnerable Republican lawmakers, urging Congress to approve a Medicare prescription drug benefit and shore up the program.

Sprinkled in the Agenda

Focusing on seniors does not necessarily mean emphasizing one generation at the expense of another. Baby Boomers, faced with caring for elderly parents, are also receptive to proposals for long-term care. Congress has already passed a bill (PL 106-4) to prevent the elderly poor and disabled from being dumped from nursing homes. (*1999 CQ Weekly, p. 713*)

"Social Security and Medicare are important to everyone — it doesn't matter if you are a senior or a 30-year-old," said Alysia Snell, senior vice president of the Democratic political consulting firm Lake, Snell, Perry and Associates.

There are important exceptions, particularly when lawmakers move from general promises to save Social Security to specific suggestions about how to do it. That is the case with legislation to ensure the long-term solvency of Social Security, which Clinton hoped would be part of his legacy.

After months of town hall meetings, White House forums and Capitol Hill hearings, Congress and Clinton all but abandoned efforts to move a bill.

There has been little willingness at the top of either party to assume the political risk of endorsing benefit cuts or tax increases that experts say are needed to keep the program solvent over the next 75 years. Social Security benefits are forecast to outpace payroll tax revenues beginning in 2014.

There are also disagreements over whether to allow individuals to invest a portion of Social Security payroll taxes in private accounts. According to a recent survey for the libertarian Cato Institute by pollster John Zogby, optional investment accounts were opposed by only about 10 percent of 18 -

to 29-year-olds, but by more than 50 percent of those 65 and older.

Some Democratic advocates of private investment said there was an opportunity to reach out to seniors, but the GOP blew it by focusing on taxes.

"When the AARP joined with the Concord Coalition and President Clinton early on to start a dialogue on Social Security, that was a good sign," said Rep. Charles W. Stenholm, D-Texas. "In the past, AARP has been knee-jerk."

Shaw has not given up. He was quietly sounding out Republicans the week of Sept. 13 to see if they would

Even though an overhaul seems unlikely this year, Commissioner Apfel, shown Sept. 13, is pleased that reserving the Social Security surplus is now "part of the vocabulary."

vote for a plan he developed with Ways and Means Chairman Bill Archer, R-Texas, to allow private accounts.

"At a time of increasing surplus, it's very hard for people to come to grips with the tough choices," Social Security Commissioner Kenneth S. Apfel said in a Sept. 13 interview.

Without the surplus, it would have been difficult for Clinton to propose a prescription drug benefit — and pick a fight with Republicans.

"The surplus, which might have tended to make it [entitlement overhaul] much easier, has moved [Congress] even further in the direction of avoiding hard decisions altogether," said Eugene Steuerle, a senior fellow at the Urban Institute, a Washington think tank.

Voting Patterns

Analysts caution against considering seniors as a monolithic voting bloc, even though Congress often does.

"Although there are issues that are very important to seniors, the senior vote is a very diverse constituency,"

said AARP's Rother.

Surveys show that a majority of voters who pollsters call "Reagan seniors" — age 60-69 — vote Republican. "Roosevelt seniors," age 70 and older, tend to vote Democratic.

"It is as much a demographic shift as it is a voter shift," said a Democratic strategist. "That's not to say that people's viewpoint won't change over time."

"They are going to be more interested in Social Security and Medicare than they were 10 or 20 years ago. That probably provides an opportunity for Democrats with a sector of voters who weren't Democrats in the past," the analyst said.

A Battleground 2000 poll released in June by Democratic pollster Celinda Lake and Republican pollster Ed Goeas of the Tarrance Group shows the diversity among older voters.

It found, for instance, that older voters were very concerned about what they saw as declining cultural values. Anger over Clinton's affair with a former White House intern may be one reason that older women voted for Republicans in 1998.

Lake has said seniors are key in the 2000 election, noting that they could play a particularly important role in many rural and small town districts.

Despite party leaders' skittishness about offending seniors, some lawmakers say there is a growing middle ground for those willing to tackle entitlements. Even the lockbox is seen as something of a breakthrough.

"Two years ago, with the larger budget deficit, the whole notion of reserving Social Security surpluses wasn't part of the vocabulary," Apfel said. "There has been a profound, bipartisan change." ◆

Veto-bound measure stalls key provisions on disclosure, portability, vesting

Rewrite of Pension Laws Handcuffed To Dead-End Tax Cut Bill

When politicians attempt to assuage the retirement concerns of the Baby Boom generation, they often discuss Social Security or incentives to shore up private savings. But another topic often overlooked on Capitol Hill is just as salient: pension law.

"It doesn't have the sex appeal, maybe, of Social Security or some other issues," said Rep. Rob Portman, R-Ohio, co-author of several pension provisions in the $792 billion GOP tax cut bill (HR 2488) that the Senate cleared Aug. 5. "But it's critically important for people facing retirement."

The Department of Labor estimates that 62.4 million of the nation's 123.9 million wage and salary workers have no kind of retirement plan. That is up from about 50 million earlier in the decade, despite incremental changes in pension law in 1996 and 1997. Only 20 percent of workers for small businesses participate in pension plans.

Social Security and private savings cannot fill in the gap for many workers, unless they are willing to live more modestly when they retire than they live now. Many analysts fear that the lack of retirement programs will affect both the Baby Boom generation, poised to start leaving the work force in 2010, and their families.

These concerns are growing as the universe of retirement plans evolves. Old-style pension plans, known as defined benefit programs, are being replaced by new accounts to which workers contribute. The traditional plans guaranteed workers a certain monthly check, often based on formulas linked to their salaries in their final years of work. The number of traditional, private plans decreased from 103,346 in 1975 to about 53,000 in 1997, according to the nonpartisan Employee Benefits Research Institute.

The newer defined contribution plans, such as tax-deferred 401(k) plans, accrue over a worker's career and are tied to the amount of money an employee invests, typically in stocks and bonds. They can generate high savings in a booming economy, but bedrock guarantees are less certain. Workers generally must contribute earnings to receive benefits.

A third plan, a hybrid pension known as a cash balance plan, is also gaining attention for its benefit to short-term workers, often at the expense of those closer to retirement. In cash-balance accounts, employees accrue benefits based on their salary throughout their working life at the company rather than in the final years.

Concerns about such new strategies, plus an awareness that many Americans are not prepared for retirement, have prompted lawmakers to endorse broad changes to the nation's pension and retirement policies. Many are included in the GOP tax package, which President Clinton has promised to veto. Some lawmakers hope pension provisions could find their way into a potential end-of-year compromise on tax cuts — although such a compromise looked unlikely as lawmakers left Washington for the summer recess. (*Tax bill, 1999 CQ Weekly, p. 1923*)

Without compromise, chances for enactment of pension changes are dim. Portman points to two other potential avenues: a minimum wage deal or a stand-alone measure. "I realize the chances for that are not very good," he said of a stand-alone bill. The problem is that "it opens up the tax code," he said, tempting other lawmakers to attach controversial tax provisions.

If Congress does not move forward this year, supporters of pension changes say they will be back next year and after the 2000 election. The issue will take on heightened prominence as the nation's Baby Boomers move closer to retirement.

Comprehensive Proposal

This year's legislation would represent the most sweeping pension overhaul since the landmark 1974 Employee Retirement Income Security Act (PL 93-406), which created federal pension protections for the nation's workers. (*1974 Almanac, p. 244*)

Most of the pension proposals in the tax bill have bipartisan support, although Democrats complain that they would not do enough for low-income workers. The proposals stem largely from a bipartisan measure (HR 1102) sponsored by Portman and Benjamin L. Cardin, D-Md., with a similar Senate counterpart (S 741) introduced by Bob Graham, D-Fla., and Charles E. Grassley, R-Iowa. Graham and Grassley also shepherded changes into the 1997 balanced-budget law (PL 105-33) aimed at making pensions more portable. (*1997 Almanac, p. 7-29*)

Quick Contents

Concerned about new-fangled company retirement plans and aware that millions of Americans have no plan at all, lawmakers have called for a broad overhaul of the nation's pension laws. They attached many proposals to the Republican tax cut bill, but President Clinton has promised to veto it — leaving the outlook for a pension overhaul uncertain.

Portman, cosponsor of several pension provisions in the Republican tax cut bill, participates in a news conference Aug. 10 on a report offering proposals to enhance retirement savings. The report was released by the American Council for Capital Formation and the Association of Private Pension and Welfare Plans.

But broad pension overhaul proposals have remained difficult to move. Adjustments have occurred recently, but in incremental provisions tacked on to larger budget bills (PL 103-66 in 1993), trade bills (PL 103-465 in 1994) or increases in the minimum wage (PL 104-188 in 1996). (*1996 Almanac, p. 7-3; 1994 Almanac, p. 123*)

Congress is reluctant to impose specific mandates on companies that are already offering benefits voluntarily. The fear is that if costs increase for employers, they might drop the coverage. Another deterrent is federal cost. Tax provisions often defer taxes, resulting in near-term loss of government revenues. This year's mammoth tax proposal would tap $35 billion over 10 years to expand individual retirement accounts (IRAs) and $15 billion to change pension law.

Pension changes are also difficult because they involve "a long-term commitment for which there is no apparent immediate gain," said Mark Ugoretz, president of the ERISA Industry Committee, which represents employer benefits plans. "And most people tend to look at these problems with one eye shut: They only see the Social Security end of it."

On the Legislative Front

This year's bill seeks to shore up retirement plans through tax-code changes.

● **Portability.** A widely supported provision would eliminate most restrictions on pension portability by allowing workers to roll over their retirement funds into different categories of plans, such as switching a 401(k) to a government plan. Current barriers often prevent people from shifting funds from one type of plan to another. In today's mobile work force, supporters say, workers should be able to carry their benefits with them to a new job.

● **Faster vesting.** Workers also would become vested — or eligible for full pension rights — more quickly. Currently, plans must allow workers to receive employer matching contributions through one of two formulas: all-at-once access to contributions after five years or a staggered schedule with full vesting after seven years. Under the bill, that timetable would move to three years or to a staggered schedule of six years.

● **Catch-up contributions.** People who left the work force at some point — such as some women who become mothers — could benefit through a provision to allow those age 50 and over to add more IRA and retirement fund contributions than normally allowed, so that they could catch up on investing.

Other provisions include eliminating certain paperwork rules for plans with assets of $250,000 or less and reducing paperwork for certain businesses with fewer than 25 workers.

Raising the Limits

One widely discussed element of the pension proposal would lift current limits on contributions, both for retirement funds and for the two types of IRAs. Some Democrats charge that Republicans are paying too much attention to increasing the contribution limits, which would help those who can afford larger contributions, and too little to broaden protection for all workers.

There are two types of IRAs: the traditional one, in which people deduct contributions at the time of investment but pay taxes on withdrawals, and the so-called Roth IRA, in which people pay taxes on contributions but not on withdrawals. Roth IRAs, named after Senate Finance Chairman William V. Roth Jr., R-Del., are often preferred by investors because both contributions and accrued earnings are tax-free upon withdrawal. Both accounts have annual contribution limits of $2,000, which would rise gradually to $5,000 under the tax bill.

Republicans would also expand IRAs. Current law does not allow people with annual incomes over a certain amount to use IRAs. The bill would raise those salary restrictions for Roth IRAs for joint filers. Current restrictions begin at $150,000 and shut people out at $160,000. The new range would be $200,000 to $210,000. The bill would permit people with incomes up to $200,000, about double the current salary cap, to convert traditional IRAs into Roth IRAs.

The bill would also alter current limits on pensions. Traditional defined benefit plans are limited by how much they can pay out to a worker in a given year. That limit in 1999 is $130,000 or the worker's total average salary, whichever is less. Defined contribution accounts are limited by how much can be added to a worker's account annually, with 1999 limits set at $30,000 or one-fourth of the worker's salary.

Congress agreed to increase those limits to $160,000 for pensions and $40,000 for defined contribution plans. The legislation would also gradually raise certain annual pre-tax contribution limits from $10,000 to $15,000.

Democrats say that instead of raising the limits, Congress should encourage more lower-income people to save money. "We're creating a system that is leaving a larger and larger number of working Americans who tend to be at the lower end of the income spectrum outside of the pension world, even though they have worked their entire lives," said a top Senate Democratic aide. "That is troubling to Democrats."

GOP leaders tout the pension provisions as a key success in their tax bill.

"If the president vetoes this bill, he vetoes these common-sense, senior-friendly tax provisions that will help American families prepare for the next century," House Speaker J. Dennis Hastert, R-Ill., said in a statement released at an Aug. 10 news conference.

"Democrats claim this bill is risky, but where's the risk in allowing workers

'Cash Balance' Controversy

A heavily lobbied issue in the battle for a pension overhaul involves new disclosure requirements for businesses when an employer switches to a retirement plan that could reduce benefits. The main target, a hybrid defined benefit plan known as a cash-balance plan, often benefits short-term workers but can cut benefits for employees with many years of service. That is because employees accrue benefits throughout their working lives and can take their benefits when they switch jobs.

Since the inception of the plans in 1985, a growing number of companies have adopted them, stirring controversy among longtime workers. Employees complain that they are often unaware of how the switch in coverage would affect them. Corporations that offer such plans include AT&T, IBM Corp., and Eastman Kodak Co.

Shorter-term workers prefer these plans because employee benefits accrue more quickly than under traditional plans, and workers who change jobs quickly often leave with more benefits than under a traditional pension. In traditional plans, benefits build slowly but balloon in the final years of work. If a company switches to a cash-balance plan, older workers may suddenly find their pensions recalculated and dramatically reduced.

Employers argue that the burden of telling each worker how the change would affect his savings is too costly. The rules could boost costs for all pension plans, companies say, which would only further erode the presence of traditional pensions.

The Senate version of the tax bill (S 1429) would have required companies moving into retirement plans that could lower the value of some workers' pensions to provide explanations of the changes. The Senate language also would have required a notice to each person who could be adversely affected if the way that benefits were determined was significantly different or if employees faced choices between plans. Sen. Tom Harkin, D-Iowa, offered an amendment to the tax bill (HR 2488) on July 30 to protect workers whose companies switch to cash-balance plans, but it was rejected, 48-52. (*Vote 245, 1999 CQ Weekly, p. 1966*)

House-Senate conferees on the tax bill sought a compromise. Rather than directly enacting disclosure proposals, Congress mandated that the Treasury Department develop disclosure rules. One result may be that companies considering a switch to cash-balance plans move quickly, before such regulations take effect.

The outcry from longer-term workers, a powerful voting bloc, is causing some lawmakers to voice concern about the cash-balance plans. "The reaction to [the plans] is forcing lawmakers to say we need to do something," said Bill Pierron, public affairs associate for the Employee Benefits Research Institute. "The political pressure is definitely there to enact something that has the appearance of being stronger enforcement."

to save more for their retirement needs?" asked Rep. E. Clay Shaw Jr., R-Fla., chairman of the Ways and Means Subcommittee on Social Security.

Unless Clinton and congressional Republicans reach an agreement, however, chances for enactment of pension changes drop off sharply. "There's no way that the pension bill by itself will be enacted," Cardin said in an Aug. 11 interview. "It has to be part of a package."

The only other likely vehicle is a minimum wage bill. The 1996 pension measure was carried by such a bill, and

advocates are looking to another one as a possibility, albeit distant.

Pension overhaul supporters understand the challenges of getting a bill passed before the 2000 elections, but remain optimistic. "We have a real opportunity to move the bill . . . this year," said James A. Klein, president of the Association of Private Pension and Welfare Plans, which represents benefit plan sponsors. Added spokeswoman Deanna Johnson Keim: "And if it doesn't happen this year, we'll be back next year." ◆

Three case studies show the political pressures of reauthorizing the education act

Education Lobbyists Mobilize for Rewrite of School Aid Law

Quick Contents

As Congress rewrites federal education law, most of the attention has been focused on broad policy issues. But a few of the act's smaller programs have brought out some big lobbyists.

There hasn't been this much hustle to enroll kids in band since Prof. Harold Hill showed up in River City. Unlike the Music Man, however, a current push by music educators to boost arts education is no false pitch, but a well-backed, highly organized effort aimed at expanding federal support for hard-pressed schools.

As Congress dives into reauthorizing the Elementary and Secondary Education Act (ESEA), the main law governing federal aid to public schools, the emerging debate offers a glimpse into the way smaller programs can put down roots and take hold in the federal bureaucracy. Once there, these entrenched programs are tough for Congress to cut or even scale back, a dynamic that is evident in both the education reauthorization and the fiscal 2000 spending bills.

Nestled within the massive ESEA are more than 30 separate programs, from the $18 million Reading Is Fundamental Inc., which distributes free books to children, to the $8 billion-a-year Title I system of aid to disadvantaged students.

While the reauthorization may not have the big-bucks cachet of a tax bill, a small army of advocates and lobbyists has descended on the Capitol to fight for preferential treatment in the law, which was last rewritten in 1994 (PL 103-382). Their efforts mean dollars and cents to school districts and private companies. They can also affect, in ways both subtle and stark, what and how students are taught.

The music push, for example, is being headed up by the National Association for Music Education, which has hired, among other consultants, the high-powered Wexler Group, a Washington lobbying firm. Wexler also represents musical instrument dealers and manufacturers as part of its coordinated campaign.

The cause has also received a boost from John Sykes, president of the the rock video channel VH1, who is leading a private drive to raise $100 million over 10 years for school music programs.

"Our parents had music and arts education available to them. You had it. I had it. Why are we taking it away from our children?" Sykes asked the Senate Health, Education, Labor and Pensions Committee in late June.

Music teachers are one just example of the special interest drives. Conservatives and feminists are at war over a $3 million program designed to ensure sex equity in schools. Architects and the Department of Education want to use $10 million a year from an existing account for grants to help communities change the way they design and use schools. The latter effort is bumping up against budget caps that are constraining fiscal 2000 spending bills.

Republicans, who are in charge of reauthorizing the ESEA for the first time since it was created in 1965, have adopted a different priority — consolidating programs and giving states flexibility.

"I have just started looking at some of the smaller programs [in the law]," said Michael N. Castle, R-Del., chairman of the House Education and the Workforce Subcommittee

Trumpeter Wynton Marsalis, shown in 1996 with Children at a Washington elementary school, has been involved in the campaign to boost music education.

on Early Childhood, Youth and Families, which has jurisdiction over the act. "That shows how big this bill is."

In 1996, Rep. Peter Hoekstra, R-Mich., counted the number of federal education programs — from pre-school to college — and came up with 760 in 39 separate agencies, departments commissions and boards. The Clinton administration tallied a lower figure. The total number was never resolved.

The GOP quest to streamline the education bureaucracy has already run into trouble. The House, which is considering the reauthorization as a series of smaller bills, on July 20 passed a measure (HR 1995) to roll three programs — President Clinton's plan to hire 100,000 new teachers, Goals 2000 grants for education quality and teacher training programs — into a single grant. Clinton has vowed to veto the bill unless the plan for 100,000 teachers remains separate. (*1999 CQ Weekly, p. 1787*)

Following is a look at three smaller programs in the act that, unlike the teacher plan, are not likely to snare the limelight, but offer case studies into the political and popular pressures that Congress faces as it considers the reauthorization.

MUSIC EDUCATION

The Senate Health, Education, Labor and Pensions Committee hosted a star witness on June 29: VH1's John Sykes.

By the end of the year, the rock channel will have raised $25 million for school music programs. Its fundraisers, including "diva" concerts with Whitney Houston, Shania Twain, Aretha Franklin and others, put local school bake sales to shame.

Sykes' testimony touted recent research showing that children who had been given structured music and arts instruction outperformed their peers in other academic subjects. Findings such as these are grabbing the attention of educators and Congress.

"I am very big on trying to increase the effort in the arts areas," said Committee Chairman James M. Jeffords, R-Vt., whose mother was a music and art teacher.

This message was echoed before the House Education and the Workforce Committee by the National Association for Music Education, which is working with other groups to put federal funds into music and arts curriculum.

A 1997 study of eighth grade arts instruction, part of the annual National Assessment of Educational Progress, which tracks student performance, found that 72 percent of schools had a state or district-ordered music curriculum, 10 percent had dance, 15 percent had theater and 64 percent visual arts.

Surveys have shown that arts programs are often the first to be cut when schools face a budget crisis. Music educators note that only 14 percent of schools offered orchestra programs in 1996, down from more than 60 percent in 1962. While music budgets have been increasing in recent years, private fundraising accounts for more than half of all aid.

"People look at the arts as frills, but they are not. They go to the core of what a person is," said Rep. Patsy T. Mink, D-Hawaii, a member of the Education and the Workforce Committee.

The music teachers' effort has created some friction in the arts community, which has been struggling to adjust to a nearly 40 percent cut in the National Endowment for the Arts since 1995.

The John F. Kennedy Center for the Performing Arts and VSA arts (formerly Very Special Arts) for the disabled, founded in 1974 by Jean Kennedy Smith, for years have had their own authorization under the ESEA. There has been some worry that a new program for music education could foster competition for funds.

When Congress rewrote the act in 1994, it authorized $11 million in annual grants for arts research, model programs and curriculum development to a broad range of institutions. If $9 million or less were appropriated in any year, the entire amount was reserved for the Kennedy Center and VSA arts, which had long received funds.

Appropriators, some of whom are members of the Kennedy Center board of directors, provided $10.5 million in fiscal 1999 — all of which went to those two institutions. Education Department officials said they have had limited success in persuading Congress to stretch aid to smaller programs.

"I worry at times that some of the other organizations see us as privileged in some way," John D. Kemp, president and CEO of VSA arts, said July 28. "Our constituents are the most poor, underserved and needy people."

VSA arts, which has its own lobbying consultant, reaches millions of disabled individuals through state affiliates and special activities. The Kennedy Center, one of the nation's premier art education centers, runs special programs for teachers in the Washington, D.C. area; conducts national training; holds touring performances and exhibitions; and sponsors an arts Web site and television programs.

Music teachers say their purpose is not to take money away from anyone.

"[Existing arts] programs are doing very special and worthy work," said Music Educators' President June M. Hinckley. "We're concerned that all children . . . have these same experiences as children in the D.C. area connected with the Kennedy Center."

Still, Hinckley insists that Congress cannot capitalize on the research linking arts to academics unless it moves past one-time enrichment programs to curriculum funding.

Education Secretary Richard W. Riley, who helped place art teachers in all South Carolina schools when he was governor, has worked to elevate arts education at the federal level. The 1994 Goals 2000 act, which provides funds to help states improve school quality, listed art proficiency as a national education standard. (*1994 Almanac, p. 397*)

The lobbying effort is well-organized. Sykes on July 14 attended a House Education caucus meeting with jazz trumpeter Wynton Marsalis. Music educators have mounted a letter-writing campaign, one-on-one meetings with lawmakers and public service announcements with stars such as pop singer Michael Bolton.

The exact goals of the lobbying campaign are still evolving. Some hope for a multimillion-dollar authorization, while others say the best they can hope for is narrower language drawing more attention to the arts instruction in existing programs.

At least four lawmakers are already hooked on harmonics. Music teachers meeting on Capitol Hill in July were treated to a concert by the Singing Senators — Jeffords, Majority Leader Trent Lott, R-Miss., Larry E. Craig, R-Idaho, and John Ashcroft, R-Mo. The senators rushed from a floor vote to the group's reception in the Hart building.

"It was the best response we've ever gotten from anybody. It really picked their spirits up," Jeffords said.

WOMEN'S EDUCATION EQUITY

As Republicans look for programs to eliminate or meld into block grants, one is emerging as a prime target: the Women's Education Equity Act (WEEA).

Sponsored by Mink and then-Minnesota Democratic senator Walter F. Mondale (1964-76), the 1974 act was designed to help schools ensure sex equity in education and comply with Title IX of the Education Amendments of 1972 (PL 92-318), which bars sexual discrimination in educational institutions that receive federal funds. (*1974 Almanac, p. 441*)

At its height in 1980, the equity act had a budget of $10 million. The current $3 million program funds grants for new approaches in instruction that remedy past inequities between girls and boys as well as a clearinghouse that publishes and disseminates gender-equity information.

For some Republicans, the issue is practicality. They say the program is just too small to be of any use. Almost since the beginning, however, the equity act has been part of a cultural battle about the women's movement.

Opponents call the program a tool of the left, mocking a WEEA-funded publication suggesting that Little League baseball may contribute to male violence. They point to data showing that boys, not girls, are the ones lagging academically and emotionally.

"It [the equity act] is very divisive, and it's clear that it operates on the assumption that girls are second-class citizens," said Christina Hoff Sommers, a scholar at the American Enterprise Institute, a Washington think tank. "The problem with that is that in most of the areas where you get really good data, the girls are ahead of the boys."

While there are more males than females in top-level math classes, there are more boys at the lower end of the spectrum as well. Women in 1995-96 made up 55 percent of those receiving bachelor's degrees; in 1970, men made up 57 percent. Three times as many boys are enrolled in special education classes as girls.

Supporters say the improved statistics are evidence that the equity act has worked. They point to a recent Supreme Court decision holding schools liable for sexual harassment, as well as the small number of women in high-technology fields, to make the case that the program is relevant.

"I don't quite understand why people are opposed to improvement in the lives of women and girls," said Katherine Hanson, director of the WEEA Equity Resource Center in Newton, Mass., and author of the paper on male violence. The federally funded center publishes research on sex equity issues, has developed special coursework and has a Web site that offers data.

A bipartisan coalition of House members on July 14 introduced a bill (HR 2505) to reauthorize the equity act and increase the number of girls in technology-related education, reduce sexual harassment in schools and gather data on girls in high school athletics.

"If girls had been part of the computer revolution, maybe there wouldn't be a Y2K problem," Lynn Woolsey, D-Calif., told a news conference .

Sponsors include Dale E. Kildee, D-Mich., Constance A. Morella, R-Md., Nancy L. Johnson, R-Conn. In the Senate, Edward M. Kennedy, D-Mass., and Olympia J. Snowe, R-Maine, have introduced a companion measure (S 1264).

Republicans have taken a number of unsuccessful runs at the program. From 1982 to 1992, Republican presidents did not include it in their budget requests. When Republicans took control of the House in 1995, the equity act was on their short list of programs slated for extinction and received no money in fiscal 1996. Under President Ronald Reagan, a member of the conservative Eagle Forum was appointed to head a board on women's education authorized under the act. The board was later abolished.

The debate over the equity act has also been fueled by practical questions about just what Congress has gotten for its money.

In 1994 at the request of Congress, the General Accounting Office (GAO) examined how the act had been carried out. The GAO found that even though the intent of the law was to develop materials that could be used nationally, half the grants from 1986 to 1992 were for local workshops or classes that did not have a broader application.

Furthermore, only about 7 percent of all projects were designed to help schools ensure that they had complied with Title IX requirements for sex equity — a major purpose of the law — and there was little coordination with states and local districts.

No major follow-up study has been carried out, partly because Congress refused to provide funding. Still, Education Department officials insist the program has been improved. The administration wants Congress to alter the women's equity act provisions in the law so that the Education Department can spend more money on technical aid to schools and less to program grants.

The education equity act was designed to ensure that girls do not get shortchanged. But opponents of the law say boys, not girls, are lagging academically.

Given its tenacious defenders, including a coalition headed by the American Association of University Women, the program could well survive.

"I would be very surprised if this Congress did not reauthorize it," said Nancy Zirkin, government relations director of the AAUW. "It is the only program that is directly aimed at women and girls."

SCHOOL CONSTRUCTION

States and school districts are in the midst of the biggest building binge since the Baby Boom generation began crowding classrooms in the 1950s.

The Clinton administration has argued that the federal government must help schools meet the need by underwriting bonds to assist districts, especially those in low-income areas. That has opened up a philosophical split with Republicans, who argue that school construction is a local or state issue.

But the Education Department, working with the American Institute of Architects, has been developing a second, less-publicized effort to guide the growth in school construction. Riley has been using his national bully pulpit to try to change the way schools are designed and used — transforming them into community centers that offer resources to a broad swath of the population.

Riley plans to use $10 million in discretionary money under the law's Fund for the Improvement of Education — the same pot the administration tapped into for its unsuccessful national testing program — for annual grants to towns and districts to develop the concept of schools as centers of communities.

The idea is to get educators, local officials and parents involved in a planning process that moves school buildings beyond the ABCs to serve as an anchor for the entire community.

Examples include schools that double as city council chambers at night, operate as senior centers on the weekends or use their gymnasiums as public recreation centers.

"Most of the time, schools are being designed with relatively small numbers of people . . . somebody gets in a back room and says, 'Go build a school,' then they put a chain link fence around it and nobody is allowed to come in except teachers and students," said Steve Bingler, president of Concordia Architects in New Orleans. He has helped draft a set of school design principles for the Department of Education that emphasize the role of community-based planning.

"The other way to do it is to take down that chain link fence. . . . Why are we building two public library systems — one in the schools and outside? The only reason anyone can think of is because we've developed this apartheid system where schools are not connected to the community," he said.

The plan does not have to go through the authorizing committee. The House Appropriations subcommittee on Labor, Health and Human Services and Education, in a draft fiscal 2000 spending bill, however, has blocked new projects under the fund because of budget constraints. Unless the White House pushes for the initiative in expected budget talks, it could die.

Even without the additional funding, the department has moved on the issue. It has held symposiums on school design, set up a national clearinghouse to disseminate information about school size, the use of technology and other design issues. The American Institute of Architects recently held a school design competition to bring more attention to the issue.

States and school districts plowed a record $15 billion into construction in 1998, up $3 billion from 1997. Half that money went toward building 700 new schools, itself a record, according to an annual survey by School Planning and Management magazine.

Nearly 53 million children were enrolled in public schools this year. That will climb to 54.3 million by 2008.

The design initiative has been overshadowed by the separate White House proposal for tax credits to leverage nearly $25 billion in school construction bonds.

In making the case for the tax credits, Clinton has focused on the other side of the school construction picture — urban schools with crumbling ceilings and suburban schools that resemble trailer parks, with students forced to shuttle outside to makeshift portable classrooms.

The GAO in 1996 estimated that there was a $112 billion backlog in school repair and maintenance.

Republicans have been lukewarm about the tax credit, though they included a provision in their tax bill (HR 2488) that would relax arbitrage rules in order to make it easier for school districts to raise funds. Democrats said the provision would do little for hard-pressed urban and rural districts. (*1999 CQ Weekly, p. 1923*)

"I recognize the need for students to have the best learning environment possible, including modern school buildings and other facilities. However, funds at the federal level are limited," Education and the Workforce Committee Chairman Rep. Bill Goodling, R-Pa., said July 16. House Democrats have started a discharge petition to force the construction bill out of committee and onto the floor. The petition is one of a series Democrats have used to put pressure on the GOP.

"If we are really serious about quality education for our kids, we had better start getting serious about the condition of our schools," said Rep. Darlene Hooley, D-Ore.

Even some who have concerns about Clinton's plans to underwrite construction bonds, however, believe there is a role for the federal government to play in encouraging new approaches to school design.

Castle said that in the wake of the April 20 shootings at Columbine High School in Littleton, Colo., he had been worried about a move among some districts to build bigger schools. Bingler said communities that engaged in an open design process often chose smaller schools.

Riley is trying a variety of methods to spread the idea, including recruiting the AARP, the nation's largest senior citizens group. That brings to the table a segment of the population that has sometimes been lukewarm to local efforts to raise taxes for schools.

"Considering that there will be more school construction over the next decade than at any time since the 1950s, it just makes sense to consider the intergenerational and community benefits of multiuse spaces," AARP Executive Director Horace B. Deets wrote in the July-August edition of the group's Modern Maturity magazine. "It's a win-win situation for everyone involved." ◆

A Guide to the Coming Debate On Campaign Finance Overhaul, From Soft Money to Issue Advocacy

The upcoming congressional debate over campaign finance legislation will feature partisan fights, procedural brinkmanship and heated rhetoric about the evils of huge and unchecked political contributions, from one side, and the threats that various campaign finance proposals pose to the Constitution, from the other.

But the central question of the debate has not changed for more than a generation: Will lawmakers revamp the fundraising system for congressional and presidential campaigns that has been integral to their success and the survival of the two political parties?

History strongly suggests the answer is no, although advocates of an overhaul remain undaunted. No campaign finance legislation has become law since the parameters of the current system were finished with enactment of a law (PL 96-187) two decades ago. (*1979 Almanac, p. 558*)

Senate opponents are confident they can continue to block such legislation with a filibuster, as they did most recently in the 105th Congress. (*1998 CQ Almanac, p. 18-3*)

The House is scheduled to take up an array of campaign finance proposals during the week of Sept. 13. But the focal point for the debate will be legislation (HR 417), sponsored by Reps. Christopher Shays, R-Conn., and Martin T. Meehan, D-Mass., which is similar to a measure that easily passed the House last year. (*1999 CQ Weekly, p. 1930*)

In the Senate, Majority Leader Trent Lott, R-Miss., has agreed to permit a campaign finance debate by Oct. 12. That will likely occur on a bill (S 26) sponsored by Sens. John McCain, R-Ariz., and Russell D. Feingold, D-Wis., that is the companion to the Shays-Meehan measure.

Both the Shays-Meehan and McCain-Feingold bills would ban "soft money," the unlimited and unregulated contributions from labor unions, corporations and wealthy individuals. That provision, along with proposals in the two bills to restrict so-called issue-advocacy advertising, will surely provoke the most vigorous debate.

Indeed, the battle has already taken a nasty turn. Sen. Mitch McConnell, R-Ky. — the leading foe of the McCain-Feingold bill and also the chairman of the National Republican Senatorial Committee — recently sent bluntly worded letters to several business executives urging them to resign from an organization that favors tightening campaign finance laws. Some members of that group, the Committee for Economic Development, suggested during the week of Aug. 30 that McConnell was trying to intimidate them.

Here is a guide to the policies, politics and process of the debate:

Q: Why has soft money become so controversial?

A: Because it is flooding the political system, say advocates of outlawing it. Common Cause, a nonpartisan group that strongly supports the soft money ban, recently released a report that found that the two parties are on pace to shatter all previous records for this sort of fundraising. The two parties raised more than $55.1 million in soft money between them during the first six months of this year — 80 percent more than in the comparable period before the 1996 presidential election.

The Common Cause report said both parties have received hundreds of thousands of dollars from groups with strong interests in pending legislation. Telecommunications and securities firms have been the leading GOP contributors; securities firms, labor unions and trial lawyers top the list of Democratic donors.

But McConnell and other defenders of the system say there is nothing intrinsically wrong with the flow of soft money into the political system. Donating to campaigns, McConnell has said, "is as American as apple pie." And many Republicans, who historically have raised more soft money than Democrats, are concerned that a soft money ban would place them at a severe disadvantage.

Q: What accounts for the increase in soft money?

A: Quite simply, the two parties have discovered it is much easier to solicit funds in large chunks rather than go after many small donations. Federal law places strict limits on the amount of money that individuals, companies and unions may donate to political candidates during each election season. Long-standing laws prevent corporations and unions from making direct donations at all — which is why they have to funnel such contributions through political action committees (PACs) that are federally regulated.

But since 1979, the two parties have been able to solicit unlimited amounts of soft money — that is, funds not covered by federal statutory caps — for party-building activities such as get-out-the-vote drives. Often, soft money finances much more than that, including issue-oriented television ads by the parties that look and sound like election ads.

Still, many observers believe the parties would not be so reliant on soft money if the federal limits on "hard money," such as the $1,000 limit on donations by individuals to candidates for each election, had been adjusted to keep up with inflation. And despite the significant increase in soft money contributions, those funds still accounted for only slightly more than 10 percent of all the money spent during the 1996 federal election campaign, according to an analysis by the Center for Responsive Politics, a nonpartisan research group.

Q: What is "issue advocacy"?

A: Any time a group or political party identifies or criticizes a position taken by a politician it is engaging in issue advocacy. The Supreme Court has ruled that such issue ads are constitutionally protected speech and may not be regulated by federal election laws. Only "express advocacy" advertisements that explicitly advocate the defeat or election of a candidate — by using so-called magic words such as "vote for congressman Smith" or "vote against Sen. Jones" — are subject to such laws.

In the campaign of three years ago, there was widespread outrage over a deluge of issue ads, particularly those that were indistinguishable from political attack ads. Both the Shays-Meehan bill and McCain-Feingold bill aim to restrict such ads, though in slightly different ways.

Supporters of the bills insist these provisions will clean up elections by eliminating some negative issue ads. Critics, including the American Civil Liberties Union (ACLU), maintain that the restrictions on issue ads are flatly unconstitutional and would force interest groups to scale back their political activity.

The Shays-Meehan bill would establish a broad, new standard on what constitutes express advocacy by imposing federal restrictions on ads that "can have no other reasonable meaning" than to advocate election or defeat of a candidate. Any issue advocacy ad that runs within 60 days of an election and refers to a candidate would also be subject to federal contribution limits under that legislation. The issue advocacy provision in the McCain-Feingold bill is narrower. Either proposal, if enacted, is sure to face a challenge on the grounds that it abridges the right to free speech.

Q: If issue advocacy restrictions are so controversial, why don't overhaul advocates drop them from their bills?

A: That is the $64,000 question in the Senate. Under an informal agreement setting ground rules for the debate, McCain and Feingold have until Sept. 14 to decide on a vehicle for the debate. It might be the original text of their bill, or a modified version of that measure.

McCain and Feingold are now considering whether and how to change their bill to overcome an expected filibuster by McConnell and his allies. In recent years, they have garnered 52 votes for their bill, eight short of the 60 needed to break the delaying tactics that otherwise scuttle legislation.

Dropping the issue advocacy provision would help McCain and Feingold neutralize the argument that their bill tramples on the First Amendment. It might also make the bill somewhat more palatable to some conservatives, who have been concerned over the potential impact of the issue advocacy restrictions on the political activities of such organizations as the Christian Coalition.

But some Senate Democrats — who have unanimously supported the McCain-Feingold bill in the past — might defect if the issue advocacy provisions are dropped. Senior Senate Democrats are concerned that millions of dollars in soft money that now flows to the GOP might simply be diverted to conservative and pro-business interest groups to help them underwrite issue ads directed against the Democrats.

Q: How will the House debate unfold?

A: The most important point to remember is that the Shays-Meehan bill received 252 votes last year. It is difficult to defeat legislation that so recently attracted such widespread support.

But the procedures House GOP leaders set for the debate clearly do not favor Shays-Meehan and their supporters. The House will consider three major alternatives to the Shays-Meehan bill and 10 other amendments. Approval of any of the alternatives means the end for Shays-Meehan. In addition, some advocates for the legislation charge that many of the 10 amendments are "poison pills" designed to fracture support for Shays-Meehan.

Q: What are the alternatives to Shays-Meehan?

A: The proposal likely to attract the most support (HR 2668) is sponsored by House Administration Committee Chairman Bill Thomas, R-Calif. That bill, which Thomas has characterized as "purposefully modest," would expand the ban on political contributions by foreigners, mandate faster and more complete disclosure of contributions and strengthen the Federal Election Commission.

Under different circumstances, Thomas' bill would probably pass the House with an overwhelming vote. Its provisions are not controversial. But since it is pitted against Shays-Meehan,

supporters of that bill will mount a furious effort to defeat the Thomas measure.

Another alternative (HR 1867), by Rep. Asa Hutchinson, R-Ark., is less aggressive in restricting soft money and issue ads than Shays-Meehan; the third (HR 1922), sponsored by Rep. John T. Doolittle, R-Calif., would take a radically different approach by removing all federal limits on political contributions and stiffening disclosure requirements.

Of the 10 other amendments, the one that has raised greatest concern among Shays-Meehan forces is another proposal by Doolittle aimed at exempting printed and on-line materials such as voter guides from the bill's issue advocacy provision.

The bill already provides some protections for voter guides, but Doolittle and other conservatives say they are insufficient. Supporters of Shays-Meehan say Doolittle's real goal is to gut their bill. Last year, a similar amendment by Doolittle was rejected by just 18 votes.

Q: What would it take to enact campaign finance legislation this year?

A: Pro-overhaul forces may well prevail in the House, but the Senate remains the stumbling block. In that chamber, the political dynamics will have to change dramatically for McCain and Feingold to succeed.

A new fundraising scandal could generate more public demand for new and tougher laws. But the 1996 campaign, with all of its sordid allegations of foreign fundraising and Lincoln Bedroom sleepovers, has not produced the needed legislative momentum.

In different ways, Hutchinson and Thomas have argued that as long as Congress is at loggerheads over more sweeping revisions, it should try to enact more modest legislation. "Too often over the years, and increasingly so it seems, the good has been seen as the enemy of the perfect when it comes to campaign finance reform," said the Administration Committee's report on Thomas' bill.

But those who back more ambitious changes argue they have already made significant concessions over the years. Besides, they say, Congress would be derelict if it enacted campaign finance legislation that does nothing to plug what they see as the biggest loopholes in current law — soft money and "sham" issue ads. ◆

Failing again to overcome filibuster, McCain and Feingold cast about for new strategy

Campaign Finance Crusaders Regroup After Latest Defeat

With the most recent demise of campaign finance legislation, proponents of changing the way money influences politics are left to ponder what for them is both a familiar and frustrating question: What, if anything, can change the seemingly static political dynamics of this issue?

This year's Senate version (S 1593) was scuttled Oct. 20 after a pair of test votes showed that sponsors John McCain, R-Ariz., and Russell D. Feingold, D-Wis., were not even close to overcoming the type of Republican filibuster that has now stopped campaign finance bills in five of the past six years.

"I think it is safe to say there is no momentum whatsoever for this kind of measure," said Mitch McConnell of Kentucky, chairman of the National Republican Senatorial Committee. The leading opponent of changing campaign finance law, he maintains that the proposals put forth by McCain and Feingold would unconstitutionally restrict political speech.

McCain, whose campaign for next year's GOP presidential nomination seems to be gaining as other money-starved aspirants drop

from the race, vowed that he and Feingold would keep up their fight. "We will take our case to the people and eventually — eventually — we will prevail," he declared.

Hoping to end years of futility, McCain and Feingold this fall dropped many of the provisions from their comprehensive package and focused primarily on banning political "soft money," the unregulated and unlimited donations that have been flowing to both parties in record amounts. (*See box, The Rising Cost of 'Soft Money,' p. 47*)

The new plan picked up the votes of three GOP senators, but that gain was nearly offset by the defections of two other Republicans, who supported the broader McCain-Feingold legislation. In the end, senators voted 53-47 on Oct. 19 to limit debate on an amendment embodying a soft money ban, seven short of the 60 votes needed to stop a filibuster. They had earlier voted 52-48 to limit debate on language copying the campaign finance bill (HR 417) that the House passed in September, again an outright majority but this time eight shy of what is required to stop a filibuster.

Opponents of changing the law insisted that the idea has gained no ground this year, despite continuing fallout from the worst presidential fundraising scandal (in 1996) since Watergate and the increasing media coverage of the proliferation of soft money.

"It is dead for the year," asserted Majority Leader Trent Lott, R-Miss.

Not enacting his proposal, McCain said, will only lead to more scandals, which in turn will ratchet up public demand for change. But campaign finance advocates have been awaiting such a surge of public outrage for years, without success. In a Gallup Poll Oct. 8-10 of 976 adults, 60 percent said overhauling campaign finance law should be a low priority or not a priority at all, while 39 percent rated the issue as either a high priority or the most important issue before Congress.

Glimmers of Hope

Still, while this year's campaign finance debate limped to a predictable impasse, there were developments that should give McCain,

CQ Weekly Oct. 23, 1999

McCain, left, and Feingold speak at an Oct. 19 news conference after their campaign finance bill was effectively thwarted on a pair of votes that kept a filibuster alive. They have threatened to try to attach their proposal to must-pass legislation that will move near the end of the session.

Feingold and their allies cause for hope, if not optimism:

● **Two in a row.** For the second year in a row, 58 percent of the House voted to pass campaign finance legislation sponsored by Christopher Shays, R-Conn., and Martin T. Meehan, D-Mass. Both times their bill got 34 votes beyond an absolute majority. The bill includes restrictions on "issue advocacy" advertising by independent groups, a provision McCain and Feingold dropped as part of their effort to keep their bill alive. The House vote did not put any identifiable new pressure on the Senate, as Shays and Meehan had hoped, but it did put 54 Republicans on record in support of such a broad measure and will provide a baseline for the House in the years to come.

● **The McCain factor.** McCain will keep campaign finance a front-burner presidential issue as long as he remains in the race. His campaign might have received a boost Oct. 20, when Elizabeth Dole said she was dropping her presidential quest because she had concluded she would never be financially competitive — a rationale that seemed to give credibility to McCain's argument that money has come to dominate politics.

As the surprisingly bitter floor debate on the bill highlighted, the down side for McCain is that his message exposes him to increased hostility from GOP colleagues at the very time he needs all the Republican support he can muster. McConnell and Robert F. Bennett, R-Utah, excoriated McCain for suggesting, in speeches and on his campaign Web site, that Congress had become corrupted by special interest money.

"This debate is being cast in the national press and over the Internet and indeed in the presidential campaign as a debate between the uncorrupt and the corrupt," McConnell said. "And I have been labeled as being on the side of the corrupt, and I don't like it."

● **Shift in the GOP?** In the Senate, a small but growing number of Republicans showed they are willing to seriously consider embracing campaign finance proposals, particularly if they are less sweeping than the Shays-Meehan bill — or previous iterations of the McCain-Feingold measure. Voting to limit debate on the soft money ban were all 45 Democrats and eight Republicans, including three who had in the past backed McConnell's filibuster: Sam Brownback of Kansas, Tim Hutchinson of Arkansas and

The Rising Cost of 'Soft Money'

Whether to stem the flow of "soft money" is the central question in the campaign finance debate. But there is no question that this type of unlimited and unregulated giving by unions, corporations and wealthy people has burgeoned in the 1990s and is now the fastest growing source of cash for the Democratic and Republican national committees and the party committees that underwrite House and Senate campaigns.

The six main national party committees took in $57.3 million in the first six months of 1999, after which they all filed reports to the Federal Election Commission (FEC) for the 2000 election cycle. That is more than quadruple the $13.6 million they collected during the first six months of 1991, the comparable period before the 1992 presidential election.

That is when the party committees were first required by the FEC to disclose soft money receipts. But this type of giving has existed since 1978, when the agency first permitted state political party committees to use non-federal money to pay for certain expenses — for example, voter drives — that benefited federal and non-federal candidates. National party committees began raising soft money during the 1980 election cycle, but since it was used for non-federal purposes it was not initially subject to federal disclosure laws.

These charts compare soft money contributions during the first six months of the current and previous four election cycles. They illustrate that, after lagging far behind for the rest of the decade, the Democrats are now approaching soft money parity with the GOP.

(in millions of dollars)

Republican National Committee vs. Democratic National Committee

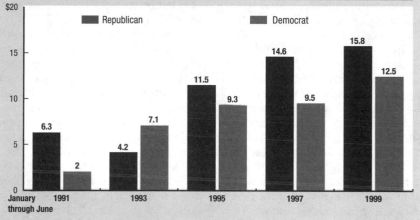

National Republican Senatorial Committee vs. Democratic Senatorial Campaign Committee

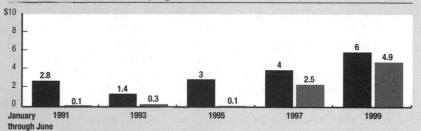

National Republican Congressional Committee vs. Democratic Congressional Campaign Committee

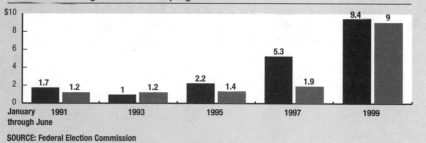

SOURCE: Federal Election Commission

William V. Roth Jr. of Delaware, who is facing a tough re-election race.

But two GOP senators who had backed more sweeping legislation in the past — John H. Chafee of Rhode Island and Arlen Specter of Pennsylvania — voted against the narrow proposal. Nor did it win over other Republicans, such as Chuck Hagel of Nebraska, who want to raise the federal "hard money" limits on direct contributions to candidates, which have not been adjusted since they were created in 1974. But Hagel's idea, which would make a ban or a cap on soft money more palatable for some Republicans, would draw objections from Democrats.

Blame Game

The biggest disappointment for McCain and Feingold was that there were never any votes on the various ideas, such as Hagel's, floated this year. Indeed, both parties seemed more interested in gaining a procedural advantage than in engaging in a meaningful legislating process.

Minority Leader Tom Daschle, D-S.D., seemed to take McConnell and other Republicans by surprise when he moved for the back-to-back test votes. That gambit enabled Democrats to control the floor, while McCain complained that Hagel and other senators had been effectively prevented from getting votes on their amendments. Democrats insisted that was not true, but Daschle's maneuver put the debate into a state of suspended animation.

McCain tried to force the action Oct. 18, with an unusual attempt to table, and thereby kill, the very amendment that included the soft money ban he and Feingold had put forward.

"There has been parliamentary maneuvering," McCain said in explaining his counterintuitive strategy. "There has been substitutes. There has been a filling up of the tree. There have been a lot of things that have been going on which have sort of not surprised me but disappointed me."

By moving to shelve his own proposal, McCain said he wanted to cut through the fog and force a "defining vote on whether or not we want to ban soft money." His maneuver came to naught, however. McConnell and the opponents of the soft money ban — confident they had the votes to sustain their filibuster — concluded there was no danger in allowing the amendment to stay alive another day. In one of the more bizarre votes on this issue in recent years, McCain and McConnell were on the same side as the Senate voted 1-92 to reject the tabling motion.

After the two cloture votes were taken the next day, it was the Democrats' turn to cry foul over procedures. Under an informal agreement reached in July, Lott had promised to allow five days of debate on the McCain-Feingold bill. And he lived up to the letter of that agreement, if not its spirit: The bill was put before the Senate on Oct. 13 and was the pending business for debate for at least part of the next four days that the Senate was in session.

But the Democrats and McCain felt cheated because the debate that began at dinnertime on Oct. 13 — a few hours after the Senate had rebuffed the nuclear test ban treaty — was brief and perfunctory. So when Lott announced he was ready to move on, they registered strong objections. "This hasn't been a debate, this has been an exercise in futility," Daschle said Oct. 19. "The majority leader is acting extremely irresponsibly in pulling this bill."

Democratic objections grew louder when Lott moved to end the debate and bring up legislation (S 1692) to outlaw "partial birth" abortions. "We have every right not to agree to withdraw campaign finance reform legislation just because we didn't get cloture on the first, second or third vote," said Carl Levin, D-Mich. "It took four votes to get civil rights legislation passed in the late 1960s and seven weeks to get that legislation passed."

But traditionally, such votes become a test of loyalty to the majority leader. Most Republicans had no interest in rolling Lott, and the motion to take up the abortion bill was approved 52-48, with the effect that the campaign finance bill had lost its place in the Senate's legislative pecking order. (*Abortion, 1999 CQ Weekly, p. 2531*)

Last-Ditch Effort

McCain and Feingold have vowed to try to attach the soft-money ban to other legislation, perhaps in the waning weeks of this session. But it is hard to see what that would accomplish, other than to slow the path to adjournment and thereby generate more senatorial ill will. Undoubtedly, they will renew the battle next year. While that might provide a platform for McCain to promote the central theme of his campaign, it is hard to imagine a different outcome from this fall.

Reflecting on the most recent debate, McCain was even-handed in assessing blame for his bill's failure. "We've not been treated fairly in this process by either side," he said, adding that he might have been too trusting in signing on to a deal that seemed to hold the promise of an open debate but in reality left supporters of his bill in the same procedural bind they have been in for years.

Feingold, buoyed by the gain of the three additional GOP votes for the soft money ban, sees some vulnerability in McConnell's position. "He's slipping," Feingold claimed.

Even if that is so, however, the debate demonstrated that Democrats have deep reservations about ending soft money absent accompanying restrictions on issue advocacy ads. "We should ban big money contributions," said Robert G. Torricelli of New Jersey, chairman of the Democratic Senatorial Campaign Committee. "But we should do it for the political parties and these fringe groups on these issue advertisements."

McCain suspects that Democrats have other reasons for insisting on the broader package — namely, that a soft money ban will deal a crippling blow to the fundraising efforts of both parties. "The fact is this is a very cynical business we're in. Very, very cynical," he said.

But there is agreement on one point from nearly all the players in the debate — including McCain, McConnell and President Clinton. Until voters determine that campaign finance is a make-or-break issue, and punish those they believe are standing in the way of change, the status quo will likely persist. ◆

Government Institutions

The articles in this section provide insight into the workings of the major institutions of American government. In this edition the focus is on Congress, particularly in its financial aspects, and the judiciary.

The first article discusses proposed changes in the House budget process. The current system has left Congress vulnerable to threatened presidential vetoes of routine spending measures, and President Bill Clinton has used the system in recent years to force Congress to agree to last-minute concessions, adding money for his priorities. A similar scenario unfolded again in the late stages of the fiscal 2000 budget negotiations in the fall of 1999. The next article, written late in the first session of the 106th Congress, describes the appropriations process in detail, emphasizing the challenges the Republican Party faces in sticking to spending caps agreed to in 1997. The article tracks various appropriations bills, such as the bill to fund the growing Labor and Health and Human Services departments, and also considers the Republicans' general spending philosophy and plans for the budget surplus.

The next article shows how a loophole in ethics laws has allowed special interest groups to influence members of Congress. Members are forbidden to accept gifts from lobbyists, but the laws forbidding gifts allow lobbyists to pay for trips, if they are relevant to congressional business, and many interest groups have repeatedly paid for expensive trips to locales such as Hawaii and Las Vegas.

The section on the judiciary begins with an article on the role of the courts in health maintenance organization reform. In the past courts have tended to protect health plans from lawsuits by patients denied coverage. But recently, just as Congress is considering legislation guaranteeing patients' rights to sue health plans, the courts have narrowed their protection of health plans and expanded the rights of patients to sue HMOs.

On October 6, 1999, the Senate rejected the nomination of a black Missouri judge, Ronnie L. White, to a seat on the U.S. District Court. The final article in this section depicts the controversy over White's nomination from the perspective of players on both sides of the aisle. Many observers, noting the intense partisan fighting, believed the judicial process to have been permanently damaged by the controversy, as the number of vacancies increases and growing acrimony ensures stalling on future nominations.

House Revamp of Budget Process Meets Discord at the Starting Line

Committees go their separate ways on overhaul, which would set up an automatic CR and require the president's signature on the annual budget resolution

Any attempt to dramatically change the way Congress conducts its fiscal business needs sweeping bipartisan support and a big push from top leaders. The current bid to rewrite the rules governing the congressional budget process has neither.

That tells most of what happened the week of June 21 to a House bill (HR 853) that would greatly alter the process Congress has used to write its budget for the past 25 years.

The measure was blasted on June 22 by the relatively bipartisan House Appropriations Committee, which saw the bill as a direct assault on the appropriations process and its prerogatives. After voting to change the one provision it has jurisdiction over, the appropriators summarily dismissed the bill on a voice vote, sending it to the full House with a recommendation that it be voted down. "The bill is so flawed that it should not pass," said Chairman C.W. "Bill" Young, R-Fla.

The next day, the House Rules Committee, meeting in a rare legislative mode because it has jurisdiction over budget process issues, just as quickly gave the bill its voice vote approval.

Why the conflicting results? The bill's progress through three committees of jurisdiction — Appropriations, Rules and Budget, which approved it June 17 — has mirrored the political dynamics of those committees. The measure went through the highly partisan Budget and Rules committees without a hint of reservation on the part of Republicans, who are looking for a way to regain leverage from a Democratic president in the wake of the 1995-96 government shutdowns.

Since those shutdowns, President Clinton has exercised extraordinary leverage over Republicans, using veto threats on routine spending measures to force Congress to add money for his favored programs.

In the more collegial Appropriations Committee, however, members of

House appropriators — led by Chairman Young, left, Regula, Jerry Lewis, R-Calif., and Joe Knollenberg, R-Mich. — dismissed the budget process reform proposals on a voice vote.

both parties had little taste for the bill's most controversial provision, which would allow for an automatic continuing resolution (CR) to fund any agency into a new fiscal year if Congress failed to pass a spending bill by the Oct. 1 deadline.

Both Republicans and Democrats on Appropriations gave solid support to Young's proposal to strip the automatic CR provision from the bill.

The bill could come to the floor the week of June 28, but with opposition so strong, it may have to wait until after the July Fourth recess. Even if the House passes the measure, the Senate has opted for a much different, piecemeal approach to budget process "reform." And the Senate's effort has little momentum.

More Provisions

As approved by the Budget and Rules committees, the bill would also:
- Give the annual budget resolution, currently a non-binding "concurrent" resolution of both chambers, the force of law by making it a "joint" resolution requiring the president's signature.
- Ease the current "pay as you go" (PAYGO) budget rules to permit non-

Social Security-generated budget surpluses to be used for tax cuts or new entitlement spending.
- Create a reserve fund so that Congress sets aside money for emergency spending in advance.
- Significantly weaken the Senate's "Byrd rule," named after Robert C. Byrd, D-W.Va., which requires 60 votes to retain non-spending items in a budget "reconciliation" bill, which implements tax and spending policies.
- Create a complicated "lockbox" procedure to try to ensure that cuts from appropriations bills made on the floor are not restored to other appropriations accounts later in the process.

With few exceptions, Democrats dislike the measure, and their leadership appears poised to aggressively oppose it. They join GOP appropriators in opposition to the automatic CR, but also have big objections to the proposed change in PAYGO procedures, which would remove a major procedural roadblock to Republican efforts to cut taxes.

The administration also opposes the bill, White House and congressional aides said.

But the immediate problem facing the measure are Republican pockets of

opposition to it. Unhappy GOP appropriators, combined with almost monolithic Democratic opposition, would be enough to scuttle the bill. On top of that, powerful Transportation committee Chairman Bud Shuster, R-Pa., also has reservations about it, said a top aide.

Response to Crisis

The bill is the product of more than a year's work by a small, bipartisan band of current and former members of the Budget Committee and GOP members of the Rules Committee. Key participants included Jim Nussle, R-Iowa, Benjamin L. Cardin, D-Md., and Porter J. Goss, R-Fla. They want to clean up an often-messy budget process, and they want to take back some of the leverage that Congress has given to Clinton.

"Make no mistake, the current budget process does not work. It is a disorganized patchwork of decades-old rules and laws," said Rules Chairman David Dreier, R-Calif. "This comprehensive bill increases efficiency, improves accountability and strengthens enforcement in the budget process."

Outside of this group and their allies, however, there appears to be little enthusiasm for tackling a complex overhaul of the budget process, which was established by the 1974 Budget Act (PL 93-344) and modified by the 1985 and 1987 Gramm-Rudman-Hollings bills (PL 99-177, PL 100-119). The addition of "caps" on appropriations and PAYGO rules against new deficit spending came with the 1990 budget deal (PL 101-508). (*1990 Almanac, p. 111; 1987 Almanac, p. 604; 1985 Almanac, p. 459; 1974 Almanac, p. 145*)

Each of those budget laws, however, came in response to a crisis: President Richard M. Nixon's impoundment of congressional spending in 1974 and the intractable deficit problems and economic crises of the 1980s and early 1990s. The process works most smoothly when a single party controls government, such as the Democrats' 1993 deficit-reduction package (PL 103-66), or when the president and an opposition party Congress both want a deal, as in

1997. (*1993 Almanac, p. 107*)

But under a divided government, the system does not work as well — witness last year, when gridlock on many of the 13 fiscal 1999 spending bills produced a bloated and unpopular omnibus spending bill (PL 105-277).

"Under today's system, there is simply no incentive for the president to come to the table and negotiate in earnest with the Congress until the last few days of the session," Goss said.

While many lawmakers and budget experts agree that the budget process could use some change, the Nussle-Cardin-Goss bill has drawn numerous critics who say its fixes would never work as intended.

"This is a very well-meaning effort by people on both sides of the aisle who don't have any real experience in trying to put through legislation that deals with the budget or with appropriations or with revenue," said David R. Obey of Wisconsin, ranking Democrat on the Appropriations Committee and its former chairman.

"Most of the fixes create more problems than they solve," added Young. "Most of the problems they create would then come home to roost on the Appropriations Committee."

The automatic CR provision would be a disaster, these critics say, because it would shift power to those defending the status quo and would permit a minority in the Senate to stall any appropriations bill and therefore block any funding changes. In effect, they said, the budget could be put on autopilot.

Interior Appropriations Subcommittee Chairman Ralph Regula, R-Ohio, who has received more than 2,700 requests from members for projects in their districts, said that committee members should remind the rank and file that under an automatic CR, such earmarking opportunities would be forfeited.

The bill would also eliminate the current rule that allows the Appropriations committees to move the annual spending bills after May 15, if the final House-Senate budget resolution has not been adopted by then.

Defending PAYGO

Among Democrats, one of the chief objections is a provision that would relax PAYGO rules to permit on-budget surpluses (those that do not depend on Social Security) to finance tax cuts or new spending. Supporters of the idea say that PAYGO was designed for an era of deficits and that it needs to be changed to permit tax cuts such as the $778 billion, 10-year cut called for under the fiscal 2000 budget resolution (H Con Res 68). (*1999 CQ Weekly, p. 881*)

But Democrats say that if revenue projections did not meet expectations, PAYGO would require across-the-board cuts in mandatory programs.

"It eliminates a useful budgetary tool [PAYGO] in order to facilitate tax cuts and, in doing so, could trigger massive across-the-board cuts in Medicare, student loans, farm price support programs, crop insurance, veterans' benefits, child support enforcement and other vital programs," said Martin Frost, D-Texas.

Requiring the president's signature on the annual budget resolution and giving that measure the force of law is seen by the bill's authors as a way to speed up the process. Currently, the congressional budget resolution sets non-binding guidelines that are fleshed out later with appropriations bills and a budget-reconciliation bill.

The idea is to get the president involved in the process earlier rather than later. If, under the new process, an impasse occurred between Congress and the executive, Congress would then pass the measure again as a non-binding resolution. In their report criticizing the bill, appropriators said the mere existence of this "escape hatch" would remove the very incentive for negotiation that the underlying provision seeks to establish.

In an attempt to assuage appropriators, Goss said, bill sponsors are leaning toward adding a "sunset" provision to the bill under which it would expire after four years. The idea is to see if the measure would work as intended and to limit the damage should it backfire. ◆

Budget gimmicks bloom as fiscal restraint is run through the reality mill

GOP Finds Caps and Cuts Cramp Its Spending Style

Quick Contents

The wrangling over appropriations is but one skirmish in a bigger battle over what to do with the budget surplus. Despite projections of a $161 billion surplus next year, lawmakers vow to stick to spending limits set in 1997. The driving factor is a bipartisan consensus that the portion of the surplus that comes from Social Security surpluses, some $147 billion, is off the table for tax cuts or additional spending.

Republicans, who came to power in 1995 vowing to cut the size of government, have made a belated discovery: They like spending money on education, medical research, aid to the elderly and other social programs.

After presiding over several years of steady increases in Labor, Health and Human Services, and Education discretionary spending, the GOP faces a problem, however, as lawmakers try to pull together a fiscal 2000 measure: Their credit line has run out.

The Labor-HHS bill — the largest domestic spending measure and traditionally the most difficult to pass — is the prime hostage in a broader debate within the Republican party over spending and taxes.

Due to tight caps on discretionary spending imposed by the 1997 balanced-budget law (PL 105-33), Republican moderates say there is simply not enough money to pay for the education and health programs that voters want and the party has defined as political priorities. (*1997 Almanac, p. 2-47*)

Though House Labor-HHS Appropriations Subcommittee Chairman John Edward Porter, R-Ill., and many of his colleagues have pushed to relax the caps, House GOP leaders, pressed by conservatives, have held tight.

Even as they scramble to find cash for fiscal 2000 programs, Republicans are staking their future on a $792 billion tax cut that could force billions of dollars in additional spending cuts. (*Taxes, 1999 CQ Weekly, p. 1783*)

"The tax package is based on the assumption that everything is going to be cut by 20 percent over five years," Rep. David R. Obey of Wisconsin, the top Democrat on the Appropriations Committee, said in an interview July 21. "They can't get moderates to vote for 5 percent reductions in defense and education, and they're assuming 20 [percent]."

President Clinton has charged that Republicans are out to decimate social spending. His rhetoric rankles conservatives, who say that Clinton agreed to the spending caps, then maneuvered around them by submitting to Congress a fiscal 2000 budget stuffed full of accounting gimmicks.

"The Democrats are trying to have a do-nothing Congress, to shut down the appropriations bills," said Rep. Randy "Duke" Cunningham, R-Calif.

Though many budget experts expect the White House and Republicans to eventually work out a tax and spending deal, that would not solve the immediate problem.

Faced with an impasse, Porter on July 21 abruptly canceled plans to mark up a Labor-HHS bill that would have frozen overall spending near fiscal 1999 levels.

The measure would have boosted the National Institutes of Health (NIH) budget by 9 percent and increased college Pell grants, special education and after-school programs, while cutting job training and the Occupational Safety and Health Administration (OSHA).

Porter postponed action after House leaders could not pull together about $11 billion in cuts from other programs and accounting changes needed to finance the measure. His panel may not meet until September.

"There is simply no sense in marking up a bill that can't pass," Porter said, resignedly.

His Senate counterpart, Arlen Specter, R-Pa., hopes to move a bill the week of July 26, but he faces many of the same pressures.

Short-Term Strategy

The House leadership's strategy for dealing with the current spending caps has been to pad smaller, less controversial appropriations bills to speed them through the floor, while delaying Labor-HHS and the spending bill for the departments of Veterans Affairs and Housing and Urban Development while a solution was worked out. Now that the time has come to write the final bills, no magic answer appears in sight.

"They [Republicans] are painting a big room and it's nearly done, and now they're stuck in that corner," said Becky Timmons, director of government relations for the American Council on Education, which represents public and private colleges and universities.

Speaker J. Dennis Hastert, R-Ill., and Appropriations Committee Chairman C.W. Bill

Spending Gap

This chart compares fiscal 1999 spending with the House and Senate fiscal 2000 allocations for three appropriations bills: the one that funds the departments of Commerce, Justice and State (CJS), the one for the departments of Veterans Affairs and Housing and Urban Development (VA-HUD), and the one for the departments of Labor, Health and Human Services, and Education (Labor-HHS). Figures are in discretionary budget authority.

(in billions of dollars)

	FISCAL 1999	HOUSE ALLOCATION	SENATE ALLOCATION
CJS	**$33.66**	**$30.07**	**$33.61**
VA-HUD	**71.95**	**65.30**	**62.36**
Labor-HHS	**88.82**	**77.07**	**80.45**

Young, R-Fla., met again on July 21 to try to find a way to move the Labor-HHS bill. The GOP leadership earlier asked Porter to write the leanest possible bill that had a chance of passing the House. In order to focus the debate squarely on spending priorities, the leadership committed to keeping social policy "riders" off the measure, with the exception of current language to ban federal funds for abortion and embryo research.

Based on those directions, Porter told House leaders that he needed about $88.5 billion in discretionary spending, roughly the same as the fiscal 1999 level but well above the amount allowed under the caps. The leadership has been trying to provide those funds, not by busting the caps, but by using accounting sleight-of-hand, rescissions and offsetting spending cuts to create more wiggle room.

"We all knew that when we came to the end of the process, there would be a shortage of money," Young told reporters.

But the leaders could not endorse a controversial package of spending cuts floated by the Budget Committee, including trimming education, welfare and the Medicaid health care program for the low-income and disabled. As details of the possible reductions leaked out, they produced an uproar among governors — a majority of them Republicans — who administer Medicaid and welfare.

"It's breaking the deal," said William Waldman, executive director of the American Public Human Services Association, which represents state social services departments.

Waldman acknowledged that states, which have seen huge declines in welfare rolls, had built up healthy — and tempting — program surpluses. But he said governors took a calculated risk in 1996 when they agreed to a welfare law (PL 104-193) that gave them a set amount of funds. (*1996 Almanac, p. 6-3*)

"Depending on the luck of the draw and

the economy, it could have been the other way around," Waldman said.

Some state officials, and many lobbyists, expect Republicans eventually will have no choice but to lift the caps. They could not understand why the House was going through the offset exercise, alienating GOP allies and providing fodder for Democrats.

"It just gets tougher from here," said Mark Sanford, R-S.C., a fiscal conservative.

In the Senate, Appropriations Committee Chairman Ted Stevens, R-Alaska, on July 20 said he wanted to lift the caps to spend $9.9 billion in surplus funds on Labor-HHS.

Stevens said he told his fellow Senate Republicans that he could adhere to the caps with one exception: the Labor-HHS bill.

Stevens and Senate Budget Committee Chairman Pete V. Domenici, R-N.M., were considering a plan under which the committee would report a bill that complied with the caps. The full Senate could then decide whether to exceed the caps.

A History of Generosity

The funding squeeze comes after years of healthy growth in Labor-HHS spending. Despite their self-described reputation for frugality, Republicans have written spending bills that have increased the NIH budget by $4.3 billion since 1995. Education spending grew by more than $3 billion in fiscal 1999 alone. (*NIH, 1999 CQ Weekly, p. 1058*)

The increase is partly the result of negotiations with a Democratic administration that has been adamant about increasing social spending. It also reflects an evolution in the Republican Party, which has moved from trying to eliminate the Education Department to pushing for hefty increases in key programs, primarily education of the disabled.

There is an army of lobbyists eager for more. The delay has bought some of them

Bumping Ever Harder Against Caps, GOP Sticks With Its Story

House Majority Leader Dick Armey invariably starts his weekly news conference with a combination of corny jokes, fishing tales and country music lyrics. Another almost weekly ritual is his public affirmation that Congress will be able to live within spending "caps" that it has repeatedly broken.

"Let me say again, the president submitted a budget that maintained the caps. . . . The House passed such a budget," the Texas Republican said July 20. "So, again, everybody in this whole town has affirmed their commitment to the caps."

That same hour, Senate Appropriations Committee Chairman Ted Stevens was painting a far different picture at a closed-door GOP meeting. "I told the conference I will have to ask for a lifting of the caps in one instance," Stevens, R-Alaska, told reporters. "It'll have to be for Labor, Health and Human Services."

Stevens is eyeing $10 billion of the budget surplus for the fiscal 2000 spending bill for the departments of Labor, Health and Human Services, and Education (Labor-HHS). It is the largest and perhaps the most vexing of the annual domestic spending bills. Without additional money, the Labor-HHS bill, which finances popular and politically sensitive programs, cannot pass.

The week of July 19 provided multiple examples of how lawmakers are struggling with the caps set in the 1997 balanced-budget law (PL 105-33) and how they inevitably will break them. (*1997 Almanac, p. 2-3*)

Perhaps the most blatant case came July 22, when the House Appropriations subcommittee that handles funding for the departments of Commerce, Justice and State and the federal judiciary approved a $35.8 billion draft bill. Panel chief Harold Rogers, R-Ky., could only win support for the bill by declaring the entire $4.5 billion cost of the 2000 census an "emergency." That means the money would not count against the caps but would tap into the fiscal 2000 budget surplus.

Also in the House, GOP leaders acknowledged that they could not pass their version of the Labor-HHS bill until after the August recess — violating Speaker J. Dennis Hastert's opening day pledge to pass all 13 annual spending bills before the recess.

The goal now is to pass 12 of the 13, but even that will prove difficult. The House so far has passed easier and less controversial spending bills, most recently the $269 billion defense bill, which passed July 22. But the next two weeks will feature difficult bills such as foreign aid, Commerce-Justice-State, and a still-to-be-unveiled bill for veterans, housing, environment and space programs (VA-HUD).

Without enough money to pass all 13 bills, action in both the House and Senate has often resembled a shell game. To an unprecedented degree, Republicans have resorted to gimmickry to advance the bills.

In the House this has included multiple transfers of money among the bills. Most significantly, Appropriations Committee Chairman C.W. Bill Young, R-Fla., has tapped the Labor-HHS bill to produce about $1.1 billion for items such as foreign aid and energy and water projects.

"We are accused on alternate days of manufacturing money out of the air or starving other bills," said House Appropriations Committee staff director James W. Dyer. "The truth of the matter is we're moving money around frantically to get as many bills out there as the leadership can get done."

The money crunch has driven GOP leaders to scour the rest of the budget to find offsetting cuts or new revenue raisers to pump additional funds into the bills. For example, a draft Labor-HHS bill scheduled for a July 21 subcommittee vote — which did not occur — included cuts in Medicaid and welfare programs. It was scrapped after protests from the nation's governors.

Surplus Battle

The wrangling over appropriations is but one skirmish in a bigger battle over what to do with the budget surplus. Despite Congressional Budget Office (CBO) projections of a $161 billion budget surplus next year, lawmakers continue to vow, at least publicly, that they will stick to the caps. The driving factor is a bipartisan consensus that the portion of the surplus that comes from Social Security reserves, about $147 billion, is off the table for tax cuts or additional spending. Only the "on-budget," or non-Social Security-generated, surplus of $14 billion is eligible for such purposes.

Over the next 10 years, CBO projects these on-budget surpluses will total $996 billion. But that assumption is built upon a shaky foundation — that Congress and President Clinton can summon the political will to live within the caps. Despite Armey's weekly admonitions, virtually no one believes the caps will not be breached. (*Surplus, 1999 CQ Weekly, p. 1673*)

But for now it is critical for Republicans to maintain the assumption they can live within the caps. The reason: tax cuts.

Every dollar of future additional appropriations is a dollar that is not available to finance the GOP's ambitious plan for a $792 billion tax cut bill (HR 2488). But if different, more realistic assumptions are made about spending, the on-budget surplus quickly evaporates. According to an analysis by the Center on Budget and Policy Priorities, a liberal-leaning think tank, the $996 billion surplus shrinks to only $112 billion after factoring in inflation-adjusted expectations about appropriations, emergency disaster spending and resulting decreases in interest savings on the national debt. (*Taxes, 1999 CQ Weekly, p. 1783*)

To stick with the fiscal 2000 budget resolution (H Con Res 68) and its assumptions about tax cuts and increases in defense spending would require huge, unprecedented cuts in discretionary programs, especially once inflation and population increases are factored in.

Even Senate Budget Committee Chairman Pete V. Domenici, R-N.M., chief architect of the budget resolution, is working, along with Stevens, on a plan to break the caps. The budget resolution was based on January estimates of a 2000 on-budget deficit of $7 billion. It contains a provision specifying that any re-estimated surplus could be directed to the Finance Committee to use for tax cuts. Domenici holds exclusive authority to make the shift. But when CBO upped its surplus estimates earlier this month to $14 billion, Domenici rebuffed a bid by Finance Chairman William V. Roth Jr. to claim the money.

When pressed, Domenici would not say that the additional almost $10 billion of on-budget surplus was slated for appropriations, specifically for Labor-HHS — although Stevens did.

Will conservatives, led by Majority Leader Trent Lott, R-Miss., give their okay? "Is he going to go along with it? I don't know," said a Lott staff aide. "Right now that's not where he is. What we made a decision to do is use $4.5 billion for tax cuts and the rest of that is unallocated right now."

Bill by Bill

The week featured House passage of the defense bill (HR 2561) on July 22 and Senate passage of the Commerce-Justice-State bill (S 1217) hours later. The Senate has now passed nine of the 13 bills and Lott

hopes to pass the transportation (S 1143) and agriculture (S 1233) bills before the August break.

Action on the agriculture bill is likely to put more pressure on the surplus: Top Agriculture, Nutrition and Forestry Committee Democrat Tom Harkin of Iowa is poised to try to claim the $9.9 billion that Stevens wants for Labor-HHS for emergency

Young, shown at the July 20 markup, tapped the strapped Labor-HHS spending bill for $1.1 billion for such items as foreign aid.

farm aid — even though Harkin is also the top Democrat on the Labor-HHS Appropriations Subcommittee.

Senate action on Labor-HHS and VA-HUD is likely to slip into September.

The House has passed seven of the 13 bills. Two more, the District of Columbia bill (HR 2587) and the energy and water bill (HR 2605), should pass with relative ease the week of July 26.

Many of the major decisions on the House process are being shaped

by GOP leaders, particularly Majority Whip Tom DeLay of Texas. The leadership, Democrats complain, has injected considerable partisanship into the process, and as a result several bills that had bipartisan subcommittee support have become partisan as panel leaders were asked to change them.

"They put together bills that have bipartisan support, and then Tom DeLay says, 'Hell no' and then orders them to . . . go after White House and Democratic priorities," said ranking Appropriations Democrat David R. Obey of Wisconsin.

Following are brief assessments of the House status of the remaining bills, excluding Labor-HHS:

● **Foreign operations.** Along with Labor-HHS, the foreign aid bill faces the most difficult floor prospects. A $200 billion cut for the International Development Association, which provides interest-free loans to the world's poorest countries, provoked heated protests from Democrats, whose help will be needed to get the bill through the House.

● **VA-HUD.** Subcommittee action is slated for July 26, but the panel faces a severe money crunch. Its fiscal 2000 allocation is more than $6 billion below fiscal 1999 and subcommittee Chairman James T. Walsh, R-N.Y., reportedly wants to use the "emergency" designation to make up much of the gap. The top candidate for the designation is veterans' health programs, a political favorite.

● **Commerce, Justice, State.** Because the bill would cut White House priorities, it faces the prospect of a veto threat and limited Democratic support on the floor. The designation of the census as an "emergency" is certain to raise hackles with some GOP spending hawks. But a fight over census sampling is over.

Above, Porter works on the Labor-HHS spending bill with staff aides, from left, Susan Firth, Francine Salvador, Tony McCann, and Carol Murphy. Porter has been urging colleagues to lift caps on spending. At right, Obey, the top Democrat on the Appropriations Committee, says the GOP tax bill is based on the assumption that Congress will have to make big cuts in future spending bills.

extra time to plot strategy.

"Certainly for the National Education Association (NEA), this [House] bill would not be acceptable. The president's budget would have been a $1.2 billion increase," said Joel Packer, an NEA lobbyist.

A Difficult Bill

Passing a Labor-HHS bill would be problematic even with more money. The fiscal 1999 measure did not make it to the floor of either the House or Senate, but was rolled into an end-of-year omnibus spending bill (PL 105-277), which gave Clinton extra leverage. (1998 Almanac, p. 2-64)

A moderate who tries to reach out to Democrats, Porter last year was told to write a bill that could pass with just Republican votes. His plan eliminated summer jobs for poor youths and the Low Income Heating and Energy Assistance Program (LIHEAP) while increasing NIH funding. The aid was restored in the omnibus bill.

Republicans felt that given the tight caps, they had no choice again this year but to write a conservative bill.

Porter's new plan would increase funding for the NIH by about $1.4 billion, from the $15.6 billion, fiscal 1999 level. A broad-based bipartisan coalition wants to double the NIH budget

over five years, and that effort is supported by hundreds of health, pharmaceutical and disease advocacy groups. (1999 CQ Weekly, p. 1058)

After being criticized last year for seeking a funding rise at the expense of social programs, the health lobby banded with education advocates this year to encourage aid for both priorities.

Porter's fiscal 2000 plan would increase the average Pell grant for low-income college students by $150 per year, to $3,275. It would roll Clinton's proposal to hire 100,000 new teachers into a $1.8 billion block grant along with teacher training and the Goals 2000 program of grants for education quality. The House on July 20 passed a bill (HR 1995) to create such block grants, which Clinton has threatened to veto.

It would also increase aid for after-school programs by $100 million, to $300 million, eliminate a slew of smaller programs, cut job training aid by 10 percent, reduce OSHA and freeze the Social Services block grant to states.

Porter's bill does not try to eliminate funding for LIHEAP, which pays the energy bills of poor people. Some subcommittee conservatives said that while they were comfortable with the plan, they wished they could put even more money in NIH.

Democrats who were briefed on the plan said they did not want to pass judgment until they saw how much money Porter got in the end.

"It doesn't make sense to focus on details when the macro picture" is unclear, said Democratic Rep. Nita M. Lowey of New York.

Some lawmakers and advocacy groups who were pleased with their portions of the bill fretted that cuts in other federal programs would hurt the very people they are trying to help.

For example, higher education groups like the increase in Pell grants. To help pay for it, Republicans were considering overturning a recent Education Department move to cut the origination fee on direct college loans. The department's move set off a battle with private lenders, who compete for business with the direct lending program.

Advocates for the disabled like a proposed $500 million increase in special education. On the other hand, Medicaid is a main source of health care for those with physical and mental impairments.

"There has to be equity," said Myrna R. Mandlawitz of the National Association of State Directors of Education. ◆

Legal, expense-paid activities create venue for lobbyists — and may open door to abuse

Hill's Privately Funded Trips: Well-Traveled Ethics Loophole

With a major aviation bill expected to move through Congress this year, a leading industry group for airports wasted no time getting its lobbying campaign off the ground. In the opening days of January, as an ice storm socked Washington, the American Association of Airport Executives flew five top congressional staff aides to Kona Beach in Hawaii.

Once there, the staff members had a choice of activities. They could listen to seminars and speeches about the airports' top legislative priority — a proposed increase in the airline passenger fees that pay for airport improvements. Or, they could take a walk on one of the world's most beautiful beaches, near the Hapuna Beach Prince Hotel, play a round on an 18-hole golf course designed by Arnold Palmer, or just put on their complimentary Japanese robes and rest up from the long flight.

No matter how they spent their time, the aides got a free ride. The airport executives picked up the $300-plus-a-night tab for each aide — staff members for House Transportation Committee Chairman Bud Shuster, R-Pa.; Senate Commerce, Science and Transportation Aviation Subcommittee Chairman Slade Gorton, R-Wash.; and House Majority Leader Dick Armey, R-Texas.

James Coon, a former aide to Shuster who went on a similar Hawaii trip with the airport executives in 1998, said: "For me, it was an invaluable tool to learn more about aviation issues and to get to know the people making the informed decisions on aviation policy." Coon is now director of government affairs for the Air Transport Association, an airline trade group.

The deluxe Hawaiian trips are not unlike hundreds of others taken by members and their aides, according to a Congressional Quarterly computer analysis of privately financed travel. Congress has rid itself of most lobbyist-sponsored perks over the last decade, but free trips by special interests remain an exception to the ban.

Even while legislators and their aides stoically turn away free lunches and baseball tickets for fear that they may exceed a $100 yearly limit per donor on such freebies imposed by 1990s reforms of the gift rule, a big loophole allows them and their staff members to accept millions of dollars in trips from corporations and other interests with a stake in the outcome of legislation before their committees. The only requirement in House and Senate rules is that the trip be related to the member's or aide's official duties.

In a 17-month period ending in May, CQ found that private interests spent nearly $3 million on 2,042 trips for leading members of Congress and their staffs. The study examined travel disclosure reports filed by the top-ranking leaders of the Republican and Democratic parties and by the chairmen and ranking members of the House and Senate standing committees. (*Methodology, 1999 CQ Weekly, p. 1601*)

The list of travel sponsors is an encyclopedia of moneyed interests on Capitol Hill, closely mirroring the top contributor lists of recent congressional campaigns. Well-represented are utilities, telecommunications firms, the computer industry, health care groups, airlines, railroads, securities firms, investment houses and agribusiness.

The travel exemption, which allows the acceptance of trips so long as they are related to the official duties, has not only created an important avenue for lobbyists, it has opened the door for possible abuses. Some trips, including the Republicans' annual policy retreat at historic Williamsburg, Va., are sponsored by foundations that are run and financed by GOP lobbyists. Some trips to foreign destinations such as Taiwan have been paid for by groups closely associated with foreign governments, even though the gift rules specifically bar quasi-governmental groups from sponsoring trips.

The analysis of records found that several staff aides on important committees are the most frequent travelers. In some cases, staff members spent up to five weeks of the year on the road on someone else's dime.

Quick Contents

A CQ computer analysis found a loophole still exists in the "gift ban" rules for members of Congress and their staffs, which limits gifts from private businesses and individuals to $100 or less per year. Corporations and special interests are still able to sponsor trips to exotic locales for "educational" purposes, providing another way to influence the people who decide what goes into legislation.

Leading the Way: The Top Five Congressional Offices

| Rep. Bill Archer, R-Texas | Sen. William V. Roth Jr., R-Del. | Rep. Thomas J. Bliley Jr., R-Va. | Former Rep. Bob Smith, R-Ore. | Rep. Dick Armey, R-Texas |

Private organizations paid for dozens of trips for members of Congress and their personal and committee staffs. Above are the members who, with their staffs, accounted for the largest totals in one 17-month period. For Archer, the total was $157,878; for Roth, $134,295; for Bliley, $133,505; for Smith, $119,885; and for Armey, $96,397. Archer and Roth totals include staff aides from Joint Taxation Committee.

In 1998, Nils W. Johnson, an energy policy aide to Senate Republican Policy Committee Chairman Larry E. Craig, R-Idaho, took 11 trips, including four January days in Las Vegas, thanks to the Nuclear Energy Institute (NEI), which promotes nuclear power; a few days in February in Denver attending the annual meeting of the National Cattleman's Beef Association; spring recess in Japan on the tab of Southern Nuclear Operating Co. of Birmingham, Ala.; and six summer days in Anchorage as a guest of the Alaska Mining Association.

This year, Johnson spent the congressional spring recess in Paris and Marseilles, compliments, again, of the nuclear industry. Like most staff members contacted for this story, Johnson declined to comment on his trips.

The travel exemption is not well-policed. While the House and Senate ethics committees review some trips before they are taken, it is left to members to decide whether to accept travel invitations to themselves and their aides.

"I almost always approve these requests by my staff to go on these trips because I don't want to go on them myself," Gorton said in an interview on June 22. "It's a way for them to be more sophisticated about the issues on which they give me advice. It's just as simple as that."

"It's the best way to get to know the issues and to get to know people on the other side of the aisle, away from the politics of the daily grind around here," said Michele Davis, a spokeswoman for Armey.

Former Rep. Lee H. Hamilton, R-Ind. (1965-99), who was ranking member of the International Relations Committee, proposed closing the loophole before he retired from Congress. The verbal drubbing he endured from his colleagues convinced him that nothing would be done about it any time soon. His proposed rules change never made it to the Rules Committee.

"It got nowhere, and it won't get anywhere," said Hamilton, now president of the Woodrow Wilson International Center for Scholars in Washington. "The trips are very popular, and members don't want to give them up."

Tightening the Rules

Since 1992, both the House and Senate have gradually revamped their gift rules after scandals of the previous decade shattered public confidence in Congress. In rethinking their rules, both chambers invoked the late Sen. Paul H. Douglas, D-Ill. (1949-67), who said in 1951: "Expensive gifts, lavish or frequent entertainment, paying hotel or travel costs . . . are clearly improper."

Although Congress banned all but token gifts by setting limits of $100 per year, members carved out an exemption that allows free trips so long as they are related to the responsibilities of the member or aide, including travel for fact-finding, speeches or educational purposes.

The House and Senate specifically banned trips paid for by "registered lobbyists." But that ban has been so loosely interpreted that the rule has done little to prevent lobbyists from being directly involved in the trips.

Under the rules, lobbyists may plan and execute the trips; they may even come along, as long as they do not pay for them out of their own pockets. The corporations, trade associations or special interest groups they work for are allowed to pay.

For example, in January, The Dutko Group, a prominent Washington lobbying firm, put on a "legislative conference" for

Frequent Travelers

These are the major trip sponsors for the top 10 traveling members and their aides, ranked by cost, as reported to the House and Senate.

Member /Sponsor	Trips	Amount
Bill Archer, R-Texas, *House Ways and Means chairman* *		
Corporate Council on Africa/ The Wilderness Foundation	1	$16,976
Tax Foundation	2	$13,600
Asan Foundation	2	$11,048
Foreign Policy Institute	1	$9,040
Nuclear Energy Institute	2	$6,869
William V. Roth Jr., R-Del., *Senate Finance chairman* *		
The Aspen Institute	2	$24,212
Tax Foundation	3	$16,004
Asia-Pacific Policy Center	2	$9,200
Japan Center for International Exchange	1	$7,472
Ripon Educational Fund	2	$7,050
Thomas J. Bliley Jr., R-Va., *House Commerce chairman*		
Edison Electric Institute	6	$8,422
Integrated Waste Services Association	4	$6,784
Microsoft Corp.	3	$5,516
Chinese National Association of Industry & Commerce	1	$3,800
SBC Communications Inc.	1	$3,696
Bob Smith, R-Ore., *House Agriculture former chairman*		
National Cotton Council	8	$12,546
Chinese National Association of Industry & Commerce	3	$11,500
Congressional Economic Leadership Institute	1	$7,717
International Dairy Foods Association	3	$6,133
American Meat Institute	4	$5,840
Dick Armey, R-Texas, *House Majority Leader*		
Citizens for a Sound Economy Foundation	16	$18,311
U.S. Asia Institute	1	$8,518
Chinese National Association of Industry & Commerce	2	$7,800
SBC Communications Inc.	2	$6,612
American Association of Airport Executives	2	$5,892
*Includes Joint Taxation Committee staff		

Member /Sponsor	Trips	Amount
Newt Gingrich, R-Ga., *former House Speaker*		
World Economic Forum	1	$16,657
Chinese National Association of Industry & Commerce	2	$12,280
Nuclear Energy Institute	2	$8,356
The Congressional Institute Inc.	14	$7,160
U.S.-Indonesia Society	1	$6,761
Larry E. Craig, R-Idaho, *Senate GOP Policy Committee chairman*		
Chinese National Association of Industry & Commerce	2	$7,750
Nuclear Energy Institute	5	$7,223
Southern Nuclear Operating Co.	1	$6,601
Tax Foundation	1	$6,482
Hong Kong & China General Chambers of Commerce	1	$4,872
Frank H. Murkowski, R-Alaska, *Senate Energy chairman*		
Nuclear Energy Institute	7	$20,060
The Aspen Institute	3	$13,160
Edison Electric Institute	3	$5,955
BP America	2	$4,548
Natural Gas Supply Association	1	$4,111
Bud Shuster, R-Pa., *House Transportation chairman*		
Intelligent Transportation Society of America	3	$23,400
American Association of Airport Executives	8	$14,012
Burlington Northern Santa Fe Corp.	3	$6,254
Union Pacific Corp.	3	$4,490
Association of American Railroads	3	$3,839
Tom DeLay, R-Texas, *House Majority Whip*		
Hong Kong Economic & Trade Office	2	$9,615
Heritage Foundation	1	$9,500
Choctaw Nation	2	$6,936
Nuclear Energy Institute	1	$6,601
Hans Seidel Foundation	2	$5,860

members and aides called "The Internet: Its History and Evolution." It was staged at the Nemacolin Woodlands Resort & Spa in Farmington, Pa., which offers skiing, swimming and horseback riding. Because the trip was paid for not by Dutko but by corporations it represents, including AT&T Corp. and SAIC/Bellcore, the aides could accept the expense-paid trips.

In March, the U.S. Telephone Association, a trade group representing the nation's major local telephone carriers, sponsored a two-day "leadership roundtable" at the fabled La Quinta Resort & Club in Palm Springs, Calif., a desert resort popular with Hollywood and sports celebrities that boasts three golf courses, five restaurants and a spa.

Once back in Washington, Lisa Costello, director of government relations for USTA, sent a note to C. Stewart Verdery Jr., an aide to Senate Assistant Majority Whip Don Nickles, R-Okla., thanking Verdery for attending and letting him know that his expenses came to $2,206.

"If you have any additional receipts that you need to submit, please forward them to us," she wrote March 23.

Though the conference lasted two days, Verdery stayed three, according to the report he filed upon his return, as regulation requires. The report in-cluded Costello's note.

Although members and their staffs comply with the rules and file their travel reports with the House or Senate, "It's really a regulation with no meaning at all," said Paul Hendrie of the Center for Responsive Politics, a Washington watchdog group that has studied congressional travel.

Out Into the 'Real' World

Members and aides defend the exemption as a way of getting outside Washington to investigate the real-world effects of legislation without draining tight congressional office budgets. That is precisely why the exemption was created, according to the aides who helped write it.

"The thinking behind it was that members of Congress and congressional staff can learn a lot by seeing things in person and by getting outside the Beltway to better understand things," said a Senate aide who helped draft the gift rules.

However, the definition of what is legitimate travel related to an aide's official duties is loosely construed in many cases.

For example, David Hobbs, Armey's chief of staff, took six trips with five different groups in the 17-month period, twice to Hawaii with the airport executives — bringing his wife, Gretchen, along on one of the trips — and to Palm Springs, Calif., with the phone industry.

Ralph Lotkin, a government ethics lawyer and former chief counsel to the House Committee on Standards of Official Conduct, said, "It seems there is nothing under the sun outside of official responsibilities, unless you are a junior LA [legislative assistant] and your issue is herpes. But if you are at least a legislative director, everything from here to Pluto is fair game."

Some groups take pains to cast their events as educational, although the actual informational value appears questionable.

The Invest to Compete Alliance, which represents the manufacturing and service industries, hosted what it billed as a "Congressional Educational Seminar" last summer. It was held for four days over the Independence Day recess on Cape Cod, Mass.

The first day, a Friday, consisted of a reception and New England-style clambake at the Wequassett Inn in Chatham, Mass. On Saturday, there was a panel at 8 a.m. and another at 7 p.m., with nothing scheduled in between. Sunday was light, too, with just two panels — one in the morning and another in the evening.

But Rep. Mark Foley, R-Fla., who attended the conference, said the printed agenda is misleading because there were several hours of discussions of issues throughout the day among members, their aides and business leaders. And, he said, he got to know Reps. Joe Moakley and Richard E. Neal, both Massachusetts Democrats, better than he had during all of their encounters on Capitol Hill.

"It was a good trip," Foley said in an interview July 1. "I fully disclose, and people know exactly where I went, and I'm prepared to discuss what I've done."

After his experiences with the travel exemption, Hamilton came to one conclusion: "My personal view is, if members and staff are going to do official travel, the government ought to pay for it. There are just too many instances in which private groups try to influence congressional opinion with very lavish trips."

Nuclear Waste

Influencing congressional opinion is just what the NEI has in mind with a program that takes 30 to 40 members and aides a year on visits to Yucca Mountain in Nevada, site of a proposed repository for the nation's stockpile of commercial nuclear waste. (*1999 CQ Weekly, p. 1466*)

NEI and and its congressional allies are locked in a battle with the state of Nevada and the state's congressional delegation over a House bill (HR 45) that would allow temporary storage of waste at Yucca. The nuclear industry also favors a permanent storage site at Yucca, which most Nevada politicians oppose.

The airport closest to the site is at Las Vegas. Although the repository tour usually takes a day and consists of back-to-back briefings at the mountain, some staff members stay over to visit the casinos on the city's famed strip.

NEI puts them up at the Hard Rock Hotel, which bills itself as the "world's first rock and roll hotel and casino" with a pool that is "lush beyond belief," according to the hotel's Web site.

William McSherry, a former aide to Gorton, stayed six days in Las Vegas last year, met his parents there and took in some shows. He said he paid for the extra nights himself. NEI picked up $1,500 for airfare, hotel and meal costs.

"I was new to the issue, so to me the trip was very valuable," said McSherry, who is now public affairs manager for the Seattle Chamber of Commerce.

The NEI's Scott Peterson, who oversees the travel program, said members and aides are driven by van the 100 miles from Las Vegas to the repository site, where the Department of Energy gives guided tours of underground alcoves where tests are under way to determine the mountain's suitability.

"You really have to take them to the place, because you can't take the place to them," said Peterson.

Nevada's officials have complained without success about NEI's congressional trips because they have tried to have state officials included in the tours. There is widespread opposition from Nevadans to the site because of health and safety concerns and because the state generates no nuclear waste of its own.

"It's a complete snow job, a total sales job," said Bob Loux, executive director of the state's Nuclear Waste Project. "Hearing both sides is the only way to get an objective view of what's going on out there."

The Energy Department insists it has no right to tell NEI whom to invite on the tours. Spokesman Allen Benson said, "If NEI wants to bring people out to the site, they are entitled to do that. If they don't want other people to go along, we accommodate that."

Auke Piersma, energy policy analyst for the liberal watchdog group Public Citizen, said, "It's ludicrous to say you're going to send congressional staff on a fact-finding trip, have them see only one side of the issue and then argue that this is good for the taxpayer."

Also popular with congressional staff is the NEI's overseas travel program. Of the key committees and leadership offices reviewed by CQ, NEI spent $39,000 to take seven aides on a tour of nuclear power plants in Japan and $22,700 to take eight aides to plants in France, Belgium and England.

NEI is promoting the commercial reuse of nuclear fuel, which has been done abroad but is currently barred in the United States.

Tax-Exempt Sponsors

A wide array of tax-exempt foundations sponsor congressional travel. Some, such as the Washington, D.C.-based Aspen Institute, are well-established think tanks. The Aspen Institute conducts seminars on topical issues around the world, selecting desirable locations such as Caribbean islands and Switzerland because they improve congressional turnout.

But some not-for-profits sponsoring trips are not free of special interest influences.

The Congressional Institute has for a dozen years picked up the tab for the House GOP's annual policy retreat, a well-attended event that members use to shape their agenda for the year ahead. In recent years, the event has been held at the Kingsmill Resort in Williamsburg, Va. Scores of aides in CQ's analysis listed the institute as their sponsor to Williamsburg earlier this year and last year.

The not-for-profit institute, however, is run almost entirely by lobbyists. Thirteen members of its board of directors are lobbyists, almost all of them Republicans and some of them among the best-known lobbyists in Washington, according to the organization's records. They represent a long list of corporate interests, including the American Bankers Association, the American Hospital Association, Shell Oil Co., Burlington Northern and Santa Fe Railway Co., Time Warner Inc., and Las Vegas casinos.

The chairman is Nicholas E. Calio, a partner in O'Brien Calio. Also on the board are Bruce Gates and Gary Andres, both top GOP fundraisers; Michael Johnson, former chief of staff to former House minority leader Bob H. Michel, R-Ill. (1957-95); Daniel J. Mattoon, BellSouth Corp.'s chief lobbyist who is close to Speaker J. Dennis Hastert, R-Ill.; David Bockorny, President Ronald Reagan's liaison to Congress; Henry Gandy, vice president of the lobbying firm run by Kenneth M. Duberstein, Reagan's former chief of staff; and Barbara Morris-Lent, vice president of federal relations for NYNEX, the phone company.

The Williamsburg retreat, as well as a bipartisan retreat held this year and in 1997 to improve relations between the two parties in the House, are the Congressional Institute's single largest costs, accounting for $377,000, or more than half, of its annual outlays for activities, according to its tax forms.

The institute also focuses on hosting private lunches at the Rayburn House Office Building and dinners at the GOP's Capitol Hill Club, where the institute's members can mingle with members of key committees.

Last month, the institute sponsored a lunch at which its members could discuss health care issues with Bill Thomas, R-Calif., chairman of the House Ways and Means Health Subcommittee; sub-

committee member Jim McCrery, R-La.; and former GOP Conference Chairman John A. Boehner, R-Ohio. The institute also recently had a lunch for House Majority Whip Tom DeLay, R-Texas, and House GOP Conference Chairman J. C. Watts Jr., R-Okla.

Membership in the institute costs $10,000 a year, which allows a dues-payer to participate in all of the organization's events, or $20,000 a year to bring a guest. The institute's mission statement says it was established in 1987 "to assist members of Congress in organization and education for their intellectual and social benefit and to provide educational information about Congress to the general public."

But participants interviewed by CQ describe its purpose as fostering "dialogue" between legislators and the private sector.

Calio said that while the institute's members may benefit from access they get, the institute provides valuable public services, including the retreats. "It does a great job with a very small staff," he said. "Does it make a contribution? Yes, because it makes Congress a better, more efficient place."

Foreign Travel

By far the most popular of the congressional trips is one to Taiwan every year sponsored by the Chinese National Association of Industry & Commerce. The organization sponsored 50 trips for leading members and aides at a cost of $203,450, according to the CQ analysis, making it the second most active trip sponsor.

Both the House and Senate gift rules bar travel paid for by foreign governments except in very limited circumstances. For instance, such travel can be done as part of a cultural exchange program if approved by the U.S. State Department. But the rules bar travel from governmental or even "quasi-governmental" organizations closely affiliated with, or funded by, a foreign government.

The trips sponsored by the association seem to brush close to the prohibition, given the group's strong ties to the Taiwanese government. The association bills itself as a privately funded

business group representing Taiwan's largest companies. But its chairman, Jeffrey Koo, is also Taiwan's ambassador at large, according to the Central News Agency in Taiwan. He has been a senior adviser to former President Lee Teng-hui and active in promoting Taiwan's case for admission to the World Trade Organization. China has insisted that Taiwan not be admitted until China is.

Koo, chairman and chief executive of ChinaTrust Commercial Bank in Taipei, also has acted as an intermediary between Taiwan and China. Forbes magazine described the association in 1998 as "one of the primary links between business and government."

Some staff members who took the trips have only a vague understanding of the association or its mission. Lisa Johnson, an aide on the House Small Business Committee who took the trip July 7-13, 1998, said, "I don't know anything about them." But the trip, she said, "was very informative. We met with military, government and business people and learned a lot about Taiwan's connection with the United States."

Several aides referred inquiries about their trips to Louis Huang of the Taipei Economic and Cultural Representative's Office, Taiwan's unofficial embassy in Washington. Huang declined comment on the group or the trips.

An itinerary for one of the trips lists stops at Taiwan's ministries of Foreign Affairs, National Defense and Economic Affairs and at the Yuan, the Taiwanese parliament. Other stops for the weeklong trip included the American Chamber of Commerce in Taipei, the National Palace Museum and the Chiang Kai-Shek Memorial Hall.

Hamilton says foreign travel in particular concerns him because of its potential impact on policy.

"Certainly foreign countries who invite you as a guest of the government — or a guest of an institution once removed from the government — can have quite an impact on policy. A better rule would be, if a member thinks taking a trip is that important, the government ought to pay for it. That's the cleanest way to do it." ◆

Hill plays legislative catch-up as patients' rights to sue HMOs are expanded

Health Plan Liability: Courts Take the Lead in Expanding Patients' Rights

While Congress is debating legislation to make it easier for patients to sue their health plans, important decisions in the federal courts, state courts and state legislatures are already changing the balance of power between patients and health care providers.

The courts generally have protected health plans from paying punitive damages in lawsuits involving the denial of coverage, but several rulings and changes in state law in recent years have narrowed that protection.

Courts have been increasingly willing to wade into the issue of health plan liability because of a perceived lack of guidance from Washington on the issue, according to industry lobbyists and many lawmakers. Supporters of legislation expressly granting patients the right to sue their health plans for damages are citing the legal trend in an attempt to sway the debate.

The House on Oct. 7 passed a measure (HR 2723), sponsored by Republican Charlie Norwood of Georgia and Democrat John D. Dingell of Michigan, that would allow people to sue their health plans in state courts. The Senate on July 15 passed a far more restrictive bill (S 1344) that included no new rights to sue. (*1999 CQ Weekly, p. 1715*)

Supporter Rep. Marge Roukema, R-N.J., said she has been warning her business constituents for a year that changes were on the way, whether they were on board with them or not. "This is something we absolutely had to do," Roukema said in an Oct. 8 interview.

Rep. Merrill Cook, R-Utah, who also voted for the Norwood-Dingell bill, said Congress' actions will help give health plans a clearer picture of what to expect in the future. "I think in some

ways we were playing a little bit of catch-up," he said.

Cook added that the legislation makes sense from a states' rights perspective: "I was convinced that there ought to be a right to sue a health plan, and that it ought to be in state court."

He said he did not believe that the legislation would provoke an explosion of litigation because the threat of being

Richard Scruggs, who handled landmark tobacco litigation, is one of several lawyers taking on health insurers.

sued would encourage health plans to reach reasonable settlements in disputes.

Opponents of federal legislation that would open the door for lawsuits against health plans, including Senate Republican Whip Don Nickles of Oklahoma, say the lawsuits already filed prove that patients already have adequate rights to sue.

Alan B. Mertz, executive vice presi-

dent of the Healthcare Leadership Council, a coalition of leading health care executives, agreed. "The courts have already addressed the quality-of-care issue," Mertz said.

Setting Precedents

Recent court rulings have undermined the notion that the Employee Retirement Income Security Act (PL 93-406), known as ERISA, provides health plans with sweeping immunity from punitive damages in lawsuits filed by patients. Because the 1974 law essentially forces patients to file their suits in federal court and limits damage awards to the cost of the denied treatment, it has long been considered a liability shield for health insurers. Patients were generally blocked from seeking punitive or compensatory damages from health plans because of the law. (*1974 Almanac, p. 244*)

However, the 3rd U.S. Circuit Court of Appeals recently rejected a request from a health maintenance organization (HMO) to throw out a malpractice lawsuit filed by the parents of an infant who died of meningitis shortly after being discharged from a hospital.

Steven and Michelle Bauman argued that the HMO's policy of routinely discharging newborns within 24 hours was not medically sound, and that it encouraged the premature discharge of some newborns in need of longer hospital care. The policy was, in effect, a medical care decision rather than a benefits judgment, the plaintiffs argued, and therefore the HMO was not shielded from the lawsuit by ERISA.

Other federal court decisions also have sided with plaintiffs by rejecting health plans' efforts to dismiss cases involving negligent supervision, negligent hiring, breach of contract and deceptive trade practices. Although such rulings do not mean that plaintiffs will win their cases, they are important because they have opened the door for plaintiffs to proceed with their lawsuits.

HMOs Playing Doctor?

The courts have continued to rule that ERISA blocks suits in which damages are sought for a denial of benefits. These rulings, observers say, have led attorneys to carefully tailor their lawsuits to focus on quality of care.

A key tactic in many of the cases has been for plaintiffs to argue that HMOs shed their malpractice protections when they make decisions or establish policies that, in effect, place the HMO in the position of making treatment decisions. In other words, the courts have found that HMOs are behaving much like doctors, and therefore they should be held accountable when medical decisions go awry.

Dictating particularly explicit and rigid policies on treatment and offering financial incentives to doctors who hold down costs are proving to be particularly dangerous practices for HMOs in this new legal context.

The Supreme Court recently stepped into the fray, agreeing to review a lower court decision that a lawsuit against Health Alliance Medical Plans of Urbana, Ill., could proceed. Cynthia Herdrich sued the HMO after she was forced to wait eight days for an ultrasound to be performed by HMO staff on her inflamed appendix. While she was waiting for the test, her appendix burst, leading to numerous medical complications.

The 7th U.S. Circuit Court of Appeals had ruled that the HMO's policy of rewarding doctors for holding down costs may have forced a conflict between physicians' interests and the needs of patients. The Supreme Court has not heard the case yet, and a decision is months away.

Federal vs. State

Another key development has been the willingness of state courts to allow malpractice suits to proceed against HMOs. Federal courts are generally considered a less hospitable forum for class action lawsuits, and insurers would prefer not to deal with a patchwork of state laws and lawsuits.

Anecdotal evidence suggests that

HMOs' fears are well grounded. Last month, an HMO was slapped with a $51.5 million judgment in an Ohio case involving a woman who died of cancer after the HMO refused to pay for her chemotherapy.

The Illinois Supreme Court late last month ruled that residents can sue their health plans for medical malpractice in some circumstances.

"Where an HMO effectively controls a physician's exercise of medical judgment and that judgment is exercised negligently, the HMO cannot be allowed to claim that the physician is solely responsible for the harm that results," the court ruled.

In the Illinois case, Inga Petrovich, who died last year of mouth cancer, sued her HMO after her doctors were slow in diagnosing her ailment. The woman, whose husband is continuing the lawsuit, alleged in her lawsuit that Share Health Plan of Illinois Inc. balked at approving an expensive test when she complained of mouth pain, which led to a delay in her diagnosis.

New Tactics

Richard Scruggs, the brother-in-law of Senate Majority Leader Trent Lott, R-Miss., is among a handful of prominent lawyers preparing a series of class action lawsuits aimed at the HMO industry. Scruggs' law firm recently was awarded more than $300 million for fees and expenses for its participation in the state of Mississippi's legal battle with the tobacco industry, which resulted in a $4 billion settlement.

Plaintiffs are trying a variety of legal tactics to pursue lawsuits against HMOs. Scruggs and other attorneys filed a class action lawsuit on Oct. 7 in Mississippi, accusing an HMO of committing mail and wire fraud and violating federal racketeering laws.

In a telephone interview Oct. 7, Scruggs acknowledged that they were using "creative legal strategies," but said they were forced to do so because of federal laws limiting their legal options. "We're doing it with one hand tied behind our back," he said.

The lawsuit alleges that the HMO committed fraud by depriving patients of "honest services," Scruggs said. When mail or wire fraud occurs across state lines, the racketeering statutes apply, he said. When asked what his brother-in-law might say about his actions, Scruggs laughed. "I bet he's screaming when he sees my picture in

the newspaper," Scruggs said. "I bet Trent's having a heart attack."

Plaintiffs suing health care provider Humana Inc. in U.S. District Court in Miami are also using the racketeering law. The HMO was accused in a lawsuit filed Oct. 4 of systematically lying to customers about how health care decisions were made. Plaintiffs are seeking class action status on behalf of Humana customers. The lawsuit alleges that Humana concealed financial incentives offered to health care providers who held down costs. The plaintiffs argue that the health plan misled patients when it told them that medical need was the sole criterion in coverage decisions.

A Changing Landscape

A handful of states have joined the fight to broaden plaintiffs' rights to sue health plans.

Texas, California and Georgia have enacted laws granting patients the right to sue HMOs for compensatory damages, and federal courts have shown some tolerance for letting these provisions stand despite ERISA's apparent pre-emption. In addition, court cases in Pennsylvania and Illinois have established some rights for plaintiffs to recover damages against HMOs.

Although the Texas law, enacted in 1997, was scaled back by a federal court, a provision allowing plaintiffs to sue for punitive damages was upheld, Fort Worth attorney George Parker Young said in an Oct. 7 telephone interview.

Young helped the state attorney general defend the law, and he has filed a handful of lawsuits against HMOs. He argues that states ought to have the right to regulate health protections for citizens, because the federal courts often are less interested in such matters.

Federal courts are already overcrowded with cases, so even if plaintiffs are allowed to seek damages in federal court, it is a difficult path for them, Young said. "If we're stuck in federal court, that's a victory for the HMOs," Young said.

But opponents of legislation to expand the rights of patients to sue say that patients are already sufficiently protected.

"There's clearly a trend in the federal courts," said Kathryn Wilber, assistant general counsel with the American Association of Health Plans. "If the case goes to quality of care, then that case will proceed to the state courts," where damages may be pursued. ◆

Clinton, Republicans trade angry charges over treatment of women and minorities

Uproar Over Rejected Jurist May Doom Other Nominations

Datafile

Judicial nominations, 106th Congress

Nominees received: 68
• 24 Circuit
• 43 District
• 1 Trade Court

Confirmed: 21
• 4 Circuit
• 17 District

Pending on floor: 8

Pending in committee: 37

Current vacancies: 62
• 24 Circuit
• 37 District
• 1 Trade Court

Source: Senate Judiciary Committee minority staff

President Clinton's chances of winning confirmation of judicial nominees in the remaining 15 months of his term are in doubt, after a week filled with charges ranging from racism to political gamesmanship.

The partisan fighting reached a fevered pitch Oct. 6, when Clinton accused Senate Republicans of racism after the chamber rejected the nomination of a black Missouri judge, Ronnie L. White, to a seat on the U.S. District Court.

Clinton's comments capped months of Democratic complaints that the GOP-controlled Senate has unfairly delayed confirmation votes on his nominees, especially women and minorities.

Republicans, in turn, accused Clinton of intentionally nominating unqualified minorities and women to the bench in hopes of painting the GOP as bigoted.

Conservative Republicans also say that Clinton is nominating judges who are too liberal, and they vow to continue delaying confirmations until more "mainstream" nominees are sent to the Senate.

Instead of prodding Republicans into quicker action, furious GOP leaders said Clinton's attack may prompt them to take even longer to review nominees for federal courts.

"They don't get my attention by slapping me in the face," said Idaho Sen. Larry E. Craig, chairman of the Republican Policy Committee. "[Clinton] has clearly tainted the water."

The bitter fighting does not bode well for the 45 judicial nominees who are still awaiting Judiciary Committee or floor action.

In the first 10 months of this session, the Senate has confirmed 21 of Clinton's nominees to the federal bench. Congress is scheduled to adjourn within a month, and observers say there is realistically only a six-month window of opportunity in 2000 before the confirmation process is stalled by election-year politics.

"This seems to be, if not the all-time low, an all-time low," said Sheldon Goldman, a political science professor at the University of Massachusetts at Amherst and author of the book "Picking Federal Judges: Lower Court Selection From Roosevelt Through Reagan."

The partisan bickering "has been ratcheted up to an extent we've never seen before," Goldman said, and it could linger into the first term of the next president.

Rising Tempers

Democratic complaints in recent months have centered on the treatment of two nominees who have been awaiting Senate action for years.

Richard A. Paez, a Hispanic, was first nominated for the 9th Circuit Court of Appeals in January 1996. He has been approved twice by the Judiciary Committee, but his nomination has never come to a vote on the floor.

Marsha Berzon was first nominated for the 9th Circuit in January 1998. She has also been approved by the Judiciary Committee, but her nomination has been blocked on the floor.

To protest the delays, Democrats in late September held a Republican-backed nominee hostage from floor consideration. Ted Stewart, a longtime GOP operative and close friend of Judiciary Committee Chairman Sen. Orrin G. Hatch, R-Utah, was nominated for a District Court seat July 27. He was approved by the Judiciary Committee three days later, and GOP leaders sought to bring him to the floor this fall. (*1999 CQ Weekly*, p. 2218)

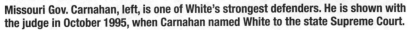

Missouri Gov. Carnahan, left, is one of White's strongest defenders. He is shown with the judge in October 1995, when Carnahan named White to the state Supreme Court.

CQ Weekly Oct. 9, 1999

On Sept. 21, Democrats defeated a cloture motion to bring Stewart's nomination to a floor vote.

Hatch attacked the cloture defeat as unprecedented and a dangerous move that could permanently taint the judicial process.

But on Oct. 1, Democrats agreed to allow the Stewart vote in exchange for floor consideration of several other nominees, including White, who was appointed by Democratic Gov. Mel Carnahan in 1995 as the first black on Missouri's Supreme Court.

But Missouri GOP Sen. John Ashcroft took to the floor Oct. 4 to attack White's dissents in death penalty cases and cited opposition to his nomination from several Missouri law enforcement organizations. Democrats countered with statements of support from Carnahan — who is set to challenge Ashcroft in 2000 — and others.

The 45-54 vote on Oct. 5 followed party lines. Several Republicans who supported White in the Judiciary Committee, including Hatch, switched on the floor. Stewart was then confirmed, 93-5.

White's rejection marked the first time the full Senate had defeated a judicial nomination since Robert H. Bork was blocked from taking a seat on the Supreme Court in 1987. (*1987 Almanac, p. 271*)

"I am hoping . . . the United States has not reverted to a time in its history when there was a color test on nominations," Sen. Patrick J. Leahy of Vermont, the top Democrat on the Judiciary Committee, said after White's defeat.

Clinton leveled his own charges against Senate Republicans in a Rose Garden ceremony the following day. "The Republican-controlled Senate is adding credence to the perceptions that they treat minority and women judicial nominees unfairly and unequally," Clinton said.

Angry Republicans responded that it was not racism, but rather a fear of overly liberal judges that led to White's defeat and the delay in action on Clinton nominees.

"These are left [wing] appointments," said Sen. Jeff Sessions, R-Ala. Sessions said he is particularly concerned about Clinton's nominations to the 9th Circuit and has placed "holds" on Paez and Berzon. A hold can indefinitely prevent nominations from coming to the Senate floor.

"I don't want them voted on, and I don't want them on the bench," Sessions said.

Sessions said that an inordinately high number of judges on the 9th Circuit Court of Appeals are liberals first nominated by Democratic Presidents Clinton and Jimmy Carter. There are eight Republican-appointed judges and 13 Democratic judges now serving on the court. There are six vacancies, although one will soon be filled by Associate Attorney General Raymond C. Fisher, who won confirmation Oct. 5 by a 69-29 vote.

"This is a legitimate thing for senators to consider," Sessions said. "I hope the White House would start sending mainstream nominees. I'm inclined to believe that until they get the message, we don't intend to vote unless we get some nominees that are more mainstream."

Minority Nominees

The flap over minority nominees has prompted both Democrats and Republicans to dig in their heels.

"We've been real sweet about it. Now we're entering a new phase," said Sen. Barbara Boxer, D-Calif. "Now we're playing hardball."

Boxer, Leahy and Minority Leader Tom Daschle, D-S.D., have threatened to use any means necessary to bring Paez, Berzon and other Clinton nominees to the floor. They have declined to say what their strategy will be, but Daschle said Democrats "will do all we can to see those votes are taken before the end of the year."

Republicans say Democrats are using the race card in order to score political points during next year's elections.

"It's the president's and his party's attempt to set up a series of scenarios that they can then charge the Senate next year as being racist," Craig said. "Maybe they're putting up a lot of nominations they know are unqualified but they think will shape this into a political issue for next year's elections."

Craig and many other Republicans insisted that they did not even know that White was black when they voted against his nomination.

"I can look you in the eye and swear on a Bible that I didn't know what his race was," said Sen. James M. Inhofe, R-Okla., who voted against White.

Senate Majority Leader Trent Lott, R-Miss., noted that of the 21 judges

confirmed this year, four were women, one was black and four were Hispanic. "Their records and the kind of judges that the men and women would make are the only thing that has been a factor," Lott said.

A recent study by the bipartisan group Citizens for Independent Courts showed that the Senate in recent years has in fact been slower to confirm women and minorities.

According to the report released Sept. 22, the GOP Senate took an average 33 days longer to confirm female than male nominees in the 104th Congress, and an average of 65 days longer to confirm women in the 105th Congress.

The study also showed that the Senate took an average of 60 days longer to act on minority nominees than whites.

But the study also levied blame against Clinton for delays in filling judicial vacancies. The study found that Clinton has taken longer to nominate judges to fill vacancies than any of his predecessors since Carter.

The Clinton administration has taken an average of 315 days to nominate federal judges to vacancies, compared with 240 days for Carter, 254 days for President Ronald Reagan and 296 days for President George Bush, the study found.

"It's silly for the Congress and the president to be pointing fingers at each other for this judicial crisis — and it is a crisis — when neither has performed well in this area on behalf of the American people," said former Rep. Mickey Edwards, R-Okla. (1977-93), co-chairman of the group.

Future Nominations

Even if Republicans and Democrats can smooth over their differences in the next several months and clear the path for Clinton's nominations, many say a dangerous precedent has been set that could hurt the judicial process for years to come.

Goldman blasted the use of holds to prevent votes on nominees as a "perversion of the judicial process." He added that stalling on nominations will likely continue — and possibly worsen — if Republicans win control of the White House.

"The Democrats are fuming," he said. "If the Republicans get the White House, Democrats will not be in any mood to cooperate — certainly not on judicial nominations." ◆

Politics and Public Policy

Articles in this section discuss major policy issues that came before Congress in the latter half of 1999. Some of these issues have been addressed by measures enacted into law. Others are still unresolved, possibly to become campaign issues in the 2000 elections.

The Senate on October 13, 1999, handed the Clinton administration a major policy defeat when it rejected the 1996 Comprehensive Test Ban Treaty, 51-48, with only four Republicans voting in favor. The first article in this section analyzes the political maneuvering that led to the defeat—the first time the Senate had rejected an international security agreement since the treaty of Versailles in 1920—and discusses strategies that arms control advocates will probably adopt to avoid future setbacks. A separate section speculates on the implications for nonproliferation efforts in Asia, particularly in light of recent governmental instability in Pakistan.

The dispute over how to spend projected budget surpluses remains unresolved, but the standoff has had a major policy consequence, planned by neither party. The surpluses will by default be used to pay down the nation's $5.5 trillion debt. One article examines reactions to this policy, which have generally been positive, and the likely economic consequences of debt reduction, compared with cutting taxes or increasing spending. A major area of contention in budget negotiations has been Social Security. A second article on the budget debate shows how Republicans have tried to seize the initiative on this traditionally Democratic issue by creating a Social Security "lockbox" that would prevent the government from using surpluses to fund other programs.

A series of articles about managed care reform traces the debate over the past months and highlights disputed areas. The first illustrates the difficulty the Republican Party faces in reconciling the demands of two traditional constituencies, doctors and insurers. The second profiles the major players in the debate, including J. Dennis Hastert (R-Ill.), Charles Norwood (R-Ga.), and John Dingell (D-Mich.). The last outlines the major provisions of the patients' rights bill that passed the House in October and was in committee as this book was going to press. Both sides are preparing for what will probably be the biggest political fight of 2000.

The next article chronicles recent attempts by Congress to regulate the Internet. For the past few years Congress has followed a laissez-faire policy toward the Internet, but this period of nonintervention seems to be over. The threat that a company such as AT&T could establish monopoly control of high-speed Internet access is spurring some members to consider taking action. Measures have recently been introduced that would ensure personal privacy, restrict unsolicited email, restrict alcohol sales across state lines, and protect children from harmful material.

After articles discussing gun control, military spending, and foreign trade, this section concludes with an in-depth analysis of the financial services overhaul. The final details of the sweeping legislation, which overturns barriers separating banks, brokerages, and insurance companies, were being hammered out as this article went to press, and the bill finally cleared both chambers on November 4, 1999. The article considers the lengthy negotiation process and the history of the restrictions, from their Depression-era origins in response to bank failures through various modifications and several attempts to repeal them. A second article on the legislation examines possible consequences of the overhaul, weighing the benefits of increased competition against possible loss of privacy and market consolidation.

Test-ban vote leaves GOP moderates groping for arms control strategy

Defeat of Nuclear Test Ban Treaty a 'Wake-Up Call' for Congress

Datafile

Test Ban Treaty Status

Ratified

Argentina	Japan
Australia	Mexico
Austria	Netherlands
Belgium	Norway
Brazil	Peru
Britain	Poland
Bulgaria	Romania
Canada	Slovakia
Finland	South Africa
France	South Korea
Germany	Spain
Hungary	Sweden
Italy	Switzerland

Have Not Ratified

Algeria	Iran
Bangladesh	Israel
Chile	North Korea*
China	Pakistan*
Colombia	Russia
Congo	Turkey
Egypt	Ukraine
India*	United States
Indonesia	Vietnam

*have not signed or ratified

SOURCE; State Department, Bureau of Arms Control

The Senate's stinging rejection of a nuclear test ban treaty signifies that any future arms control agreement will require the active — and early — support of a small but influential group of Senate moderates who voted "no" on Oct. 13.

Tactical blunders by the Clinton White House and Senate Democrats put "internationalist" Republicans such as John W. Warner of Virginia, Pete V. Domenici of New Mexico, Richard G. Lugar of Indiana and Ted Stevens of Alaska squarely in the camp of their more isolationist GOP colleagues.

All opposed the Comprehensive Test Ban Treaty because of serious doubts that it could be enforced or that it provided enough assurances for U.S. national security interests. When it became apparent that they could not sidestep or put off a ratification vote, however, they chose to reject it outright, all but scoffing at the attendant worldwide outcry over the Senate's repudiation of a major international agreement.

Yet these lawmakers and a handful of other centrist Republicans believe the United States should play a key role in international agreements. They are now trying to pick up the pieces in the backwash of bitter partisan recriminations. A bipartisan group of senators had dinner together after the vote to discuss how to cooperate.

"We really talked very frankly about how we pull together a very strong bipartisan majority for not only arms control, but for very constructive foreign policy activity," Lugar said Oct. 14 on PBS's NewsHour with Jim Lehrer. "I think that is the majority [view], and it has to be nourished. We have to get together and visit more often."

Sens. Chuck Hagel, R-Neb., and Joseph I. Lieberman, D-Conn., also have begun talks about how to better negotiate such terrain.

The subject of nuclear non-proliferation "is very much alive, and I think embraced . . . by a majority of members of Congress, including the Senate, if it's presented in the right way," Lieberman said at an Oct. 14 news conference.

Hagel, a Foreign Relations Committee member who voted against the treaty but strongly advocated delaying the vote, said he and Lieberman want to find "a way to come at this with some more accountability. This thing got snagged and dragged into the political swamp, and we couldn't rescue it."

Meanwhile, conservative Republicans were celebrating one of their few clear triumphs over President Clinton this year.

After months of careful groundwork, Majority Leader Trent Lott, R-Miss., and Foreign Relations Chairman Jesse Helms, R-N.C., found themselves with a clear shot at two things they despise — an arms control treaty and President Clinton — and the result was never in doubt.

Ratification of the pact (Treaty Doc 105-28) was rejected, 48-51, with only four Republicans voting in favor.

"What today's treaty rejection does say . . . is that our constitutional democracy, with its shared powers and checks and balances, is alive and well," said Jon Kyl, R-Ariz., one of the pact's most outspoken opponents, in an Oct. 13 written statement. "Today's Senate action sends a clear message that the United States will not sign on to flawed treaties that are not in our national interests."

Arms Control Challenges

To the treaty's supporters, such objections should be interpreted as "a wake-up call," said John D. Steinbruner, a senior fellow at the Brookings Institution, a nonpartisan think tank.

Ted Stevens (R-Alaska) talks with reporters the day before the treaty vote. He believes the United States will need nuclear weapons indefinitely but could support a test ban agreement.

The next challenge for lawmakers on arms control, Steinbruner said, will be amendments to the Anti-Ballistic Missile (ABM) Treaty, which limits the scope of anti-missile systems. Helms has repeatedly called on the administration to submit revisions to that 1972 agreement for his committee's consideration.

The rejection of the test ban treaty "is sort of like an early infection that could kill you, that could really kill you," Steinbruner said in an interview. "Are you going to go to work on it, or are you going to mess around with it?"

If the ABM treaty revisions meet a fate similar to the test ban, arms control experts warned, it could imperil the 1968 Nuclear Non-Proliferation Treaty, which bans the transfer of nuclear weapons to nations that do not already possess them. (*1969 Almanac, p. 162*)

The test ban vote "has raised the prospect of the [non-proliferation] regime gradually unraveling, perhaps beginning at the April 2000 [treaty] review conference, with nuclear weapons spreading widely around the world," said Thomas Graham Jr., president of the Lawyers Alliance for World Security and a former Clinton administration arms control aide.

Opponents of the test ban treaty, however, dismiss the notion that the pact's defeat will have any negative ramifications. In fact, they countered, it should strengthen the hand of U.S. negotiators in future arms talks.

"Our negotiators will be able to say in the future, when they're negotiating treaties, 'We can't agree to that, because we can't get the Senate to confirm it,' " Lott told reporters.

Partisan Twilight

Lott was among the test ban treaty's staunchest opponents, creating an atmosphere where confrontation trumped cooperation.

The treaty aroused deep-seated partisan tensions that had remained buried since Clinton's impeachment trial over his involvement with former White House intern Monica Lewinsky. Helms even alluded to Lewinsky on the Senate floor in his closing remarks against the test ban.

Former Sen. Alan K. Simpson, R-Wyo. (1979-97), said such partisanship reflects his party's mistrust of Clinton, as well as its unwillingness to hand him any major foreign policy accomplishment in the twilight of his final term.

"The bitterness toward Clinton from a majority of Republicans, you couldn't even measure," Simpson said. "Some of them say, 'He has foiled us so many times, we look like a circus act.' "

The White House, Senate Democrats and arms control activists, in denouncing the vote, made it clear that they intend to try to resuscitate the treaty even as they attempt to use its defeat as a political weapon against the Republicans.

"We will continue to force it, in as many ways as we know how," Minority Leader Tom Daschle, S.D., told reporters Oct. 14.

Despite such talk, most advocates agree that action is unlikely as long as Clinton is in office. Several Republican presidential candidates, including the current front-runner, Texas Gov. George W. Bush, have spoken out against the test ban, but some arms control activists held out hope that if Bush or another Republican is elected, the treaty will get another chance. They cited Bush's stated willingness to continue Clinton's seven-year moratorium on nuclear tests.

Until then, the arms control activists promised to exert political pressure on Republicans who opposed the treaty, particularly incumbents up for re-election next year such as Michigan's Spencer Abraham and Montana's Conrad Burns. Vice President Al Gore has joined them, running television advertisements blasting the Senate's action the day after it occurred.

"We will certainly try to make [opponents] pay a price in the coming weeks and months before the 2000 election," said John Isaacs, executive director and president of the Council for a Livable World, one of the groups that lobbied for the treaty.

Nuclear Stewards

Opponents of the treaty said they voted on the merits of the treaty, not the politics. Lugar and other moderates agreed that if lawmakers are to be coaxed into revisiting the treaty, their concern over protecting the U.S. nuclear arsenal will have to be addressed.

In particular, some lawmakers worry about the Energy Department's stockpile stewardship program as an alternative to nuclear testing. The ambitious and costly program uses computer modeling and simulations to verify the safety and reliability of the weapons inventory. Critics of the treaty have said stockpile stewardship remains unlikely to be fully operational for another decade or so.

"Stockpile stewardship is as yet unproven," Domenici said. "We still do not fully understand the aging effects on our nuclear arsenal."

The directors of the three Energy Department weapons laboratories — Los Alamos and Sandia in New Mexico and Lawrence Livermore in California — told senators at an Oct. 7 Armed Services Committee hearing that the nuclear stockpile remains safe and reliable without testing under the program. But some lawmakers said the officials were more equivocal in private.

"Privately, they will say, 'If this [treaty] goes down, it's fine, because

Pakistani soldiers guard the Punjab Assembly in Lahore a day after an Oct. 12 army coup. Tension between Pakistan and India has increased fears of an eventual nuclear clash.

Treaty Rejection Casts a Shadow Over Non-Proliferation Efforts in Asia

As the Senate considered the Comprehensive Test Ban Treaty (CTBT), the true battleground was in Asia. There, last year's nuclear tests by India and Pakistan and North Korea's recent threat to test fire a long-range missile capable of carrying a nuclear warhead have brought new relevance to the decades-old debate.

Pakistan's military leaders further raised the stakes by staging a military coup Oct. 12 and effectively imposing martial law three days later. Secretary of State Madeleine K. Albright said the military putsch had injected a new level of uncertainty into the already tense relations between Pakistan and India.

It also clouded relations with the United States, which had been on the mend after Pakistan, at President Clinton's insistence, pulled its troops back from a border clash with India this summer. Before the coup, the Clinton administration had hopes of persuading both countries to sign the test ban treaty.

That possibility was one reason Senate Democrats gave for refusing to agree not to bring up the treaty during the rest of President Clinton's term — a refusal that removed any hope of delaying the Oct. 13 vote. Senate Minority Leader Tom Daschle, D-S.D., said Clinton wanted the door left open for a quick vote on the treaty if it were needed to make sure that countries did not bolt the non-proliferation regime.

"What happens in Pakistan, what happens in India, what happens in North Korea, what happens in the Middle East, what happens in Iraq and Iran, what happens in an awful lot of those countries could have a profound effect on the decisions made in the Senate over the course of the next 14 months," Daschle said during the Oct. 13 debate.

Democrats and some Republicans also warned that rejecting the treaty would send a disastrous signal to nascent and would-be nuclear powers.

"We no longer have standing, when we defeat this treaty, to tell China or India or Pakistan or any other country, 'Don't test nuclear weapons,'" said Carl Levin of Michigan, ranking Democrat on the Armed Services Committee.

Clinton made the same claim after the treaty was defeated.

"By this vote, the Senate majority has turned its back on 50 years of American leadership against the spread of weapons of mass destruction. They are saying America does not need to lead, either by effort or by example. They are saying we don't need our friends or allies," he said Oct 14.

No Deterrence

Most Republicans dismissed that argument, saying the treaty and its sanctions would not deter proliferation.

"This treaty will not stop or slow down the development of nuclear weapons if a nation deems these weapons as vital to their national interests," said Armed Services Committee member Pat Roberts, R-Kan.

And Foreign Relations Chairman Jesse Helms, R-N.C., scoffed at treaty supporters: "If we vote the CTBT down, they warn, India and Pakistan may well proceed with nuclear tests. . . . Give me a break! That horse has already left the barn. India and Pakistan have already tested."

At a hearing of that panel's Near Eastern and South Asian Affairs Subcommittee, Chairman Sam Brownback, R-Kan., and Karl F. Inderfurth, assistant secretary of State for South Asian Affairs, agreed that previous sanctions on Pakistan for its nuclear activities may have harmed the United States' ability to prevent the coup and pushed Pakistan to accelerate its nuclear program.

Before the coup, Congress had been rushing to grant the Clinton administration permanent authority to lift economic sanctions on India

and Pakistan imposed after last year's tests. In addition, the fiscal 2000 defense appropriations bill (HR 2561) would give Clinton authority to waive a longstanding ban on aid and military sales to Pakistan.

House and Senate conferees on the defense bill also had agreed to permit exports to Pakistan of dual-use items — those with both a military and civilian application.

Administration officials now say any rollback of sanctions is on hold until a civilian government is in place in Pakistan. Officials said they would abide by a provision in the fiscal 1999 foreign operations appropriations law (PL 105-277), which bans most U.S. aid to countries in which a military coup has taken place against a democratic government. (*1998 Almanac, p. 2-45*)

U.S. officials stressed, however, that they hoped Pakistan could move quickly to civilian rule so positive relations could resume. "It is not our hope or interest to see Pakistan further isolated," Inderfurth said.

Testifying before the House and Senate Foreign Affairs committees Oct. 12 and 13, former Defense Secretary William J. Perry made a similar argument in unveiling the administration's new approach to curbing North Korea's nuclear ambitions.

The goal of Perry's step-by-step proposal is normalization of trade and diplomatic relations with North Korea in exchange for an end to Pyongyang's nuclear and long-range missile programs.

"The year 1999 may represent, historically, one of our best opportunities for some time to come, to begin a path to normalization," Perry told members of the House International Relations Committee on Oct. 13.

But many Republicans were skeptical, arguing that U.S. food and fuel aid has bought time for a shaky and dangerous regime and its nuclear program. Further easing, they say, would only extend its shelf life.

we've got a ways to go,' " said Gordon H. Smith, R-Ore., who put aside his concerns and joined Arlen Specter of Pennsylvania, John H. Chafee of Rhode Island and James M. Jeffords of Vermont as the only Republicans to back the treaty.

A related concern for lawmakers was continued funding for the stockpile stewardship program. House members tried to cut the program in the fiscal 2000 energy and water appropriations bill (PL 106-60) as part of an overall $1 billion reduction in the Energy Department's budget, but Domenici and Stevens worked to restore the cuts in conference. (*1999 CQ Weekly, p. 2299*)

"Senator Domenici and I had to fight like banshees to get the $1 billion this year," Stevens said.

While Stevens said he thinks the United States will need nuclear weapons indefinitely, he said he has no trouble backing a test ban in theory. Nevertheless, he added, stockpile stewardship could be proven to work at a faster pace if Clinton abandoned his argument that any tests should be "zero yield," with no release of radiation.

But perhaps the main stumbling block to arms control treaties in the Senate is verification — how to keep other countries from cheating.

Lugar and other moderate Republicans said the test ban treaty lacked a common definition of an actual nuclear test but contained a process for on-site inspections that would require the consent of 30 members of the treaty's 51-member executive council.

By contrast, Lugar noted, the Chemical Weapons Convention, which the Senate overwhelmingly adopted in 1997, requires an affirmative vote to stop an inspection, not permit one. Lugar, Warner, Stevens and Domenici all supported that treaty — negotiated by former President George Bush — despite opposition from Helms and other conservatives. (*1997 Almanac, p. 8-13*)

Rescue Squad

When other arms control agreements have run into trouble in the Senate, a bipartisan group has been able to rescue them, or at least shelve them for another day.

During the 1979 debate over the SALT II arms-reduction treaty with the former Soviet Union, Warner sent President Jimmy Carter a letter, signed by Domenici and 17 other senators,

Sen. Jesse Helms' opposition to the test ban treaty drew this protest from anti-nuclear activitists at a Capitol Hill rally Sept. 14. Helms had held the treaty in his committee.

letting him know of their concerns. The letter became a factor in Carter's subsequent decision to ask the Senate to defer action on SALT II. (*1979 Almanac, p. 411*)

When it became clear that the test ban treaty would fail, it again fell to Warner to seek a deferral. He joined Daniel Patrick Moynihan, D-N.Y., in circulating a letter to Lott and Daschle urging a "statesmanlike initiative" to delay the vote until the 107th Congress. That letter was eventually signed by 62 senators — 24 Republicans and 38 Democrats.

But the rules of the Senate, as well as the tradition of senators' deference to their leaders, helped give the treaty's critics the upper hand in what escalated into a political game of chicken.

After Warner began circulating his letter Oct. 12, Daschle agreed in writing not to push for a vote until after a new president and Congress take office in 2001, "absent unforeseen changes in the international situation," such as renewed testing by nuclear-capable nations. He later agreed to change the language to "extraordinary circumstances."

Under Senate rules, however, Lott had to obtain the unanimous consent of all senators. And treaty critics such as Helms and Kyl told him they wanted to see the pact voted down. Those critics, as well as Lott, had reservations with the vagueness of the "extraordinary circumstances" language.

"You can drive a Mack truck

through that," Lott said.

In addition, no matter what their views on delaying the treaty, all of the Republicans — including the internationalist moderates — felt compelled to support a procedural motion by Lott to turn from the agriculture appropriations conference report (HR 1906 — H Rept 106-354) back to the treaty. The Democrats objected, and the Senate returned to the treaty on a 55-45 party line vote.

"We should never be put in a spot where we have to challenge the Republican leader," Warner said. "Our party's going to stick with our leader."

Before he could bring up the treaty for the final vote, however, Lott was subjected to a harsh rebuke on the Senate floor from Robert C. Byrd, D-W.Va., the Senate's guardian of rules and customs. Byrd complained that Lott would not permit him 15 minutes to speak on the non-debatable motion.

After Byrd spent more than 15 minutes criticizing Lott, he shook Lott's hand, and the march toward the treaty's defeat proceeded. Byrd voted "present," for the first time in more than 40 years, citing procedural concerns.

The results left some of the treaty's opponents jubilant, but the older GOP veterans were considerably more sober about the turn of events. An unusually subdued Stevens summed up his feelings in an interview just before he entered the chamber to cast his vote.

"I'm sad," he said. "I'm sad." ◆

Congress finds itself defaulting into agreement on how to use projected surpluses

Buying Down the Debt: Policy by Stalemate

Quick Contents

Congress and President Clinton have dramatically reshaped national economic policy — albeit by default — in determining to use most of future budget surpluses to start paying down the national debt. Now the question is how much that will benefit the economy.

Little noticed in all the quarreling over the budget this year, Congress and President Clinton appear to have set a major element of U.S. fiscal policy for the next decade and beyond: The bulk of future budget surpluses will be used to start paying down the nation's $5.5 trillion debt.

They are not necessarily doing this by design.

In fact, the operative policy to continue running surpluses and buying down the cumulative national debt has remarkably little to do with economic argulments in favor of the idea. Rather, years of partisan skirmishing over who is the guardian of Social Security, plus immense distrust between Republicans and Democrats in this Congress, have produced a stalemate with extraordinary consequences.

The outcome appears to be a commitment to stop the practice of borrowing from Social Security surpluses to fund other government programs. Instead, those surpluses — projected to total $1.9 trillion over the next decade — would be dedicated to paying down the national debt. With remarkable ease and with little substantive debate, national economic policy has been dramatically reshaped.

"This is the most fundamental development in the last decade," said former Congressional Budget Office (CBO) Director Robert D. Reischauer, now a senior analyst at the Brookings Institution, a Washington think tank. "Without a great debate and without much controversy . . . our measure of fiscal rectitude is balance in the non-Social Security portion of the budget."

Now the question is to what extent paying down debt would be beneficial to the public and the economy.

The de facto decision to pay down debt has its roots in a small band of lawmakers, including Sen. Ernest F. Hollings, D-S.C., who have for years protested the practice of using Social Security trust funds — where revenues regularly exceed expenses — as a piggy bank to hide the size of the deficit in the rest of the budget. Democrats have used the politics of Social Security to stymie Republicans on taxes and twice to kill a proposed constitutional amendment requiring a balanced budget. Now Republicans have taken up the call in an effort to thwart Democrats on spending. As the parties play to a draw, the surpluses continue to pile up. (*Social Security, p. 76; budget, 1999 CQ Weekly, p. 2369*)

"Because we're at a stalemate on everything else, largely for political reasons and particularly because of a lack of trust at either end of [Pennsylvania] Avenue, retiring the debt becomes in this case a good default," said Martin Corry, top lobbyist for the the AARP, which represents senior citizens. "It's one time

Sen. Ernest F. Hollings, D-S.C., at microphone, and other lawmakers speak Oct. 1 at a news conference, sponsored by the Concord Coalition, highlighting the growing national debt.

Federal Debt Held by the Public

The federal budget showed a surplus for most of the nation's first 200 years. World War I brought a $23 billion deficit from 1917 through 1919, but the budget was in the black through the 1920s. The Depression and World War II, however, resulted in a long string of unprecedented deficits. The federal debt held by the public grew from less than $3 billion in 1917 to $16 billion in 1930 and to $242 billion in 1946. This same pattern of incurring debt during war and recession persisted through most of the postwar period, as shown in this chart. But that pattern changed during the 1980s, when constant deficits drove up the debt from $785 billion in 1981 to $3 trillion in 1992.

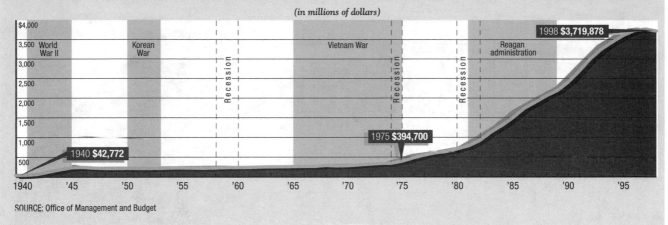

(in millions of dollars)

SOURCE: Office of Management and Budget

when inaction has a potentially good outcome."

Added a senior White House official: "We got backed into it because it is not an offensive position for either party to be in. Both are comfortable with it, even if it is not their favorite position."

As Clinton and Republicans battled last year over tax cuts, the projected surplus kept growing. The once unimaginable prospect of balancing the budget without relying on Social Security became a reality. Indeed, on Oct. 12, the CBO announced that for the first time since 1960 the government did not need to borrow from Social Security to finance the rest of its general operations, because it ran a $1 billion surplus on those operations in fiscal 1999.

But even earlier this year, surplus projections had become so large that lawmakers across the spectrum could put forward plans that isolated the Social Security surplus. No agreement was ever likely, but lawmakers fell over themselves to pledge fealty to budget caps, debt reduction and protection of Social Security. "Part of it is classic Capitol Hill. We all got wrapped up in our own rhetoric," said Sen. Joseph I. Lieberman, D-Conn.

Economic Merits

Mostly missing from the debate has been a serious dialogue about what debt reduction would mean for the economy and for the budget choices confronting future policy-makers. There has been little discussion about the relative economic merits of paying down debt, cutting taxes or adding to government spending.

The stakes are huge. The Social Security system is projected to produce a $1.9 trillion surplus from fiscal 2000 through fiscal 2009, according to CBO. The rest of the surplus, which would come from the general operating budget, is predicted to total about $1 trillion. But surplus projections are tricky, and this $1 trillion surplus may fluctuate, depending on such factors as the economy's health and pressure for more federal spending. Once more realistic assumptions about future spending for annually appropriated programs such as defense and education are taken into account, projected operating surpluses shrink dramatically. (*Surplus, 1999 CQ Weekly, pp. 1673, 1603*)

Lawmakers hope to use the non-Social Security surplus for their tax and spending plans, but debt reduction — in the name of Social Security — would get first claim on the surplus.

There is one politically palatable use for the Social Security surplus, lawmakers and staff aides say: using it to finance a structural overhaul of the retirement system. However, the bulging surpluses have taken away any significant sense of urgency for a Social Security overhaul.

"The problem hasn't gone away. The clock is ticking," said Wayne Struble, majority staff director of the House Budget Committee. "We've spent so much time this summer dealing with the fact that we're not going to spend the Social Security surplus . . . on other programs that we've lost sight of the fact that we need to reform Social Security."

The prevailing view among economists is that reducing debt is probably the best single use of the budget surplus, especially now that the economy is doing well.

"I think that the reduction that is occurring in the federal debt at this stage as a conse-

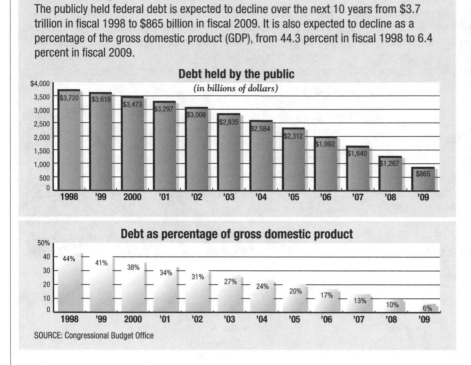

Declining Debt Projections

The publicly held federal debt is expected to decline over the next 10 years from $3.7 trillion in fiscal 1998 to $865 billion in fiscal 2009. It is also expected to decline as a percentage of the gross domestic product (GDP), from 44.3 percent in fiscal 1998 to 6.4 percent in fiscal 2009.

Debt held by the public
(in billions of dollars)

1998	$3,720
'99	$3,618
2000	$3,473
'01	$3,297
'02	$3,006
'03	$2,835
'04	$2,584
'05	$2,312
'06	$1,992
'07	$1,640
'08	$1,267
'09	$865

Debt as percentage of gross domestic product

Year	Percent
1998	44%
'99	41%
2000	38%
'01	34%
'02	31%
'03	27%
'04	24%
'05	20%
'06	17%
'07	13%
'08	10%
'09	6%

SOURCE: Congressional Budget Office

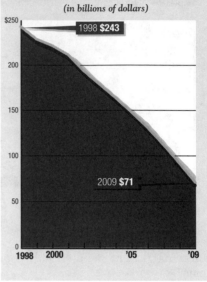

Net Interest Outlays

Net interest payments on the debt, the fastest-growing category of spending in the 1980s, are expected to decline from $243 billion in fiscal 1998 to $71 billion in fiscal 2009.

(in billions of dollars)

1998 $243
2009 $71

---

quence of the ongoing surplus is an extraordinarily effective force for good in this economy," Federal Reserve Board Chairman Alan Greenspan said in July.

Greenspan's views are not universally shared. Economists on both the left and right believe there are better uses for the surplus than cutting the federal debt.

"Reducing the debt is a good idea if you have nothing better to do," said former Labor Secretary Robert B. Reich, now a professor of economics at Brandeis University. "Public investment in education, job skills, public infrastructure that both supports industry and also makes people more productive, publicly supported research and development . . . are all vital components of a vital economy in the future."

Supply-side economists say tax cuts aimed at spurring economic growth are the best way to use the surplus to boost the economy. "There's so many more useful things that you can do with the money than reducing the debt," said Stephen Moore, an economist at the libertarian CATO Institute. "The economic impacts of reducing marginal tax rates, the payroll or income tax, eliminating the death [estate] tax or cutting the capital gains tax would be significantly higher than the economic impact of reducing the national debt."

Economists who favor debt reduction over tax cuts or new spending say the chief benefit to the economy is that debt reduction helps keep interest rates low and promotes savings and investment. Thus, the government and the economy would be better able to absorb the demands of Baby Boomers when they retire.

Even economists who prefer spending to debt reduction acknowledge that running a budget surplus and reducing debt are good ideas.

"Paying down debt should increase national savings and result in modestly but nevertheless noticeably greater economic growth over the long term and also improve our fiscal position for when the Baby Boomers retire," said Robert Greenstein, executive director of the Center on Budget and Policy Priorities, a liberal-leaning Washington think tank.

Economists say, however, that assessing how much good a surplus will do for the economy is difficult. Opinions vary.

"The basic belief, and I use the word 'belief' advisedly, bolstered by a lot of both theory and common sense — but by surprisingly little empirical evidence, that's an important point — is that lower national debt . . . will lead to lower real interest rates and all that brings," said Princeton University economics professor Alan Blinder, former vice chairman of the Federal Reserve. "Empirically, that turns out to be surprising-

ly hard to demonstrate, though every bit of logic points in that direction."

Others say the impact of surpluses and debt reduction on a $9 trillion economy is small and that other economic forces can easily swamp the effects of running a surplus.

"Over time, properly modeled, you will find very, very little correlation between deficits, Treasury debt and interest rates when you control for economic cycles, monetary policy and inflation," said Mickey Levy, chief economist for Bank of America. "In terms of economic effects — I'm serious about this — you're not going to get much at all."

The Basics

Paying down the debt was once unthinkable, a notion buried in economics textbooks. The theory is relatively simple.

When the government is running a deficit, it must sell Treasury bonds to the public to finance its operations. When the government runs a surplus, the opposite is true: It buys back bonds. Bonds then become more scarce, and their price goes up. As the price of a bond rises, its interest yield drops. This phenomenon puts downward pressure on interest rates.

According to Harvard University economics professor Benjamin M. Friedman, when the government runs a surplus, "that reduces the supply of debt being offered and that leads interest rates to go down."

Still, countervailing forces such as inflation, the Fed's monetary policy and the condition of the economy also combine to affect interest rates, making it difficult to isolate the effect of running a surplus. And frequently enough, interest rates move in the opposite direction from what analysts expect. For example, rates dropped as deficits skyrocketed in the 1980s. And recently, rates have inched up — along with surpluses.

"Interest rates move in cycles that frankly have not a whole lot to do with the federal budget," said Ward McCarthy, a principal of Stone & McCarthy Research Associates, an economics research company based in New Jersey. For example, during a recession the deficit typically rises as tax collections fall and social welfare payments rise. But recessions also usually spur the Fed to lower interest rates.

"Whenever rates are moving around, there are a lot of things going on simultaneously," Friedman said. "There's monetary policy. There's investor mood. So you don't have an isolated experiment in which fiscal policy moves and nothing else happens."

Another benefit to running budget surpluses, advocates say, is that it boosts national savings and investment. When the government runs a surplus it redeems debt held by businesses and the public. Bondholders get cash. Opinions vary as to what they do with the cash, but supporters of debt reduction say they are more likely to reinvest it than to spend it.

"If I own some public debt and the government calls it . . . then part of my wealth has been transferred from an interest-earning asset into cash, and the most natural and very reliable reaction is for people to say, 'Well, I'm not going to spend this,' " said Robert M. Solow, professor emeritus of economics at the Massachusetts Institute of Technology. "So I will be inclined one way or the other to put this money at the disposal of business and corporations."

Sure enough, said Harvard's Friedman, as the deficit declined in the 1990s, the amount of investment went up. In 1992, the percentage of the gross domestic product (GDP) devoted to net investment in plant and equipment was 1.4 percent. By 1997, it had more than doubled, to 3.4 percent of GDP. "That's what you would expect to see happening

in a world where there's a surplus instead of a deficit," Friedman said.

But economists who prefer tax cuts say when debt is paid down, the government is merely putting back what it took away in taxes. "All that has really happened is that you're taking a dollar out of the private sector [in taxes] and then you're returning it by redeeming debt," said Aldona Robbins, an economist with the Institute for Policy Innovation, a free market think tank. "That transaction is a zero."

The prevailing view among most economists is that when the economy is humming, as it is now, tax cuts should wait. "We're at full employment. We don't need a demand-side stimulus of a tax cut," said David Wyss, chief economist for Standard & Poor's DRI economic forecasting unit.

And even supply-side economists see the most popular tax cut proposals, such as eliminating the "marriage penalty" or taking other steps aimed at the middle class, as less beneficial than pro-growth proposals they favor, such as reducing capital gains taxes or lowering estate taxes. Those cuts, supply-side economists say, would encourage more investment.

Should the economy hit the skids, however, many economists say they would rethink a policy of debt reduction.

"If we had a depressed economy right now or if we had a recession, this would not be a great time to be paying down the debt. This would be a better time for cutting taxes or spending more to keep the economy humming," Blinder said. "Most of us think that if you were to cut taxes now you would just end up with a tighter monetary policy to cancel out the demand effects. And that's not a very good idea."

Public Opinion

Lawmakers and pollsters say voters do not understand nuanced economic arguments about debt reduction, such as its impact on interest rates or national savings. But they know that the government has been rolling up a huge debt over most of the past 20 years. And they know the Baby Boomers are going to retire soon. Instinctively, the public thinks debt reduction is a good idea.

But voters, when offered specific choices, also support using the surplus for tax cuts or for new spending on Medicare, Social Security and education, opinion polls show.

For example, an NBC News-Wall Street Journal poll taken July 24-26

found 22 percent of respondents favoring debt reduction as the single best use of the surplus. But 24 percent favored increased social spending, 22 percent favored a Medicare prescription drug benefit and 20 percent favored tax cuts.

"Many voters, particularly with the strong economy, understand the importance of the debt in terms of economic growth in the long term," said GOP pollster Linda DiVall, whose polling indicates a combined 27 percent favoring debt reduction, with 13 percent favoring debt reduction and 14 percent in favor of a Social Security "lockbox," which amounts to the same thing. DiVall said, however, that voters do not understand the connection between Social Security surpluses and debt reduction.

Among the most fervent supporters of paying down debt are fiscally conservative "Blue Dogs." House Blue Dogs focused on the issue as they toured their districts in August — and found that some of the most receptive constituents were Republicans. Rep. Baron P. Hill, D-Ind., who wrote an opinion piece in favor of debt reduction for his local newspaper, said that after it ran, "I literally had dozens of phone calls from Republican friends of mine . . . saying 'This is the right thing to do.' "

CATO's Moore, a regular on conservative radio talk shows, reports the same phenomenon: "Some of the loudest clamorers for retiring the debt are conservatives, conservative voters, conservative Republicans."

Democratic pollster Mark Mellman says he has not detected a "tremendous gain in traction for paying down the national debt" but said he thinks "what is on the rise is that tax cuts are a relatively low priority for the people right now."

One way lawmakers tried to explain debt reduction to their voters was to equate it to a family that has run up credit card bills. When money comes in, it is a good idea to pay those debts off. Or as Rep. John Tanner, a Blue Dog who represents a rural, small-town district in West Tennessee, put it: "Where I come from, it's considered to be very poor form if you owe a fellow some money and if you come into some money and you don't pay him and you do something else with it.' "

For economist Wyss, the complex subject of debt reduction can be explained simply: "The best advice is what Joseph told the Pharaoh about 3,000 years ago: 'Save up the corn in the good times and use it in the bad.' " ◆

Social Security rules the budget debate as parties fight for high ground

Debate Over Social Security: The Weapon of Choice

Since Republicans took over Congress in 1995, Democrats have used Social Security to club the GOP over the budget. It was the decisive factor in killing the balanced-budget amendment to the Constitution in 1995 and 1997. And last year President Clinton had only to say "save Social Security first" in his State of the Union address to smash any Republican hopes for a tax cut.

Then Clinton and his Democratic allies blithely extracted billions of dollars in extra fiscal 1999 spending — all of it borrowed from surplus Social Security revenues.

This year, Republicans want to turn the tables and use Social Security against Democrats. They have carefully sought to avoid the appearance of tapping into Social Security when crafting their budget plans. They have pressured Democrats and Clinton to support a Social Security "lockbox." The National Republican Congressional Committee has run attack ads on the issue in the districts of vulnerable Democrats.

As Republicans seek to prevent Clinton from claiming his annual end-of-session victory on appropriations, they are the ones using Social Security as a foil, this time against Clinton's demands for more spending.

"The Democrats have a risky scheme to finance big government spending on the backs of seniors' retirement plans," House Majority Leader Dick Armey, R-Texas, said Oct. 6. "Republicans want to lock away every penny of Social Security for seniors."

Whether Republicans will succeed in using Social Security to stem Clinton's appetite for spending is by no means a sure thing. After all, Republicans have participated for more than three decades in the very practice — borrowing from Social Security surpluses to finance other federal programs — for which they are lambasting Clinton. And they lack the White House's bully pulpit to make their strategy resonate with the clarity or power of "save So-

NATIONAL REPUBLICAN CONGRESSIONAL COMMITTEE

The National Republican Congressional Committee has run attack ads in the districts of vulnerable Democrats, charging that Democrats are "raiding" Social Security.

cial Security first."

Moreover, the Congressional Budget Office (CBO) estimates that the GOP-drafted spending bills are already on track to dip into Social Security. That is, despite GOP claims, the bills would spend more than the projected $14 billion non-Social Security surplus for fiscal 2000.

And the point that Republicans are trying to drill home — that borrowing from the Social Security trust funds is a threat to beneficiaries — is disputed by virtually every budget expert.

"Whether discretionary spending is $500 billion or $800 billion in 2000 has no impact on Social Security whatsoever," said former CBO Director Robert D. Reischauer, now a senior fellow at the Brookings Institution, a Washington think tank. "It does not affect the revenues flowing into the Social Security system. It has no impact on the trust funds' balances."

Lawmakers and staff aides acknowledge that a few billion dollars borrowed from fiscal 2000 Social Security surpluses to fund other spending would

not harm the retirement program.

But stopping the practice of tapping Social Security to finance general government operations would be a major political coup for a generation of lawmakers reared on the politics of deficit reduction. "The issue is more one of principle than of substance in the near term," said G. William Hoagland, majority staff director of the Senate Budget Committee.

Political Battlefield

Instead of a fight about substance, this year's budget debate has been waged on the battlefield of politics, with Social Security as the most powerful weapon. Congress achieved the goal of the 1997 budget law (PL 105-33) to reach a balanced budget by 2002, and replaced it with promises not to borrow from Social Security to pay for tax cuts or more spending. (*1997 Almanac, p. 2-18*)

So instead of having a debate on taxes and programs, or trying to deal with the long-range solvency of Medicare and Social Security, lawmak-

Budget Experts Follow the Paper Trail Of Social Security Trust Funds

Economists and budget experts say congressional Republicans' crusade to stop relying on Social Security to help finance the rest of the government represents a noble goal. But they also say that the Republicans' chief argument — that this "raid" on Social Security somehow threatens beneficiaries and the solvency of the program's trust funds — is simplistic at best.

Budget experts say the only relationship between Social Security and the budget surplus is an indirect one involving the health of the economy and the government's fiscal strength when it comes time to deal with the retirement of the Baby Boom generation.

Virtually every budget expert and even some proponents of a Social Security "lockbox" believe that there is no direct link between Social Security and the size of the surplus. Whether Congress and President Clinton "save" the Social Security surplus or whether they dip into it yet again by tens of billions of dollars has virtually no impact on the system's solvency.

"No one's raiding the trust funds. You can't raid the trust funds," said Martin Corry, top lobbyist for the AARP, which represents senior citizens. "All we're doing is what we've been doing since [President] Lyndon Johnson's day, if not before, which is borrow. Is that great? No, it's not great, but it's not the end of the world, either."

At the center of the debate are the two Social Security trust funds and their role in the way the federal government keeps its books.

The trust funds — one pays Social Security retirement benefits and the other pays benefits to the disabled — are currently estimated to be worth almost $900 billion. They consist entirely of special issue Treasury securities that are supposed to be socked away to pay benefits to the wave of Baby Boomers when they start to retire in 2010. They are pieces of paper

in a file cabinet at the Bureau of Public Debt in West Virginia.

Opinions vary as to what these trust funds actually represent. Some lawmakers argue that the money is gone, that it has already been spent and that the trust funds are filled with IOUs. In its fiscal 2000 budget documents, the Clinton administration acknowledged that the trust funds contain balances "only in a bookkeeping sense. . . . They do not consist of real economic assets that can be drawn down in the future to fund benefits."

This characterization reflects the fact that regardless of bookkeeping, Social Security is based on a "pay as you go" system: Current revenues from payroll taxes pay current benefits and, unless the system is overhauled, future revenues will pay future benefits. The difference is that, at present, Social Security payroll taxes are sufficient to do the job. In the future, payroll taxes will have to be supplemented with additional money from the non-Social Security budget. To budget experts, that is not a big deal.

The trust funds are "an accounting device," said a senior Congressional Budget Office official. "It helps one assess current and future situations but it doesn't provide any real resources. All it is is a promise to yourself."

A second — and not necessarily opposing — view among budget experts is that the trust funds are real. Yes, they consist of paper promises, but those promises are rock-solid Treasury bonds. The government has never defaulted on its obligations, and it is inconceivable that any policy-maker would permit the government to default on the Social Security bonds. It would be political suicide.

Under current projections, Social Security benefits will exceed payroll taxes starting in 2015. At that point, general fund revenues will be required to help pay benefits. In essence, the government will have to start paying

back all the money it has borrowed from Social Security. Just as Social Security has subsidized the rest of the government for so many years, the rest of the government will then have to start subsidizing Social Security.

At that point, lawmakers will face a menu of choices: They can raise taxes or cut benefits or both. And they almost certainly will begin borrowing again from the public to pay benefits.

Opinions Converge

Virtually every economist and budget analyst agrees that the most important factor in the long-term health of Social Security is the capacity of the government and the economy to subsidize retirees' benefits.

This is where two links can be drawn between Social Security and paying down the national debt. First, if the government has reduced the amount of debt held by the public, it will be easier to borrow again to pay benefits. Second, the positive effect that paying down debt will have on strengthening the economy will make it easier for society to subsidize the swelling population of retirees.

"Down the road in 30 years, we're going to have a hell of a lot of old people," said Robert M. Solow, an economist at the Massachusetts Institute of Technology. "The idea of generating some savings and investment now is to make the economy more productive 30 years from now so that it is better able to handle that situation."

The more debt that is retired, added Senate Budget Committee Majority Staff Director G. William Hoagland, "the better the country will be prepared to fund future Social Security beneficiaries."

What is impossible to measure is just how helpful debt reduction in 1999 will be 15 years from now. Some economists argue that given the size of world capital markets and growth in the economy, the benefits of debt reduction would be negligible.

ers of both parties are clobbering each other with charges and countercharges on Social Security, using the arbitrary $14 billion non-Social Security surplus as the new litmus test of fiscal purity.

The resulting gridlock ensures that surpluses will go almost entirely for debt relief — a favorable outcome according to many economists. (*Debt, p. 72*)

But does paying down debt help Social Security? Not directly. Preserving Social Security-generated surpluses for debt reduction does not shore up the long-term solvency of the Social Security system. Most budget analysts, however, link the two by arguing that if the government has a smaller national debt when it comes time to start redeeming the bonds in the Social Security retirement trust fund in 2015, it will be on a stronger fiscal footing to do so.

"If we do not begin to retire debt held by the public, and if holding off on that is the result of spending the Social Security surplus, then we will make it harder to address the program's future demands," Hoagland said.

But in this year's maelstrom over the budget, such nuanced arguments have mostly given way to exaggerated claims about what impact surpluses or deficits would have on Social Security. (*Budget, 1999 CQ Weekly, p. 2369*)

The debate is laced with charges that borrowing Social Security-generated surpluses to finance other government spending or tax cuts amounts to a "raid" on retirees' benefits or stealing from Social Security.

"Stop the raid. Stop the raid on Social Security. That is our simple message," said Dave Weldon, R-Fla., in one of many "one-minute" speeches on the House floor that have addressed the topic. "For 40 years Democrats controlled this body and they never put one thin dime of the Social Security surplus aside."

But the situation is far more complicated than that. Borrowing from Social Security trust funds to finance spending on other programs has no effect on the Social Security system itself, experts say. By law, every penny of surplus Social Security revenues must be invested in Treasury bonds, which are deposited in the trust funds. Treasury uses the cash either to run the rest of the government or to buy down debt, or some mixture of the two. In either instance, the amount of money deposited into the trust funds is the same. (*Trust funds, 1999 CQ Weekly, p. 2431*)

The bitter politics that has produced gridlock in all likelihood means that future lawmakers will also keep their hands off the Social Security-generated portion of the surplus — instead of using it for priorities such as tax cuts or new spending. When a politician makes a promise, such as Armey did, that "we will not schedule any legislation that spends one penny of the Social Security surplus," it is difficult to reverse course.

"The White House and the congressional Republicans have created a fiction and have unfortunately sold it to the American people," said former Clinton administration Labor Secretary Robert B. Reich, now an economics professor at Brandeis University. "[The fiction] is that Social Security is in crisis and that if we touch the Social Security surplus we are jeopardizing Social Security for the future."

Historical Precedents

Republicans will be lucky if their Social Security strategy works as well against Clinton as it has when Clinton and Democrats used it against them.

Even before Clinton weighed in, Senate Democrats had vividly demonstrated the political power of protecting the Social Security surplus. They used it twice to scuttle Republican efforts to pass a constitutional amendment to require a balanced budget. (*1997 Almanac, p. 2-66*)

And in early 1998, after budget projections unexpectedly showed surpluses for the upcoming fiscal year, many Republicans started to see favorable prospects for an election-year tax cut. But Clinton stopped them cold — even though he has never concealed his support for borrowing from Social Security to finance his pet programs. He has always held that after overhauling Social Security, he would like to use the surplus for additional spending.

To be sure, politicians on both sides have been inconsistent in their votes on whether to protect Social Security. Many of the same Republicans who unanimously voted this year to put Social Security surpluses in a "lockbox" rejected the idea during the 1995 and 1997 debates on the balanced-budget amendment.

And several Democrats who voted against the balanced-budget amendment in 1997 because it would have kept Social Security as part of deficit calculations turned around and sup-

ported the 1997 tax and spending bills, which relied heavily on Social Security surpluses to reach balance.

Only months after hammering Republicans last year about "saving" Social Security, Clinton hammered them again — with spending demands requiring more borrowing from Social Security.

Same Difference

Among the ironies of the debate is that over time, the amount of money spent is unlikely to vary much with or without "protecting" Social Security. To stick within the $14 billion limit, Republicans have resorted to an unprecedented amount of fiscal gimmickry. On the defense appropriations bill (HR 2561) alone, according to calculations by top House Appropriations Committee Democrat David R. Obey of Wisconsin, such gimmicks total $21.6 billion in outlays. These gimmicks either underestimate the costs of the bill or push fiscal 2000 spending into future years.

Democrats say they are not threatened by the GOP's offensive on Social Security. They say it is up to Republicans to pass all 13 appropriations bills and ship them to Clinton. Even after the GOP stretches budget rules with scorekeeping adjustments, Democrats doubt that Republicans will be able to pass all the bills without touching the Social Security surplus. According to a recent CBO analysis, lawmakers are already on track to use perhaps $18 billion of the Social Security surplus. (*Appropriations, 1999 CQ Weekly, p. 2444*)

"You have Republicans leading with the message that we have to save Social Security, and then you get news story after news story leading with the fact that they are indeed spending the Social Security surplus that they have vowed to protect," said a senior White House aide. "We're not nervous."

To Reich, the debate is dispiriting because the back and forth over Social Security has drowned out any effort at genuine dialogue.

"For years, Social Security has been demagogued. It's the weapon that Democrats have used to intimidate the Republicans," Reich said. "If you are going to create the impression in the public's mind that Social Security is somehow threatened by Republican tax-cutting plans, then you are inviting the Republicans to play a demagogic game back." ◆

House leaders, struggling to keep troops in line, put off floor action until after recess

Managed Care Fight Finds GOP Torn Between Doctors, Insurers

Shortly after he arrived in Congress this year, Rep. Ernie Fletcher, R-Ky., was handed a spot in the limelight that is rare for a freshman. A family physician, he was chosen by House GOP leaders to be a top spokesman for their position on managed care.

But now, as Republicans scramble to overcome deep schisms within the party over the politically volatile issue, Fletcher has come to regret all the attention.

On July 27, the American Medical Association (AMA) faxed letters to every physician in Fletcher's central Kentucky district accusing him of choosing "to ignore the concerns of local patients and physicians."

"Tell him that you are his constituent and a physician or a physician's spouse, resident or medical student," the letter said. "Ask him to support real reforms."

A day after the letter went out, Fletcher was clearly no longer a spokesman for his leadership. He was reluctant to discuss the issue, and he refused to say whether he would still support the GOP package (HR 2041-2047; HR 2089) that he helped steer out of subcommit-

CQ Weekly July 31, 1999

tee June 16. (*1999 CQ Weekly, p. 1453*)

"It's not realistic" to discuss the package, which will likely never reach the House floor, Fletcher said. "I'm just trying to bring consensus with a focus on what's good for patients."

The pressures on Fletcher are emblematic of those facing the House GOP leadership as it tries to find a compromise in the stalemate over managed care. The GOP is caught between two powerful, longtime constituencies: doctors, who want a broad bill to increase their leverage with health maintenance organizations, and the insurance industry, which argues that new regulations will raise health care costs and increase the number of people who are uninsured.

After months of trying to sell their plan, House Republican leaders are still struggling to keep their troops in line and are scrambling for ways to avoid what could quickly turn into an embarrassing floor defeat at the hands of their own rank and file. They conceded the week of July 26 that they would not be able to bring a managed care bill to the floor before the August recess, a goal of Speaker J. Dennis Hastert, R-Ill.

Democrats and their allies, including the

Quick Contents

With Democrats united against them and an increasing number of Republican members breaking ranks, House GOP leaders were left with a choice on managed care: bring to the House floor a bill that might be defeated, or put off a floor debate until after the August recess. They chose the latter.

Boehner and Bilirakis, members of the House task force writing managed care legislation, walk to a GOP Conference meeting July 29 at which several members voiced opposition to the leadership's approach.

CQ PHOTO / DOUGLAS GRAHAM

AMA, have vowed to continue their attack on the Republican majority and to focus on the issue in next year's campaigns. They want a broad measure that would allow doctors — not insurers — to decide which treatments are medically necessary and would allow patients to sue for damages if they are injured by health plans' coverage decisions.

Republican leaders have been pushing less strict bills they say would allow the marketplace and consumer choice to weed out health plans that do not provide adequate patient protections.

A new survey by the Kaiser Family Foundation and the Harvard School of Public Health will likely bolster the Democrats' position. The survey of nearly 2,000 doctors and nurses, released July 28, found a high level of conflict between medical professionals and health insurers, with nine out of 10 doctors reporting that health plans have denied coverage of needed services over the past two years. About three-quarters of the doctors and nurses said managed care has decreased quality of care. Health insurers played down the report, saying it did not look at the appropriateness of coverage decisions or at patient satisfaction with their health plans. (*Chart, next page*)

Meetings With Democrats

In a sign of growing trouble for the leadership, an increasing number of rank-and-file Republicans — led by several other House GOP doctors — have started to actively work with Democrats on the issue.

Republican Greg Ganske, a reconstructive surgeon from Iowa, met with House Democratic leader Richard A. Gephardt of Missouri twice the week of July 26, while Charlie Norwood, a Republican dentist from Georgia, held continual discussions throughout the week with John D. Dingell of Michigan, dean of the House Democrats.

Norwood and Ganske say that in their medical practices, they have seen devastating injuries caused when health plans cut corners in order to save money.

Hastert also broke his pledge to use "regular order" and move a health care bill through the committee process. Instead, on July 27 he hastily appointed a task force of subcommittee chairmen to draft a limited patients protection bill that could garner enough Republican votes to pass the House.

In contrast to the deeply divided Republican Conference — Norwood and Ganske say they have the support of 30 to 60 Republicans — House Democrats appeared unified in their legislative efforts.

Marion Berry, D-Ark., a member of the conservative Democratic "Blue Dog" caucus, said about a dozen Democrats are wavering in their support for a bill that would allow patients to sue their health plans for damages.

"I will vote with whatever my leaders put up," said Berry, who is chairman of the Blue Dogs' task force on health care. "There are not that many [Democrats] who won't."

With a united Democratic front, and a slim majority in the House, Republican leaders cannot afford to lose many of their members.

Hastert is trying to keep his troops in line, but has been unwilling to compromise his opposition to broad government regulation and expanded liability for health insurance companies.

As former chairman of the GOP health care task force that drafted a narrow package that passed the House last July by just six votes, Hastert has a personal interest in moving the bill this year and a political desire to remove the issue as a potential campaign weapon for Democrats in the 2000 elections. (*1998 Almanac, p. 14-3*)

Hastert has not only been forced to put the debate off until September, he now faces the prospect of having to use the August recess to attempt to unify his conference, a challenge that some say is impossible.

Norwood and Ganske say that if Hastert does not compromise on managed care legislation, they will sign a Democratic discharge petition in September to bring a broad patients protection bill to the floor.

"It's not easy," said Porter J. Goss, R-Fla., a Rules Committee member on the Hastert task force. The group spent 10 hours July 28 trying to piece together a package, but found themselves in a frustrating exercise of trying to balance competing, and often conflicting, demands. It became almost impossible, participants said, to write a bill that could win support from both moderates and conservatives in their conference.

"If you pick the wrong piece, you get two votes but lose four," Goss said. "We want to pick the piece where you win four votes but lose two."

Few were surprised when Republican tensions boiled over into public view the week of July 26. Norwood had bumped heads with Hastert last year over the leadership's managed care bill and only grudgingly voted for it in hopes of expanding its provisions in conference committee.

Ganske was one of 12 Republicans to vote against the GOP bill last year, and this spring he began making weekly after-hour floor speeches to call for a broad patient protection bill.

"For two years, I have argued to my own Republican leadership that the best action would be a bipartisan agreement," Ganske said in a recent interview. "Hastert's cover for months was, 'Well, you know, we'll just let the committee process do its job.' But when it became obvious that we had the votes to bring out a good bill, all of a sudden that just goes by the wayside."

Bliley-Dingell Talks Fail

In recent weeks, Ganske and Norwood had pinned their hopes for a bipartisan agreement on intense negotiations between Commerce Committee chairman Thomas J. Bliley Jr., R-Va., and committee ranking Democrat Dingell. Staff aides for the two met throughout much of July and appeared close to agreement on the most controversial of the managed care issues — allowing patients to sue their health plans for damages in state court.

Under current law, patients can only sue in federal court, where awards are limited to attorneys' fees and the cost of the denied treatment.

"They came within a gnat's blink of having an agreement," Norwood said of the Dingell-Bliley negotiations.

Earlier this year, Bliley told Norwood he would accept right-to-sue language. Norwood, in fact, said he was told the two had reached a deal on July 23. But by July 27, Bliley and Dingell declared the negotiations dead.

"It is very disappointing that the House Democrat leadership has decided to play partisan politics with the managed care issue, pulling the rug out from negotiations at the eleventh hour," Bliley said after the talks were called off. "At the last minute, Democrats insisted on including costly provisions that would significantly increase the number of uninsured Americans. This was unacceptable and ultimately the reason negotiations failed."

But Ganske, Norwood and other rebellious Republicans blame their own leadership for halting the talks.

"This was jerked out from under

Doctors' Impressions of the Impact of Managed Care

In a recent survey, the Kaiser Family Foundation and the Harvard School of Public Health asked 1,053 doctors and 768 nurses about their experiences with managed care. Respondents said that managed care has had a primarily negative effect on health care, with some exceptions. This chart shows the responses to some of the questions posed to doctors.

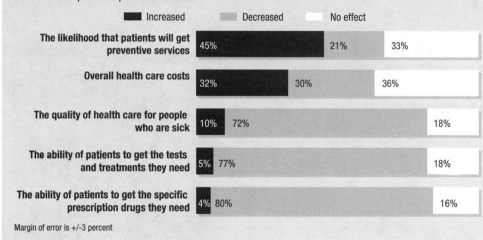

■ Increased ■ Decreased □ No effect

	Increased	Decreased	No effect
The likelihood that patients will get preventive services	45%	21%	33%
Overall health care costs	32%	30%	36%
The quality of health care for people who are sick	10%	72%	18%
The ability of patients to get the tests and treatments they need	5%	77%	18%
The ability of patients to get the specific prescription drugs they need	4%	80%	16%

Margin of error is +/-3 percent

SOURCE: Henry J. Kaiser Family Foundation Survey of Physicians and Nurses, July 28

them," Tom Coburn, R-Okla., an obstetrician who is working with Norwood, said of the bipartisan talks. "The bill coming out of the committee was not something the [Republican leadership] wanted."

Soon after the negotiations ended, Hastert announced the creation of a task force of several subcommittee chairmen who have long opposed expanding liability. Bill Thomas, R-Calif., chairman of the House Ways and Means Health Subcommittee, is heading the task force, and he is working with Goss, Michael Bilirakis, R-Fla., chairman of the Commerce Subcommittee on Health and Environment, and John A. Boehner, R-Ohio, chairman of the Education and the Workforce Subcommittee on Employer-Employee Relations.

Although the task force members oppose language that would expose health plans to large court damages, they have not ruled out a limited liability provision. For example, they might consider expanding the awards patients could win in federal court, or capping compensatory damages.

Task force members and leadership aides say the group will try to draft a bill that borrows elements from last year's House-passed bill, and from the managed care package that passed the Senate on June 15. (*1999 CQ Weekly, p. 1715*)

The Senate plan was passed largely along party lines and stuck to the Republican philosophy of limited government. It expanded patient protections in areas such as emergency room treat-

ment and women's health care but limited those provisions to the 48 million patients who belong to health plans that are exempt from state regulation.

Leadership aides said the House task force wants to extend the protections to an additional 113 million patients in plans that are regulated by the states.

The task force is also looking at a proposal by John Shadegg, R-Ariz., that would create a variety of tax incentives aimed at making health insurance more affordable.

Shadegg said conservative members of the Republican Conference would not likely support a broad patient protection bill if it did not contain financial breaks such as expanded medical savings accounts, tax credits to help self-insured workers buy health coverage, and association health plans to allow groups of workers to purchase insurance at lower costs.

Looking for Compromise

The task force, members say, will also likely look to legislation approved by Boehner's subcommittee on June 16. The eight-bill package would provide a limited number of expanded protections for managed care patients, including allowing a woman to see her gynecologist without first getting a referral from her primary care physician; allowing parents to choose a pediatrician as their child's primary care provider; and establishing an external review process to which patients could appeal their health plans' treatment decisions. The package, however,

would not allow patients to sue plans for damages.

Soon after Hastert appointed his task force, the Republican rebels let it be known that they were negotiating with Democrats.

"I made a plea for [Democrats] to consider a bipartisan effort when we get to the floor," Ganske said of his meetings with Gephardt. "I told them it would be in the best interest for patients to do that, and it would be a politically wise move for them."

Norwood on July 28 said that he and Dingell had reached a tentative agreement on a bipartisan package and were planning to spend the next several days lobbying their respective party members to sign on.

"I'm looking for 300 good men and women," Norwood said. "I would like to go to the Speaker and say, 'Here's your opportunity to pass a good piece of legislation, but you'll have to share the credit with the Democrats.' "

Democrats said they were willing to talk but agreed with the GOP doctors that they would not compromise with Republican leaders on two issues: allowing patients to sue and letting doctors decide medical necessity.

"If I compromise on those two issues, there's no sense having a bill," Gephardt told reporters July 29. "We really shouldn't spend any time on the floor fooling around with a fraud bill."

Even if a compromise is reached, many do not believe Hastert would allow such a bill to come to the floor. ◆

Asserting a common goal, key lawmakers take dramatically different approaches

The Many Faces of Managed Care Reform

*F*or years, both parties have talked about passing "patients' rights" legislation, but the phrase has had different meanings for different members. The fault lines have never been sharply drawn: some lawmakers insist on patients' ability to sue their health plans. Others focus more on expanding coverage. Some are pushing for tax breaks to help the uninsured buy coverage. Alliances begin to take shape, only to fall apart over the details. As the House takes up managed care legislation, the views of several lawmakers at the center of the debate dramatize the diverse — and often contradictory — points of view.

J. DENNIS HASTERT, R-Ill. ▲
Speaker Finds Himself in a Tough Spot

*D*uring his 13 years in Congress, J. Dennis Hastert has shown passionate interest in health care. In 1993, he served on Hillary Rodham Clinton's health care task force, and in 1996 he played a key role in passing a law that allows workers to keep their health insurance when they change jobs. In 1998, he headed a task force

that developed managed care legislation that passed the House.

So it is with a little irony — and a lot of frustration — that the 57-year-old former wrestling coach has been unable so far to forge a compromise in the managed care debate now that he is Speaker of the House.

Hastert who has promised a vote on managed care legislation during the week of Oct. 4, but it is unclear what course the debate will take. House Republicans, concerned that a bipartisan plan (HR 2723) by John D. Dingell, D-Mich., and Charlie Norwood, R-Ga., could drive up health costs and possibly cause employers to drop benefits, want a leadership alternative. Hastert has not offered one. The simplest explanation is that it is clear that he does not have the votes to defeat the Norwood-Dingell bill, so he has instead focused his efforts on limiting the damage.

Hastert has tried to find a compromise. In September, he hoped that that Republicans Tom Coburn of Oklahoma and John Shadegg of Arizona would develop alternative legislation, but after they released their plan (HR 2824), the Speaker did not endorse it. He is opposed to a provision that would allow patients to sue their health plans in federal court, proving again that liability is the defining issue in the debate.

Hastert has said he is focused on three As: accessibility, affordability and accountability. But patching together a bill that satisfies those criteria has proved difficult. Adding provisions demanded by one faction invariably leads to the loss of support from another.

Some say that resolving the health care dilemma may prove to be the toughest task of Hastert's congressional career — no small challenge at a time when the two parties are at war over spending and taxes. His predecessor, Newt Gingrich, R-Ga. (1979-99), was willing to ruffle egos to get his way. He would often then turn to the congenial Hastert to repair the damage and find a compromise. Now, the question is whether Hastert can

JOHN A. BOEHNER, R-Ohio ▲
Looking Out for Business

use his skills as a consensus builder to lead his fellow Republicans out of a potentially embarrassing defeat.

*I*t is telling that the only major House option on managed care that would not expand patients' rights to sue their health plans is sponsored by Ohio Republican John A. Boehner. That is his bottom line.

Boehner took on the role of point man for the business community on managed care this session when he inherited the gavel of the Education and the Workforce Employer-Employee Relations Subcommittee.

Boehner, 49, a former plastics and packaging executive, has pushed measures that are roundly applauded by business allies — many of whom cultivated him when he served until last year as the GOP Conference Chairman. Some members accuse him of being too close to the insurance industry.

"It's the industry bill," said Shadegg, a conservative who has cosponsored a rival measure.

Boehner smiles at the suggestion that he is a mouthpiece for insurers.

"Some people may call me a sop for the insurance industry, but anything else that includes liability — and could lead to an increase in the number of uninsured — is irresponsible," he said in a Sept. 28 interview.

As subcommittee chairman, Boehner pushed an eight-bill package (HR 2041-2047; HR 2089) through his panel June 16, but was blocked at the full committee by Norwood and his supporters. When it became clear that support for Boehner's package would collapse in competition with Norwood's approach, committee Chairman Bill Goodling, R-Pa., indefinitely postponed a full panel markup. (*1999 CQ Weekly, p. 1453*)

Boehner retooled his legislation and introduced a new bill (HR 2926) that included a demonstration project of medical savings accounts.

Boehner, who is serving his fifth term, is praised by House leaders, notably Speaker Hastert and Majority Leader Dick Armey, R-Texas. But most analysts predict that Boehner's bill could not win the needed support to pass the House.

Even Boehner concedes, with his trademark shrug, that the Norwood-Dingell bill is the one to beat.

TOM COBURN, R-Okla. ▲
Doctor Seeks a Compromise

Once the 106th Congress adjourns, Rep. Tom Coburn plans to return to his Oklahoma district and resume the medical practice where he has delivered more than 3,000 babies, even during weekends away from Washington.

The conservative Republican is spending his third, and last, term in Congress pushing for limits on the power of health maintenance organizations, which Coburn says routinely interfere with doctors' decisions — including his — about patient care.

Coburn, 51, who described himself to The New York Times in August as "a pain in the butt," has smacked heads with Hastert over the issue. Although Hastert courted Coburn to work with him to draft a managed care bill that the House GOP leadership could endorse, a disagreement over how to broaden liability for health insurers caused a rift.

Coburn recently threatened to throw his support to the Norwood-Dingell bill and did nothing to quell speculation about his next move. As a dozen reporters huddled around him in the Speaker's lobby Sept. 28, Coburn repeated the same answer he had given during the past week. He was talking to everyone and committing to no one. When the reporters groaned, Coburn tried to assure them that he was being honest.

"I'm not trying to be coy," he said before escaping back to the House floor.

Coburn has been at odds before with the GOP leadership. In May, he brought the House agriculture appropriations bill to a halt by waging a one-man crusade to cut more than $250 million from the measure. In 1997, he tried to block a cost of living increase for lawmakers and said Republican leaders had given President Clinton too much money for certain programs.

Coburn said the upcoming managed care vote will be a "definer" for Republicans, a test of "whether or not you really believe in Republican principles" such as personal responsibility and accountability.

In seeking a compromise, Coburn has noted that if too many Republicans vote for the Norwood-Dingell bill — 21 have so far endorsed it — the party will suffer.

Republicans who back a broad overhaul such as Norwood-Dingell, he says, are taking a politically risky step because they may have problems later if a more conservative proposal emerges and they want to support it.

"Once you go that far," he said, "I think you'll have trouble getting back."

CHARLES NORWOOD, R-Ga. ▲
An Unlikely Rebel

Charlie Norwood came to Washington in 1995 to battle "big government" health care, Hillary Rodham Clinton's 1,342-page proposal that conservatives feared was a tome of terror for the nation's health care system.

Now Norwood, 58, is the prime sponsor of a largely Democratic managed care proposal that has the backing of Clinton.

What happened? Last year, Norwood was willing to work on a House Republican task force, headed by now Speaker Hastert. The Georgia dentist stopped pushing his own bill, which had more than 200 cosponsors, and worked with his colleagues to draft a bill that passed the House last year mostly along party lines.

This year, different dynamics created different results, Norwood said. The Senate had passed its own bill, putting pressure on the House to act. And Hastert's reluctance to accept provisions Norwood wanted renewed his drive to build enough support to force a floor vote on his measure.

"When the leadership just refused to work with us, after trying all year, I made a personal decision. I know there are 300 votes out there. I'm going to talk to the voters," Norwood said.

His alliance with Dingell has resulted in a bipartisan bill that has wide backing in the House, and from a slew of interest groups representing consumers, patients and health care providers such as nurses, allergists and, of course, dentists.

Norwood believes his bill has enough support to pass the House, but he wants a margin greater than the 218 required for passage. He is hoping for a much larger majority, perhaps 300 or more, so Senate Republicans will feel pressure to modify the significantly different measure (S 1344) they passed in July. (1999 *CQ Weekly*, p. 1715)

Norwood's own troubles with managed care in his practice, coupled with stories he heard from dentists and doctors back home in Georgia, influenced him to take on the issue. He has questioned why federal law exempts many health plans from facing the threat of costly punitive damage awards and believes insurers have far too much clout in determining what medical treatments are best for patients.

The ultimate irony, however, is that now Norwood is almost singly identified with an issue he never imagined he would tackle when he came to Washington five years ago.

"I did not leave my dental practice to run for Congress on this," he said.

GREG GANSKE, R-Iowa ▲
The Renegade Physician

If the managed care debate is, as some maintain, essentially a war between insurers and doctors over treatment decisions, Greg Ganske has served on the front lines.

As a reconstructive surgeon in Iowa, Ganske often took on insurers who re-

fused to cover a procedure because they deemed it cosmetic rather than medically necessary. One case he cites is that of a 50-year-old woman who wanted breast reconstruction surgery after she was treated for cancer.

Angry over the insurance company's denial, she appealed. During the hearing, Ganske said, the insurer's medical director asked: "Of what functional use is a breast, anyway?" Women on the insurance company's appeal panel overruled their male colleague and decided to pay for the reconstructive surgery.

While that patient won, Ganske said, thousands more lose every day because they do not have the money, the stamina or the will to take on their insurer.

"Insurance companies rely on that," he said, adding that he thinks patients have lost their lives because of such decisions.

Such memories motivate Ganske, 50, as he heads full-force into the House debate. Elected in 1994, he parted ways with House GOP leaders long ago on managed care, and was the first to push legislation to stop insurers from using so-called gag clauses to curb communications between doctors and their patients.

In 1997, he voted against the Balanced Budget Act (PL 105-33) because he thought the Medicare cost-cutting provisions were too draconian and he has also opposed his leadership's attempts to ban needle-exchange programs, agreeing with advocates that they can stop the spread of AIDS.

His efforts have not come without cost, however. He resigned from the bipartisan commission on Medicare in 1998, saying his positions on managed care would cause "disharmony" that could interfere with the panel's work. This year, he landed in the doghouse — and was pushed out of leadership strategy sessions on managed care — after he released provisions of proposed legislation before they were ready, upsetting what some participants said were delicate talks. (1999 *CQ Weekly*, p. 1025)

Last year, he shared the stage with Clinton and Richard A. Gephardt, D-Mo., during an American Medical Association (AMA) event to promote Democrats' managed care legislation.

Ganske rejects claims that he is pushing the bill for doctors rather than patients. He recently told AMA delegates not to accept GOP overtures to put malpractice caps into legislation, a

provision doctors have wanted for years. Instead, he said, they should focus on passing a patients' rights bill and worry later about lowering their malpractice premiums.

BILL THOMAS, R-Calif. ▲
An Expert in the Shadows

As chairman of the Ways and Means subcommittee on Health, Bill Thomas, R-Calif., is considered the health policy guru of the House. He spearheaded the Medicare overhaul that was contained in the Balanced Budget Act of 1997 (PL 105-33). Within that package, he passed a number of patient protection provisions for Medicare recipients enrolled in managed care plans, including expanded access to emergency room treatment and a prohibition on so-called "gag clauses" restricting the advice that doctors could give their patients.

But during this year's managed care debate, Thomas, who is serving his 11th term, has stayed mostly in the shadows. In early August, he was named by Hastert as a member of a leadership task force charged with developing a broad managed care overhaul. Thomas hosted several meetings of the task force in his Capitol office, but has yet to add his name to any legislation that has since emerged. Nor has he offered any proposal of his own.

"I've been facilitating and coordinating," Thomas, 57, says about his role so far. He says he is trying to find a "reasonable position in the middle."

He said the Boehner proposal — which has won the support of Majority Leader Armey — cannot win a majority of votes in the House. He also said the Norwood-Dingell approach could not win support of the Senate.

"I'm trying to find something that meets both policy and politics," Thomas said.

Thomas has so far refused to detail what he thinks could pass Congress and win the president's signature.

Unlike many members of the GOP leadership, Thomas has not ruled out expanding the liability of health plans.

He believes state courts should have jurisdiction over suits filed when patients are physically harmed, and federal courts should have jurisdiction over health plan contractual disputes. He would not, however, say whether managed care plans should be held liable for physical harm.

Thomas does believe legal damages should be capped for both plans and doctors. He admitted that the insurance industry may not agree with his proposal, but "after Boehner's bill is defeated, they will find [it] more attractive."

JOHN D. DINGELL, D-Mich. ▲
A Realistic Veteran

After 44 years of pushing a family legacy of health care legislation, the 73-year-old Michigan Democrat is close to victory. Still, Dingell, the man who used to make wit-nesses tremble when he was chairman of the Energy and Commerce Committee's Subcommittee on Oversight and Investigations, is humble.

"I've been around here a long time and I'm not impressed with myself," said the dean of the House as he maneuvered his 6-foot-3-inch frame down the Capitol steps on the way to a news conference about domestic violence. "And I don't spend a lot of time reading my press releases. . . . What is important is what we do and how the public is served."

Certainly, the measure he sponsors with Norwood is a far cry from the national health insurance bill (HR 16) he introduces each Congress, carrying on a tradition his father, former Rep. John Dingell Sr. (1932-55), started in 1943 when the younger Dingell was a 16-year-old House page. Today, he jokes that if Republicans are so concerned about uninsured Americans, they could simply accept his national program.

" I think their sincerity in that matter is slightly open to question," he said of the GOP's efforts to ensure health care coverage for the nation's 44 million uninsured Americans.

His measure with Norwood, he says, is "a good bill . . . what the public needs" and he has so far not had to rely on his famously strong arm to win support for his legislation, which has 133 cosponsors.

In 1994, Dingell tried, but failed, to shepherd Clinton's massive Health Security Act through the Commerce Committee, and he battled Republicans the following year when they tried to curb the rate of growth of Medicare.

Most recently, Dingell served on a bipartisan commission charged with strengthening Medicare for future generations. At times, he looked weary as panel members rehashed Medicare's perennial problems: too many people, too little money and an abundance of political pitfalls. Perhaps, as the veteran of the health care wars, he knew from the beginning the panel would go nowhere. (It disbanded after failing to win the needed supermajority vote for an overhaul plan.) (*1999 CQ Weekly, p. 703*)

This time he is similarly realistic, pointing out that House passage of his managed care bill does not mean enactment. The Senate-passed bill has very little in common with his, meaning the conference committee will be the real challenge.

MARION BERRY, D-Ark. ▲
Rounding Up the Blue Dogs

Rep. Marion Berry, a soft-talking ex-farmer from Arkansas, refuses to take any credit for the Dingell-Norwood bill. But as the health care point man for the conservative Democratic "Blue Dog" caucus, Berry played a key role in securing the group's much-needed endorsement of the plan.

Democratic unity on the measure is important not only because every vote counts, but because support from moderates helps counter industry characterizations of the bill as a product of liberals who want to expand the reach of government.

Berry, 57, spent most of his life as a farmer, but he worked as a pharmacist for several years in the 1960s, and is still licensed as one. He came to Washington in 1993 as a special assistant to Clinton on agriculture issues. and served in the White House during Clinton's failed 1994 health care overhaul, though he did not work directly on that effort.

After his election in 1996, Berry was named by Gephardt to serve as one of three co-chairmen of the Democratic Caucus' health care task force, a position he still holds. At the start of this year, Berry invited insurance industry spokesmen, business people and doctors to talk to the group about a managed care overhaul.

Dingell and Norwood, he said, "accommodated the Blue Dogs on a number of provisions" and the group officially endorsed the bill in August. ◆

Settling differences with Senate bill won't be easy, and tax provisions could prompt veto

House Passes Patients' Rights Bill as Reformers Claim Momentum, for the Moment

Norwood celebrates with Judith L. Lichtman, president of the National Partnership for Women and Families, after passage of his managed care bill Oct. 6.

Patients' rights legislation passed by the House Oct. 6 is significantly different from a Senate-passed measure, indicating a difficult conference ahead. Most of its provisions are opposed by both the House and Senate leaderships. And the White House is adamantly opposed to tax provisions that have been attached to the bill.

But, as the week of Oct. 4 showed, the politics of health care is complicated, unpredictable and dynamic. The broad patient protection bill (HR 2723) whose fate was uncertain right up until the vote on Oct. 7 ended up winning the support of almost a third of House Republicans.

Sponsors of the legislation are hoping that the sheer momentum of their victory will propel the legislation through to enactment. At a time when Democrats have tapped into voters' concerns about managed care, a stalled conference committee could make Senate Republicans vulnerable to charges of obstructionism on an issue that has wide public appeal.

But sponsors of the measure face numerous, possibly overwhelming, obstacles before their bill could become law. For starters, the measure, which passed 275-151, is completely different from its Senate counterpart (S 1344). The cornerstone of the House bill, which is cosponsored by Charlie Norwood, R-Ga., and John D. Dingell, D-Mich., is a provision that would give patients the right to sue their health plans in coverage disputes. The Senate measure has no liability provision.

The House bill is also much wider than the Senate's in scope. While the Norwood-Dingell bill would apply to all 161 million Americans in private insurance plans, the Senate bill parcels out its protections. For example, the Senate provision requiring insurers to pay for emergency medical care when a prudent layperson thought it necessary would apply to 48 million patients enrolled in health plans that are exempt from state regulations.

These policy differences could be easy compared to the political ones. President Clinton and Democrats are opposed to a package of so-called access provisions (HR 2990) passed by the House on Oct. 6, which Republicans said are critical to helping the 44.3 million Americans who have no health insurance. The patient protection bill was melded with the tax provisions and sent to the conference committee as HR 2990.

The president and the Democrats also accused Republicans of not finding budget offsets for the package and charged that the GOP will be forced to use the Social Security surplus to pay for the provisions, which include tax deductions and insurance pooling arrangements. Clinton even threatened a veto should the bill reach his desk.

"I will not sign it unless its costs are fully offset by the conference committee," the president wrote in an Oct. 7 letter to House Minority Leader Richard A. Gephardt, D-Mo. Republicans said the criticisms were a sign that Democrats and Clinton were more interested in keeping managed care as a campaign issue for the 2000 election campaigns than in passing a managed care overhaul measure to help patients.

House Ways and Means Health Subcommittee Chairman Bill Thomas, R-Calif., a veteran of Capitol Hill health care wars, said trying to merge the two approaches in conference will be highly difficult. "You don't see too many crossbreeds between a Chihuahua and a Great Dane," he said.

Key Managed Care Provisions

Patient protections passed by the House on Oct. 7.

Issue	Provision
Scope	The bill would cover all privately insured Americans, about 161 million people.
Liability	The bill would allow patients who claimed that they had been physically or mentally injured when wrongly denied care by their health plans to sue in state court for damages. Plans that had complied with the decision of an independent, external reviewer would not be subject to punitive damages, and any state caps on damages would apply. Employers could not be sued unless they made a decision on a benefits claim.
Emergency Care	Health plans that covered emergency room care would be required to pay for it without prior approval if a "prudent layperson" would deem it necessary. The patient could seek care at any hospital. The care would include medical screenings as well as any treatment needed to stabilize the patient's health.
Gag Rules	The bill would bar plans from restricting what a doctor could tell a patient about treatment options. Even if a treatment was not covered by a plan, medical professionals could not be prevented from discussing that option.
Internal Appeals	Plans would be required to respond within 14 days (with a possible 14-day extension) to a patient's internal appeal of a denial of coverage, and within 72 hours in urgent cases. The reviewer would be chosen by the plan but could not have made the initial denial. If the decision involved medical judgment, the reviewer would have to be a doctor. Any patient whose internal review was rejected could appeal to an independent reviewer.
External Appeals	Any patient whose internal appeal was rejected could appeal to an independent, external reviewer who would have to issue a binding, final decision within 72 hours in case of an emergency or 21 days otherwise. Penalties could include federal court action such as civil fines of up to $1,000 per day. Plan officials who repeatedly violated external review decisions could be fined up to $500,000.
Medical Necessity	The bill would guarantee that doctors, not health plan officials, determined what treatment was medically necessary. Patients could appeal a decision that found a treatment medically unnecessary or experimental.
Women's Health	Women in plans that covered obstetrical and gynecological care would be able to visit ob/gyns without going through a "gatekeeper" primary care physician.
Access to Specialists	The bill would require plans that cover specialty care to provide referrals for such care when needed, including treatment by out-of-network providers if no appropriate specialist was available in the network. Parents could designate pediatricians as primary care doctors for their children. Patients with ongoing special conditions would have continued access to their specialists for up to 90 days after a health plan dropped that specialist for reasons other than fraud or failure to meet quality standards. In cases such as pregnancy, scheduled surgery or terminal illness, patients could see the doctor throughout the duration of the experience.
"Whistleblower" Protections	Medical professionals who reported any actions by a plan affecting quality of care for patients would be protected. No health plan could retaliate against a protected health care professional who disclosed health plan abuses to a regulatory agency or other oversight officials.
Choice of Plans	The bill would permit patients to choose a point-of-service option if their health plan did not offer access to non-network providers. The patient could pay additional costs associated with this option.

Gephardt also acknowledged that prospects for a final bill are slim. "I'm worried that this bill goes into file 13 . . . into a conference that never ends," he said.

On a Roll

The biggest weapon Norwood and Dingell have in the fight, however, is momentum. Their ability to win the support of 68 Republicans, they say, could help them put pressure on a House-Senate conference committee to move the discussions more toward the bipartisan House bill.

"Ladies and gentlemen, we are now on top of Hamburger Hill," Norwood told supporters shortly after his victory, referring to a bloody battle 30 years ago in the Vietnam War. The metaphor was fitting for Norwood, who served as a combat medic in Vietnam after graduating from dental school.

Supporters of the Norwood-Dingell bill acknowledge that getting to the president's desk is a long shot, but as Dingell noted, the political dynamics of conference committees can be strange and unpredictable.

Senate Republicans facing tough reelection races may want political cover on the managed care issue and push Senate GOP leaders to give ground in negotiations with the House. House Republicans, not wanting to look as if they are content to pass managed care legislation and then let the issue go, may also push their leadership to find compromise.

The certainty that Democrats and Clinton will continue to use a managed care overhaul as a cornerstone of the agenda for the 2000 elections may give Republican leaders incentive to pass a law. With the centerpiece of its legislative agenda, their tax package, having failed, the GOP may want an achievement going into 2000. Democrats may agree to accept some sort of tax breaks in exchange for patient protections.

At an Oct. 7 news conference crowded with reporters as well as doctors, nurses, therapists and others representing the 300 groups that had endorsed the Norwood-Dingell bill, the legislation's two cosponsors were jubilant. Norwood was gracious, thanking House Speaker J. Dennis Hastert, R-Ill., for permitting the measure to receive a floor vote.

"The Speaker could have stopped this and you know it," he said. But moments later, Dingell likened the campaign for passage to "pushing a great wheelbarrow up a hill" because "we didn't get a great deal of help from the leadership."

While the crowd of supporters relished their victory, Dingell, the 44-year Capitol veteran who understands the lengthy battle ahead, urged restraint. "The time for rejoicing is really not here," Dingell said, telling supporters to "go back to work" to help push for a bill that Clinton would sign. "And then we'll have a wingding," he said.

Defining Issue

The defining line between the Norwood-Dingell measure and the three other substitutes considered by the House during the week of Oct. 4 was liability. In many patient protection areas, such as guaranteed access to emergency care or appeals procedures, the plans were quite similar.

The fact that House Republicans were debating how patients should be allowed to sue their health plans — rather than on how to block lawsuits — was a watershed moment for the GOP, which directed its efforts to restrict rather than expand liability for industry.

A 1974 law known as the Employee Retirement Income Security Act (PL 93-406), known as ERISA, permits health plans to be sued in federal courts and damages are generally limited to the cost of denied care. (*1974 Almanac, p. 244; legal issues, 1999 CQ Weekly, p. 2363*)

Porter J. Goss, R-Fla., whom Hastert appointed to build a GOP consensus on managed care legislation, does not favor widening health plans' liability. But including it in a leadership-backed bill (HR 2824) sponsored by Goss, John Shadegg, R-Ariz., and Tom Coburn, R-Okla., was inevitable because a large number of House Republicans wanted it.

"I know that my bill is not my first preference, but it's the best choice for the House," Goss said. It was, he said, "the middle ground of all the pieces I could get."

John A. Boehner, R-Ohio, pushed a measure (HR 2926) that would have not allowed consumers to sue their health plans. It failed 145-284, with 76 Republicans opposing their former GOP Conference chairman. Boehner, who played the role of protector of business interests in the debate, warned that widening health plans' liability would expose employers as well to costly lawsuits.

"Expanding lawsuits against employer-based health plans means expanding lawsuits against employers," he said. "And if employers are exposed to lawsuits, they're going to stop providing coverage for their employees. It means millions of workers are going to lose their health insurance at the very time Congress should be working to expand access to coverage."

Opponents of ERISA changes argue that federal and state judges are interpreting the federal law to allow health plans to be sued, so Congress does not need to make sweeping changes that have unintended consequences.

"Right now, members of health plans all around the country have the right to sue if something has gone wrong in the quality area," said Karen Ignagni, president and chief executive officer of the American Association of Health Plans, a trade group representing managed care insurers.

The Dingell-Norwood bill would make the broadest changes to ERISA, widening it so that health plans could be sued in state courts over coverage disputes. Proponents said the change was necessary to make insurers accountable for their actions, and to think twice before denying needed medical care.

"Understand this: The value of the right to sue is not in the lawsuit. It is in the deterrence," Albert R. Wynn, D-Md., said during floor debate Oct. 6. "Because when HMOs understand that they can be sued, they have a strong deterrent to provide . . . the best quality of health care."

The proposal Goss and other leadership members advocated was a revised version of legislation first proposed by Coburn and Shadegg. Fine-tuning by Goss, Thomas and James C. Greenwood, R-Pa., broadened the bill's liability provision to allow lawsuits in both federal and state courts, if states had their own laws to allow such lawsuits, as in Texas and California, for example.

While the measure would have permitted lawsuits in federal courts, patients would first have had to meet a tougher test than in the Norwood-Dingell bill, proving to a third party that they had been injured.

Despite Hastert's assessment just before the vote that the Coburn-Shadegg bill was "an excellent product," it failed 193-238, with 29 Republicans opposing it. Coburn, who had been at odds with Hastert over his reluctance to embrace the bill earlier, said political dynamics played a part in the bill's defeat.

"Party politics is what's driving this,"

Coburn said just after the vote. "The House is going to pass a bill that protects patients, even if it's a poor one."

Another liability proposal from Republicans Amo Houghton of New York and Lindsey Graham of South Carolina would have allowed individuals to sue in federal court, or, if they chose, select binding arbitration. Like the Goss-Coburn-Shadegg measure, the Houghton-Graham bill would have capped damages. The measure failed on a 160-269 vote.

her view of the day's events.

The group launched a new television ad campaign Oct. 6 to continue their message that the Norwood-Dingell bill's liability provisions would benefit trial lawyers more than patients. The ad uses an old lawyer cliché — swimming sharks — to stress the point.

The spot features a shark mouth open, inching toward the camera then jumping out of the water to devour bait. An announcer urges viewers to call Congress and "tell them to protect

communications strategy" after the House vote and will "prepare for the next phase of activity."

Seeking Middle Ground

It is unclear when conferees will be appointed for a joint House-Senate conference to merge the two bills, but GOP leaders in both chambers said they wanted to convene a conference.

Ganske said the fact that his bill won 275 votes is a sign that there is enough bipartisan support to push for a bill to send to Clinton.

"Once in a while, when it's a really important issue, we can come together to address the needs of our constituents," Ganske said. Goss said Hastert wants a conference to convene quickly and Senate Republican leaders echoed that sentiment after the vote.

Boehner said he would be surprised if Congress could produce anything that Clinton would sign because "it's beyond my imagination that both sides of Congress would support" the liability provisions of the Norwood-Dingell bill.

Greenwood, a co-author of the revised Coburn-Shadegg bill, predicted their liability provision would be the one that comes out of the conference.

"We've established middle ground and I think the center will hold," he said.

Senate Democrats, including Edward M. Kennedy of Massachusetts, said they welcomed a second crack at the issue. The Senate Republican bill passed along party lines, 53-47, on July 15.

Kennedy and other Democrats want to strip the tax and insurance provisions in the conference bill, arguing that they are not paid for and will not benefit the uninsured.

Republicans want to revive the tax measures that were part of the tax bill (HR 2488) that Clinton vetoed Sept. 23. Medical savings accounts, tax-exempt accounts used for medical expenses, are backed by GOP members in both chambers but strongly opposed by Democrats, guaranteeing a conference showdown. (*1999 CQ Weekly, p. 2213*) ◆

In the Democrats' "war room," Gephardt, center, is interviewed on a nationally syndicated radio show as Jay Inslee, D-Wash., and Gephardt's director of radio, Julianne Corbet, listen.

Industry Opposition

Business and insurance groups that had battled both expanding liability for health plans and giving the federal government power to regulate health plans pledged to continue their opposition. Those efforts will be pushed with a renewed vigor in light of the large number of House Republicans voting for the Dingell-Norwood bill.

Ignagni, for instance, lingered outside the hallway of the news conference where Norwood, Dingell, Greg Ganske, R-Iowa, and dozens of their supporters talked with reporters about their victory. As the event ended, Ignagni greeted reporters as they trailed out, ready to give

your family's health care from the trial lawyers' feeding frenzy."

Another insurance trade group executive, Chip Kahn, president of the Health Insurance Association of America, issued a memo to members calling the Norwood-Dingell vote "not a good day for the home team."

Kahn, a former Capitol Hill staff aide, told his membership — the chairmen, presidents and chief executive officers of insurance companies — that politics paid a key part in the outcome.

"That the national elections are a mere 13 months away of course played a part in this result," Kahn wrote. The group is now examining its "policy and

Despite avowed hands-off policy, piecemeal efforts at intervention are taking shape

Regulating the Internet: Congress Asserts Domain

Quick Contents

Lawmakers are struggling to deal with, as Senate Majority Leader Trent Lott put it, "this incredible phenomenon called the Internet." So far, Congress has adopted a hands-off policy. But it is under increasing pressure to regulate everything from how Americans access the Internet to the content they see on their computer screens.

While most of official Washington was riveted on the Clinton impeachment hearings late last year, two members of the House Judiciary Committee found themselves in the hallway trading thoughts on an issue closer to their hearts: the future of the Internet.

Virginians Rick Boucher, a Democrat, and Robert W. Goodlatte, a Republican, shared a common concern that AT&T Corp. was gobbling up cable television companies in order to dominate the high-speed Internet access business.

A national grid of upgraded cable television networks and telephone lines is expected to be able to deliver high-speed Internet access at up to 100 times the speed of standard telephone service, allowing Americans to keep pace with the rising tide of electronic information, including new services such as on-line movies, music and video games.

Boucher and Goodlatte see AT&T's move into the cable networks across the country as a threat not only to their rural constituents — most of whom do not live in the company's cable territory and might not be able to receive high-speed access for years — but also to one of their state's biggest employers, America Online Inc. (AOL), the nation's largest Internet service provider. They decided to introduce legislation (HR 1686) in May that would force AT&T to allow Internet providers to use its cable lines to deliver high-speed access to customers.

Boucher and Goodlatte thus became part of a movement that wants Congress to take sides in a battle over the future shape of the Internet, specifically how high-speed Internet service will be delivered to Americans' homes.

The issue has become one of the most heavily lobbied in Washington, with big telecommunications companies forming coalitions and hiring top communications attorneys and high-priced lobbyists to make their case in Congress and the courts. Consumer groups have also pressed the Federal Communications Commission (FCC) for action, arguing that without regulatory intervention, AT&T will gradually gain undue control of the Internet.

The pressure to act will test Congress' stated policy of taking a hands-off approach to the Internet. Although the outcome of the access debate is uncertain, it may open the door for

CQ Weekly Sept. 4, 1999

Boucher helped found the Congressional Internet Caucus in 1996. He now hopes his Internet access measure will become the centerpiece for a broader debate on Internet regulation.

Congress to extend its reach into cyberspace.

Many Internet strategists believe the government's best approach would be to avoid imposing new regulations on the worldwide computer network so as not to stifle its growth. And so far, lawmakers appear to be adhering to that philosophy, saying they will impose regulations incrementally, when specific needs arise.

But as the Internet gains prominence in the everyday lives of Americans, the legislative impulse has grown along with it. In the 106th Congress, dozens of bills have been introduced on a variety of fronts — to protect children, fight crime, establish business standards, set privacy standards and protect intellectual property.

"Every lawmaker takes the pledge: I won't regulate," said Stephen I. Jacobs, a vice president and senior counsel for the Computer and Communications Industry Association, a Washington group that represents about 40 telecommunications and high-tech companies. "But everyone is talking about exceptions this year. They want to regulate this corner or that corner of the Internet."

Seeking a Broad Debate

Boucher and Goodlatte see their effort to force AT&T to open up the high-speed Internet access business not as a regulatory measure, but one to ensure competition. But they also say their bill could serve as the centerpiece for a broader debate to answer some key questions that so far have eluded consensus: Should the government take steps to protect the personal information supplied by consumers to on-line vendors of products and services? Should regulators make efforts to restrict nuisances on the Internet, such as unsolicited electronic mail? How can Congress protect children from harmful material without contradicting the First Amendment?

Senate Majority Leader Trent Lott, R-Miss., said in an interview Aug. 6 he wanted to encourage a broader debate of the Internet's future, and he suggested a bipartisan committee to develop policy recommendations. The panel would be similar to the Special Committee on the Year 2000 Technology Problem.

"We're trying to figure out how to deal with this incredible phenomenon called the Internet," Lott said. "I may need to create a special committee. We have to give some thought to the long-term implications of the Internet in addition to the tax ramifications."

Sen. Harry Reid of Nevada, the Democratic assistant minority whip, agreed. "We are struggling with how to deal with this," he

Goodlatte, shown in his office Aug. 25, has been working with fellow Virginian Boucher on legislation he says will ensure competition among companies that provide Internet service to American homes.

FCC Chairman Kennard, center, has resisted pressure to require cable companies to open their lines to Internet service providers. He is shown at a House subcommittee hearing in March listening to Washington attorney Peter Huber testify on the FCC reauthorization.

said in a recent interview. "This is like trying to deal with the invention of the automobile. Who ever dreamed of a stop light or a speed limit?"

In the House, Thomas M. Davis III, R-Va., chairman of the National Republican Congressional Committee, has also urged a longer view.

"People have not thought this through," he said in an interview. "They are not thinking about how bills will affect the Internet or [electronic commerce], they are thinking about how bills will affect this group or that group."

A broader debate would help Congress set its priorities and could lead to a re-evaluation of its past decisions to avoid legislation on controversial issues such as privacy.

"The Internet's regulatory honeymoon will eventually end," said Paul Glenchur, a telecommunications analyst for the Schwab Washington Research Group, a branch of the brokerage firm Charles Schwab Corp. "We may be seeing some signs of that already."

Dealing With Access

With billions of dollars in revenue at stake for the nation's biggest telecommunications companies, Congress will return from the summer

recess to face the question of how to contend with the high-speed access issue.

Goodlatte and other lawmakers believe future control of the Internet will be determined by companies that own the "pipe," the cable television and upgraded telephone lines used to provide high-speed Internet access.

Although they were on opposite sides of the impeachment fight, Boucher and Goodlatte quickly found common ground on ways to check the power of the new pipe's owners, specifically AT&T.

Their vision became a slogan: "He who controls the pipe, controls the Internet."

Their bill would prevent cable companies from shutting out rival high-speed Internet service providers.

House Judiciary Committee Chairman Henry J. Hyde, R-Ill., is expected to decide this month whether to mark up the Goodlatte-Boucher bill, which would expand antitrust law to prevent discrimination by telecommunications companies against Internet service providers.

Meanwhile, the House Commerce Committee is considering another bill (HR 2420), sponsored by Reps. W.J. "Billy" Tauzin, R-La., and John D. Dingell, D-Mich., that would loosen

restrictions on the regional Bell companies' entry into long-distance telephone service in order to permit them to transmit data from coast to coast.

Senate Commerce, Science and Transportation Committee Chairman John McCain, R-Ariz., has introduced a bill (S 1043) that would eliminate regulation of the Internet by the FCC. The measure would have a similar effect as the Tauzin bill in allowing the Baby Bells to transmit high-speed data. But McCain's bill will likely face strong opposition from key lawmakers, including Lott, a strong supporter of the Mississippi-based long-distance giant MCI WorldCom Inc.

All three bills are now at the center of the lobbying. The Baby Bells have launched a new iAdvance coalition to push Tauzin's bill. The group hired two well-known co-chairmen: former Republican Rep. Susan Molinari of New York (1990-97), and Mike McCurry, President Clinton's former press secretary.

AOL has recruited Clinton's private lawyer, David E. Kendall, to join the campaign. The OpenNet Coalition formed earlier this year by AOL, MCI WorldCom and GTE Corp. is actively lobbying on the open access issue. The coalition has hired a bipartisan team that includes Greg Simon, former chief domestic policy adviser to Vice President Al Gore, and Rich Bond, former Republican National Committee chairman. (*1999 CQ Weekly, p. 331*)

Meanwhile, AT&T has been strongly lobbying against both bills. Its general counsel, James W. Cicconi, a former aide to President George Bush, is leading the fight. Mark C. Rosenblum, an AT&T vice president, told the House Judiciary Committee on June 30 that his company strongly opposed HR 1686 because it would hurt competition by stifling investment in the cable television industry.

"We cannot legislate technology," he said. "To do so would distort not only the workings of markets, but the development of technology itself."

AT&T is also part of a newly formed group, the Hands Off the Internet Coalition. Other members of the group included Net.Action, a California-based Internet users group, and the taxpayer watchdog group, Americans for Tax Reform.

"The Internet has succeeded beyond our wildest dreams," said Christopher Wolf, a spokesman for the coalition. "Unfortunately, we are increasingly seeing a variety of short-sighted government mandates that threaten this success. That's why our message is straightforward: hands off the Internet."

Nurture or Regulate?

For the past several years, Congress has been content to follow the admonitions of AT&T and other technology companies to stay out of the business of regulating Internet access.

Hoping to nurture more competition in the telephone industry, the Republican-controlled Congress passed the landmark Telecommunications Act of 1996 (PL 104-104). The law established rules designed to encourage competition in both long-distance and local service, and it decreed that rate regulation of the cable television industry would end March 31, 1999. But the law made scant mention of the Internet, except for a provision designed to prevent children from getting access to on-line pornography. (*1996 Almanac, p. 3-43*)

The section of the law known as the Communications Decency Act imposed criminal penalties for on-line companies that exposed youth to "patently offensive" material. The law

was later overturned by the Supreme Court as a violation of free speech. (*1997 Almanac, p. 5-25*)

Congress last year returned to the issue by including the Child On-line Protection Act in the fiscal 1999 omnibus spending law (PL 105-277). It was a second attempt to protect children from pornography by setting penalties for companies that expose them to material that is "harmful to minors." The law also barred companies from soliciting information from children without the consent of their parents. (*1998 Almanac, p. 22-10*)

A federal judge's preliminary injunction Feb. 1 prevented enforcement of the 1998 law. The judge cited concern it would violate free speech. The Justice Department has appealed his decision. (*1999 CQ Weekly, p. 334*)

Other than that, lawmakers have generally sidestepped Internet-related issues. The fiscal 1999 omnibus spending law included the Internet Tax Freedom Act, which calls for a moratorium until 2001 on new taxes on monthly Internet service bills. (*1998 Almanac, p. 21-19*)

After the contentious telecommunications overhaul of 1996, many lawmakers are loath to put Congress in the middle of the open-access dispute. Foremost among those opposing congressional intervention is House Commerce Committee Chairman Thomas J. Bliley Jr., R-Va. The FCC has also resisted pressure to act, with Chairman William Kennard arguing that the Internet via cable is in its nascent stages, and government regulation could stifle its growth.

A Legislative Strategy

After the summer recess, Boucher and Goodlatte, and a potential ally, Tauzin, will face their first major challenge as they try to develop a strategy for moving a bill in the House and for dealing with a staunch opponent, Bliley.

From the start, Boucher and Goodlatte have recognized that any effort to pass legislation on the open-access issue would require a compromise with Bliley. Goodlatte, who played doubles tennis with Bliley every Wednesday morning, knew his fellow Virginian would be a formidable foe.

Bliley opposed the Goodlatte-Boucher bill partly because of his passionate defense of the 1996 act. He said the law had not yet been in effect long enough to nurture competition in

high-speed Internet service.

Boucher said in an interview Aug. 19 that he envisioned a two-part strategy for passing legislation. First, his own bill to require open access to cable television networks and to upgraded telephone lines for providers of high-speed Internet service must pass the Judiciary Committee. It now has 20 cosponsors including George W. Gekas, R-Pa., and Lamar Smith, R-Texas, but the panel's chairman, Hyde, has not indicated whether he will support it.

The second step would require passage by the Commerce Committee of the narrower Tauzin-sponsored bill to loosen long-distance telephone restrictions on the Baby Bells in the 1996 act. The bill would allow the Baby Bells to provide high-speed data transmission and encourage them to upgrade telephone lines to deliver high-speed Internet service.

In Boucher's view, the approval of bills by two committees would increase pressure on Bliley to cut a deal and clear the way for both bills to be melded together in negotiations between Bliley and Hyde.

It is a complicated scenario, but Boucher says he is optimistic that a compromise can be reached.

"I think we will pass the first comprehensive Internet legislation," he said. "Internet time moves very quickly. There is a need for Congress to act now."

For now, the main battle appears to be in the House, unless McCain can reach a compromise of his own in the Senate on revisions to his bill (S 1043) to prevent regulation of high-speed Internet access by the FCC. The bill is strongly opposed by long-distance companies, including AT&T and MCI WorldCom. They argue that without FCC regulation, the Baby Bells would be able to carry high-speed data from coast to coast without opening local telephone systems to competition. The 1996 act requires Baby Bells to open their local telephone lines to competitors before they can enter any long distance telephone business.

Suggesting that he was sympathetic to considering open-access legislation, Judiciary Committee Chairman Orrin G. Hatch, R-Utah, said July 14 that competition was critical to the Internet's future. But he did not say what he would do on the access issue.

"No single company should control

who can access or develop applications or content for the Internet," he said.

In the House, it remains unclear how successful Boucher, Goodlatte and Tauzin will be in cutting a deal with Bliley.

The maneuvering began in early May when Boucher and Goodlatte unveiled their open-access legislation. Their main bill was developed as an expansion of antitrust law, over which the Judiciary Committee has jurisdiction. It was part of their strategy of dealing with Bliley by skirting his committee, at least initially. The second bill (HR 1685) had a similar antitrust provision, but was intended to move through the Commerce Committee.

To broaden the appeal of HR 1685, Boucher and Goodlatte included consumer privacy provisions. The measure would require companies to post on their Internet sites their policy for using the personal information of customers. It would also authorize the Federal Trade Commission to set rules to protect the privacy of users of commercial Internet sites. Finally, they included provisions in both bills to set restrictions on unsolicited e-mail, or "spam."

They hoped the consumer protection provisions would help win support from lawmakers of both parties, including members of the 134-member Congressional Internet Caucus, a policy study group that Boucher helped found in 1996. Goodlatte joined Boucher as a co-chairman of the group in 1998.

Boucher urged lawmakers to support the bills as a means of setting Internet standards that could eventually become global.

"If we do not act, we will have a patchwork quilt of regulation that could disrupt the seamless quality of the Internet," Boucher said.

For his part, Tauzin rejected the open-access requirement. He said it could fetter the cable television industry, which is still adjusting to the end of rate regulation March 31. (*1999 CQ Weekly, p. 545*)

Tauzin knew the Baby Bells would be able to muster strong support for his bill to permit them to provide high-speed data transmission. And he hoped to find an ally in Speaker J. Dennis Hastert, R-Ill., and to win Democratic support with Dingell's help.

Referring to Bliley, Tauzin said: "I want to set aside our differences and deal with policy issues."

Four of the five Commerce subcommittee chairmen have backed HR 2420: Tauzin, Michael Bilirakis, R-Fla., Michael G. Oxley, R-Ohio, and Joe L. Barton, R-Texas. The fifth, Oversight and Investigations Subcommittee Chairman Fred Upton, R-Mich., refrained from taking a stand.

For now, Bliley has declined to comment on how he will deal with the challenges posed by the bills. Tauzin, Boucher and Goodlatte are hoping he will make concessions this month.

Finding a Balance

While the House prepares to deal with the issue of high-speed Internet access, lawmakers are searching for a middle ground between companies that want little or no federal regulation and consumers groups that are urging Congress to take action to prevent fraud, ensure privacy and nurture competition to help keep Internet service rates low.

From the Internet's inception as a research project in 1969 through the early 1990s, Congress found itself in the role of trying to be a nurturing, and indulgent, patron.

Regulation of content and access was not required because the network was used mainly by academics and the Defense Department for study. For the most part, Congress was focused on encouraging growth of the network.

In 1992, for example, Boucher won passage of a provision in a NASA authorization law (PL 102-588) to allow the main trunk of the Internet, a computer network controlled by the National Science Foundation, to carry commercial information, as well as research and educational materials. (*1992 Almanac, p. 305*)

"The Boucher bill opened the Net to commercialization in a way that was not possible before," said Robert Kahn, one of the inventors of the information transfer protocol used to move data on the Internet.

But as the Internet emerged as a mass medium both for communications and for direct sales, Congress found itself under pressure from two opposite sides: from some on-line businesses to leave the Internet alone and from consumer groups to set rules of the road.

Typical of the sentiment among on-line entrepreneurs against government regulation is John Scheibel, a lobbyist for Yahoo!, the California-based Internet search engine company. His company belongs to the new trade group NetCoalition.com, which represents a half-dozen other on-line businesses including bookseller Amazon.com.

The group strongly advocates voluntary measures by companies to set standards for electronic commerce, instead of government regulation.

"We support market-driven policies to address issues that confront the Internet," Scheibel said.

On the opposite side of the debate, Mark N. Cooper, research director for the Consumer Federation of America, a consumer watchdog group, argued against allowing Internet companies alone to establish policies for doing business on the Internet.

"Congress and agencies need to get much more active to establish rules to protect consumers," Cooper said. "The danger is everyone will exert maximum pressure, and we will have legislative gridlock."

Some legal experts now say Congress should begin to deal with the Internet as it would with any other legislative issue, by carefully weighing arguments on both sides.

Jack L. Goldsmith, a professor at the University of Chicago Law School, advocates no specific regulation of the Internet by Congress. But he argues that federal and state governments are justified in weighing the costs and benefits of reasonable regulations in order to prevent "cyber-anarchy" and to protect consumers.

Goldsmith said that, as with all regulation, Congress will have to find a balance between the need for regulatory control and the harms that could result from government intervention.

Richard Jay Solomon, a researcher specializing in Internet-related public policy for the University of Pennsylvania, compares the debate in Congress with the evolution of the nation's railroad system after the Civil War.

Solomon said Congress helped to establish rules for a national rail system, including a standard width for railroad tracks. In addition, he noted that Congress took action to curb the power of railroad companies with the Sherman Antitrust Act of 1890.

"We should not repeat mistakes of the past with too much regulation," he said. "But if we have no regulation, there will be monopolies. And monopolies will dictate rates and conditions." ◆

'Soccer moms' take their place alongside NRA as a voting bloc to be feared

Lawmakers Rethink Assumptions About Politics of Gun Control

On recent trips home to northern Michigan, Bart Stupak has noticed something different. Women in his district have suddenly become more receptive.

Stupak, a conservative Democrat who represents Michigan's previously Republican 1st District, says that has never polled well with women — a fact he attributes to his opposition to abortion rights. But on June 18, he did something that earned him new kudos from at least some female voters. He abandoned his long-held opposition to gun control and voted for the strictest of three versions of legislation to require background checks at gun shows. The measure, by Rep. Carolyn McCarthy, D-N.Y., was narrowly defeated anyway. (*1999 CQ Weekly pp. 1426, 1430*)

"Women overwhelmingly have come to me and said, 'Thank you for that vote,'" says Stupak, a lawyer and a former state trooper who will be seeking a fifth term next year.

To the congressman's dismay, his female constituents are not the only ones who took notice of that vote. At many of his stops, Stupak is dogged by a group called Brass Roots, an anti-gun control organization with a take-no-prisoners attitude. Members of the group have followed him to public meetings in the Upper Peninsula, asking hostile and pointed question and generally striving, in Stupak's words, to "make my life impossible."

Stupak's situation is not unusual. Throughout the country during this year's summer congressional recess, members of the House from swing districts have been engaging in a new round of political calculations, weighing the relative strengths of those who favor and oppose gun control and trying to figure which side will be able to exercise more sway over the 2000 election.

Finding the politically appropriate position on gun control in a competitive House district has always required a difficult calculation. Until this year, many lawmakers had decided to oppose gun restrictions — even those that a majority of constituents supported — on the grounds that supporters of unfettered gun rights are more passionate on the issue, and also more likely to base their votes on their convictions.

Stupak, at an Aug. 19 ceremony in a national park in Calumet, Mich., says his recent reversal to favor gun control drew both protests and kudos as he traveled his district during the summer recess.

But the April 20 shootings at Columbine High School in Littleton, Colo. — and a series of shootings around the country since — have caused a wholesale re-evaluation of the political assumptions surrounding gun control. Tom W. Smith, a pollster at the National Opinion Research Center at the University of Chicago and the author of a report on public attitudes on guns, says the Colorado shootings have put a new spotlight on the issue.

"The main thing it did was shift public attention to the gun issue at a time when some other issues, like drugs, are not particularly hot," Smith said.

In the aggregate, Democrats are convinced that pushing for tighter gun controls

During the summer congressional recess, members of the House from swing districts recalculated the political consequences of their positions on gun control. Most constituents favor tighter curbs, they say, but defenders of gun rights appear to be more passionate. The same dynamic may be at work in Congress, where conferees are ready to resume talks on a juvenile justice and gun control package. Absent another incidence of violence that grabs the headlines, however, there are few signs that a deal is at hand.

works to their electoral advantage. Polls show that clear majorities — often in the neighborhood of 75 to 80 percent — support some gun restrictions, such as requiring that new guns be sold with trigger locks and that background checks be conducted on all gun show customers.

But on a district-by-district basis, the issue can work to Republican advantage as well. In 1994, the GOP swept back into control of the House in part because of conservative ire at the assault weapons ban enacted as part of an omnibus anti-crime package (PL 103-322). About a half-dozen House members, including Judiciary Committee Chairman Jack Brooks, D-Texas (1953-95), suggested that their support for gun control had yielded their margins of defeat. (*1994 Almanac, p. 273*)

"I think everyone recognizes that guns are a huge political issue that cuts both ways," said Rep. James C. Greenwood of Pennsylvania, a moderate Republican who supports most gun restrictions.

Those crosscurrents were in evidence as the congressional summer recess drew toward a close the week of Aug. 30. With the lawmakers still away, aides were working on drafting recommendations to conferees on legislation (HR 1501) drafted principally to curb juvenile crime. But there were no initial signs that they had found any way to settle the principal disagreements on the measure: The Senate version contains some modest gun restrictions — including mandatory background checks at guns shows, mandatory trigger lock sales with handguns and a ban on imported large-capacity ammunition magazines — but the House version has none at all, that chamber having defeated a gun control bill (HR 2122) by a lopsided margin. (*1999 CQ Weekly, p. 1944*)

Top Republicans remain split. House Majority Whip Tom DeLay of Texas is in the forefront of the opposition to any new gun controls. House Speaker J. Dennis Hastert of Illinois and the chairmen of the Senate and House Judiciary committees all are in favor of some new curbs.

Their point of view gained potential momentum Aug. 27 when the frontrunner for the Republican presidential nomination, Gov. George W. Bush of Texas, who has generally opposed gun curbs, said he favored some provisions before Congress. One, a version of

which is in the Senate bill, would outlaw large-capacity magazines. Another, which the House endorsed as an amendment before defeating the underlying bill, would expand background checks at gun shows but set a 24-hour limit for the review. The third would raise the minimum age for handgun purchasers to 21 from 18, an idea favored by the Speaker but not voted on in Congress this year.

Rogan's Switch

California Republican James E. Rogan is in a situation that has many similarities, and many dissimilarities, to Stupak's case halfway across the country. Like Stupak, Rogan cast his first vote in favor of strict gun control when he voted for the McCarthy measure. But unlike Stupak, who worries that his new position could hurt him, Rogan's biggest concern may be whether he made the shift early enough.

Rogan represents the San Gabriel Mountains east of Los Angeles, an area that has long been represented in the House by Republicans but has been trending Democratic in the 1990s because of immigration and redistricting. In the past two presidential elections, the 27th District was a national bellwether, with President Clinton, the GOP nominees and Ross Perot garnering percentages there that were nearly identical to their nationwide numbers.

The district does not have the types of gun-rights activists that populate northern Michigan. And if gun restrictions were not already popular, the Aug. 10 shootings at a Jewish community center in nearby Granada Hills focused greater attention on them.

Until the McCarthy vote, Rogan had such a pure record of opposing gun control since coming to the House in 1997 that the National Rifle Association (NRA) presented him its Defender of Freedom award, given to those whose opposition to gun restrictions is considered exceptional.

So it is not Rogan's most recent vote but his previous support of the NRA's position that has come under attack from state Sen. Adam Schiff, his likely Democratic opponent next year and one of the best-financed and most highly touted challengers in the nation. "He now realizes what a strong issue this is," Schiff said in an interview. "He, for instance, tries to ignore the fact that he is a [Defender] of Freedom winner."

Schiff plans to cite both Rogan's

gun rights record and his role as a manager of the House impeachment case against Clinton in portraying the incumbent as too far to the right for the district. The NRA, meanwhile, is not rushing to the support of its erstwhile hero. "It is probably unlikely he would be considered for the award again, at least in the near future," said NRA spokesman Bill Powers.

Gun Control Foes Feel the Heat

Political risk is not limited to those lawmakers who have switched their position. Many longtime gun control opponents realize that in the post-Columbine world their positions can be a liability.

Republican Jack Kingston, who has represented a conservative constituency in southeastern Georgia's 1st District since 1993, opposes most gun restrictions. But he is hearing from more and more gun control supporters, particularly from the same pivotal demographic group — women — that has given some succor to Stupak.

"What has happened is that a suburban soccer mom doesn't have a handgun in her house and does not have an interest in, or knowledge of, handguns," Kingston said in an interview. "And this is such a critical voting bloc."

Kingston argues that his opposition to gun control is the correct choice, both substantively and politically. But he laments that his party has been forced to spend more time explaining its opposition to gun restrictions — at a time when the GOP would rather stick to its message of tax cuts and health care issues.

"Having voted for some difficult bills in my time, I know that when you take a difficult stand it's going to take a lot of maintenance; you are going to have to go on the offensive."

Gun Control Support Is Sky-High

Given the focus on gun issues since Columbine, one might think the event dramatically changed poll numbers in support of gun restrictions. This is not true, but only because support has always been sky-high.

In a May Gallup/CNN/USA Today poll, 65 percent said the nation's gun laws should be stricter. At least three in five of those polled have answered that way in a series of similar polls dating to 1990, when the number peaked at 78 percent. When specific policy options are examined, the public is even more supportive. Background checks at gun shows were supported by 89 percent in an ABC News/Washington Post poll in May, while mandatory trigger locks were supported by 75 percent and a ban on assault weapons was backed by 79 percent of those surveyed. These numbers, too, are consistent with prior polls.

Looking only at numbers such as these, it might be difficult to fathom why Congress has not adopted a series of gun measures already. The answer lies in the makeup of the electorate, experts say. In a tight race with low turnout, a candidate could be elected with the support of just 15 percent of the registered voters. In a situation like that, a relatively small bloc of committed anti-gun control voters could have a determinative impact. Even if they constitute less than 10 percent of registered voters, if they turn out on Election Day (which they generally do) and vote en bloc for the candidate most committed to gun ownership rights (which they generally do) they could constitute more than half of the people voting for the winning candidate.

In a primary, gun control foes could make an even bigger impact. In such a race, 15 percent might not represent the amount of registered voters that backed the winning candidate; instead, it might represent the amount that voted.

But some pollsters suspect that, while the overall numbers have not changed, those who support gun restrictions are growing firmer in their convictions and more likely to make gun issues an important part of their evaluations of candidates. With episodes of gun violence in the headlines several times this year, the public is growing more and more concerned, said Karlyn Bowman, a resident fellow at the American Enterprise Institute, a conservative think tank. "There is something about the randomness of these violent events that may contribute to change," she said.

Crime Rate Down

Contrary to the impression that may have been left by the recent spree of highly publicized shootings, violent crime is down. Juvenile crime is down. Even suspensions of students for possessing firearms in schools is down, the Education Department reported Aug. 10.

The homicide rate in 1997, the last year for which complete data have been compiled, was 7.4 for every 100,000 people, the lowest since 1968.

It is still considerably higher than it was during the 1950s but is lower than during Prohibition. (*Chart, below*)

The murder rate for juveniles between 14 and 17 and for young adults 18 to 24 spiked up in the mid-1980s, but has been declining since 1994.

Many major cities have reported significant drops in crime. And while the front-page shootings this spring and summer in the bedroom communities near Denver and Atlanta might suggest a boomlet of violent crime outside urban centers, this is not so, say crime experts. "Juvenile violent crime involving firearms continues to drop," said Richard Rosenfeld, a criminologist at the University of Missouri at St. Louis. "I know of no information to suggest it is on the rise in small towns and suburbs."

No one seems ready to declare victory over crime. But the drop in crime rates had been sufficient to take crime off the front burner as a political issue until the Columbine shooting.

Since enactment of the 1994 law to combat crime, Congress has moved on the issue only in reaction to major news stories. In 1996, a year after the bombing of an Oklahoma City federal building, Congress enacted an anti-terrorism law (PL 104-132), and later that year, in response to a bombing at the Olympic games in Atlanta, it added more anti-terrorism provisions as part of an omnibus spending measure (PL 104-208). (*1996 Almanac, pp. 5-18, 10-20*)

Legislation directed specifically at youth crime stalled in the 105th Congress even though it had been identi-

fied by the leadership of both houses as a priority. Under attack from both left and right, it suffered because there was little public pressure to do anything. (*1998 Almanac, p. 17-15*)

In the 106th Congress, House Republicans had all but given up on producing juvenile crime legislation. The bill that had been introduced before Columbine was a minimalist, consensus measure that did little more than authorize $1.5 billion for states to spend on crime-fighting programs.

Issue May Remain Unresolved

In politics, it is perception that counts most. Most Republican leaders clearly feel under pressure to put some sort of gun measure in the conference report on the juvenile crime bill. But that task will be made tougher by uncertainty over how gun politics will play out in the 14 months before the election.

The fact that the House version has no gun provisions provides little cover for failing to act. House Judiciary Committee Chairman Henry J. Hyde, R-Ill., admitted as much at the outset of a conference committee meeting Aug. 5. At the same time, neither he nor his Senate counterpart, Orrin G. Hatch, R-Utah, believe they can go all the way and include the Senate-passed gun language. This leaves little room for compromise with Senate Democrats, who have threatened to filibuster anything that falls short of that Senate language.

In the end, the issue may be as unresolved come the 2000 election as it is now. ◆

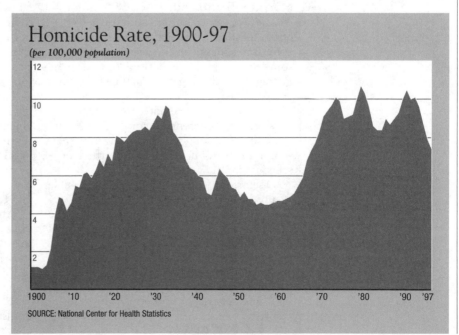

Homicide Rate, 1900-97

(per 100,000 population)

SOURCE: National Center for Health Statistics

Added funds go for upkeep, construction, and recruiting and keeping personnel

Conferees Boost Defense Budget, Stressing Readiness, Innovation

Quick Contents

A plan to create a nuclear security agency within the Energy Department could lead President Clinton to veto the defense authorization bill, but most of the legislation should remain intact, including $8.3 billion more for personnel, maintenance and research than Clinton asked for. Congress hopes the money will ease the growing strain on the military services and improve combat readiness.

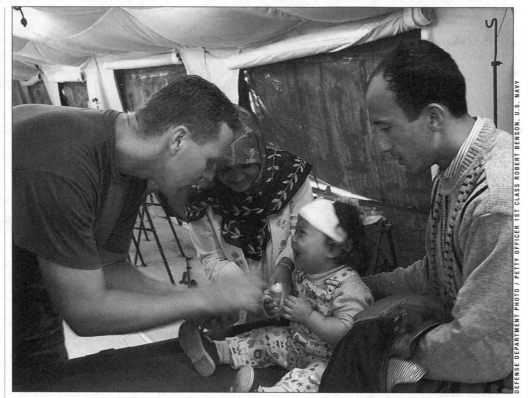

When an earthquake struck Turkey on Aug. 17, some U.S. military forces shifted from helping Kosovo refugees to aiding quake survivors. Navy Lt. Jeff Bledsoe, an operating room nurse, treats a Turkish child.

Conferees on the fiscal 2000 defense authorization bill added $8.3 billion to President Clinton's military budget request, most of it aimed at improving military combat readiness. But the lawmakers included some money and instructions to nudge the Pentagon into buying more high-tech weapons and equipment.

The House and Senate are expected to vote on the conference report (S 1059 — H Rept 106-301) soon after returning from their summer recess, but it was not on the House schedule for the week of Sept. 6.

Discussions were continuing over possible White House opposition to the proposed creation of a nuclear security agency within the Energy Department to keep tighter control of the national nuclear weapons laboratories. Energy Secretary Bill Richardson thinks the semi-autonomous agency would undermine his authority. (*1999 CQ Weekly, p. 1959*)

While defense authorizers sought to foster innovation in the services, they did not go so far as canceling the Air Force's F-22 fighter — something the House included in its version of the fiscal 2000 defense appropriations bill (HR 2561) to force the services to take a closer look at their big-ticket weapons programs. (*1999 CQ Weekly, p. 1992*)

Instead, the authorizers proposed accelerating the purchase of some high-tech weapons already in service, such as electronic warfare planes and precision-guided missiles and bombs. They also agreed to authorize more money for research and development, including a lighter and more transportable Army tank.

And the conferees approved several provisions aimed at encouraging innovative thinking in the military and among defense contractors, including proposals to:
- Require a quadrennial Pentagon report to Congress on new warfare concepts.
- Add $10 million to the $42 million the administration requested for multiservice exercises to test new concepts.

CQ Weekly Sept. 4, 1999

● Require the Pentagon to consider whether changing the rules on profit margins for defense contracts might encourage greater innovation by contractors.

● Allow the Pentagon to spend as much as $10 million annually on cash prizes to companies that develop promising military technologies.

Here is a closer look at the main elements of the conference report:

Military Personnel

The focus of the report's $72 billion authorization for military personnel is improving recruiting and retention.

In hopes of inducing experienced personnel to remain in uniform, the conferees approved a 4.8 percent raise in basic pay, rather than the 4.4 percent Clinton requested. The higher increase was in both the House and Senate bills.

The conference report would deduct from Clinton's budget request the $1.8 billion cost of a 4.4 percent raise, because it was paid for in the supplemental appropriations bill (PL 106-31) enacted in May. Since those were emergency funds, they did not count against the spending cap set by the 1997 balanced-budget act. (*1997 Almanac, p. 2-18*)

The 0.4 percent additional pay raise required another $156 million. The conference report also mandates that future annual pay raises through 2006 be 0.5 percent larger than the increase in private-sector wages, as measured by a government survey.

Both versions of the bill had approved the administration's request for additional targeted raises of up to 5.5 percent for mid-career officers and enlisted personnel.

Pension changes. The conference report would replace a 1986 law (PL 99-348) that reduced pensions for service members retiring after 20 years of active duty, from 50 percent of basic pay to 40 percent for those who joined up beginning in 1986. The conference report would offer members a choice: They could retire under the 50 percent formula or stay with the 40 percent pension, in which case they would receive a $30,000 lump-sum payment after 15 years of service.

Because the new pension system is expected to save money, the conference report offsets some of its add-ons by trimming $161 million from the personnel budget request. Conferees cut an additional $270 million from the total authorized on grounds that the services will start the fiscal year with fewer personnel than the budget assumed.

Military 401(k). The conference report would authorize military personnel to contribute up to 5 percent of their pre-tax basic pay to a tax-sheltered investment fund, similar to civilian 401(k) plans. This option would be available only if Congress enacted measures next year that would offset the loss in federal revenue.

As a retention incentive, the Pentagon would have discretion to match such contributions, as many private companies do.

Pay raise for generals. The services' 150 highest-ranking officers, who hold the ranks of general, admiral, lieutenant general or vice admiral, would get a hefty pay raise under the conference report, since it raises the $110,700 limit on military pay. The limit is set to keep military officers from making more than their civilian bosses.

The conference report would increase the pay cap to $125,900, so pay for the 35 generals and admirals would climb to that level, while pay for the next tier of senior officers would increase to nearly $120,000, the full amount provided by the Pentagon's pay formula.

Recruiting benefits. To accelerate the transition to more liberal military housing allowances, the conference report would add $225 million to the budget request. It does not include several Senate-passed provisions that would have provided more GI Bill education benefits.

The final bill would renew authority for enlistment and re-enlistment bonuses and extra pay for personnel in key, hard-to-fill specialties. It also would increase some existing bonuses and create new ones, such as a bonus for lawyers and Navy officers specializing in surface warfare.

It would add $71 million to the amount requested for recruiting and advertising, and increase from $150 to $200 the monthly stipend for college students enrolled in senior ROTC programs. It also would add $32 million to Clinton's request for high school ROTC programs, from which 40 percent of the graduates eventually join the service.

In their report, the conferees urged the Pentagon to review the medical and physical standards for joining the services, with an eye to easing the requirements.

"Persons with conditions heretofore considered disabling today make significant contributions in all walks of life," the conferees said.

The measure would also direct the Army to test a program allowing recruits to defer the start of their full-time service for up to two years and collect a stipend while they complete college or technical training.

To better understand why military personnel are leaving, the conferees directed the Pentagon to survey all those departing between Jan. 1 and June 30, 2000.

Addressing one likely reason — long overseas deployments — the conferees approved a slightly revised version of a Senate-passed provision that would require a general or admiral to approve any deployment of more than 220 days and would give anyone sent overseas for more than 250 days a daily bonus of $100. Each service chief could suspend this provision, for his service, on grounds of national security.

The conference report would reduce the active-duty force by more than 10,000, setting a ceiling for fiscal 2000 of 1.39 million personnel. This is slightly larger than Clinton requested, with most of the increase aimed at providing more Marine guards at U.S. embassies.

Operations and Maintenance

The view of many lawmakers that far-flung peacekeeping missions have undermined the combat readiness of U.S. forces underpinned several provisions of the conference report.

The $2.4 billion Clinton requested for operations in the Persian Gulf and the Balkans was cut by $508 million. The conferees justified the cut by citing the Pentagon's decision to greatly reduce the number of U.S. troops deployed in Bosnia.

To prevent the cost of operations in Bosnia or Kosovo from siphoning funds from training and maintenance, the conference report would require Clinton to request a supplemental appropriation to pay for the deployment of U.S. forces in Kosovo and for any costs of the Bosnia mission in excess of the $1.82 billion Clinton requested.

The administration planned to unveil such a request the week of Sept. 6.

The Pentagon also would be required to report on how severely deployments in the Balkans would affect the avowed goal of having U.S. forces

Anti-Missile Debate Deferred

The defense authorization conference report would provide $4.2 billion for anti-missile programs in fiscal 2000, which is 9 percent more than President Clinton requested.

However, GOP conferees did not present the increase as a challenge to the administration, even though acceleration of anti-missile defenses is a prominent issue in the Republicans' critique of Clinton's defense program.

In 1995, Republican efforts to use the fiscal 1996 authorization bill to force the pace of the anti-missile programs came to naught when Clinton vetoed the first version of the bill at no apparent political cost. (1995 Almanac, p. 9-3)

This year, the GOP-led drive for a system that could protect all 50 states against a limited number of missiles has gained strength from evidence that North Korea and Iran are developing long-range ballistic missiles. But the anti-missile advocates hitched their political effort to a separate bill (HR 4), which Clinton signed in May. The bill declares a national policy to deploy defenses "as soon as technologically possible," but mandates no specific change in the budget or timetable for Clinton's program for developing a national missile defense. (1999 CQ Weekly, p. 1223)

The conference report on S 1059 (H Rept 106-301) would provide $867 million for national missile defense, which is $31 million more than Clinton requested. The first attempt to intercept a long-range missile using key components of this system is scheduled for late September, but it will test only part of the system.

The interceptor missile is designed to get directions from ground-based radar as it flies to within a few hundred miles of an enemy missile, at which point an infrared telescope in the interceptor will take over and steer the weapon into a collision with the oncoming enemy warhead. In the first test, the ground radar will not

be used. The interceptor and its target will be aimed to come within a few hundred miles of each other, at which point the onboard, infrared homing system will take over.

Two additional tests — which will use the ground radar — are slated before June 2000, when the Pentagon is scheduled to decide whether the system is worth pursuing. To meet the planned deployment date of 2005, Clinton would have to approve the system by September 2000.

A decision to deploy would likely provoke a diplomatic blowup with Russia, since it is all but certain that the system would require changes to the 1972 treaty limiting anti-ballistic missile (ABM) weapons. Russia adamantly rejected any such moves in discussions with senior administration officials in August.

The conferees approved $528 million, $84 million less than was requested, for the Army's THAAD, which is intended to intercept medium-range missiles. After missing target warheads in its first six flight tests, THAAD scored direct hits on the next two tests, in June and August. Though additional tests of the prototype missile were scheduled, top Pentagon officials have recommended that they be dropped so that the Army and THAAD contractor Lockheed Martin can get to work on the modified version of the missile that would go into production. The conference report would give the Pentagon that discretion.

Among the other missile defense initiatives in the conference report are the following authorizations:

- $420 million for the Navy's long-range counterpart of the THAAD, $90 million more than requested.
- $309 million, as requested, to develop an airborne anti-missile defense by mounting a powerful laser in the nose of a jumbo jet.
- $149 million, $10 million more than requested, to develop a laser-armed space satellite.

ready to win nearly simultaneous wars, for instance in Korea and the Persian Gulf.

Haiti withdrawal. The conference report would terminate by May 31, 2000, the deployment of U.S. forces in Haiti, a mission that began in 1994.

Though fewer than 500 active-duty U.S. troops remain in Haiti, most Republicans consider their presence an example of the type of humanitarian mission, peripheral to U.S. security, on which they contend that Clinton is frittering away military strength. Their opposition gained strength early this year when Marine Corps Gen. Charles E. Wilhelm, commander of U.S. forces in Latin America, recommended withdrawing the troops from Haiti because growing domestic turmoil in the country put them at risk.

The administration has announced that it will replace the current U.S. force with small contingents sent for brief periods to carry out specific projects, such as road building.

Targeting readiness. As has been customary in recent years, the conferees approved additions to budget accounts Congress deems particularly relevant to combat readiness. They agreed to authorize $868 million more than the $5.2 billion Clinton requested for facilities maintenance and $380 million more than the $13.8 billion requested for day-to-day base operating costs. They also proposed to add $184 million to the $7.3 billion requested for equipment overhauls and $145 million to the $1.3 billion requested for aircraft spare parts.

The conferees also added $110 million to amounts requested for major combat training ranges.

Those increases would be partly offset by reductions that lawmakers routinely make in Pentagon budgets, including:

- $205 million because the dollar's strength has reduced the cost of supplies and services purchased overseas.
- $176 million to reduce the number of people assigned to various headquarters.
- $100 million because the Pentagon has been reducing its civilian payroll faster than the budget assumed.

Ground Combat

The dilemma lawmakers face in wanting to upgrade current weapons while encouraging faster development of new arms is evident in their treatment of several types of land warfare

U.S. Army military police man a checkpoint in Vitina, Kosovo. The United States has 5,500 military personnel in Kosovo as part of a NATO-led peacekeeping force and 6,900 in nearby Bosnia. Critics say such deployments are wearing down the military's combat readiness.

equipment.

To upgrade early-model M-1 tanks with larger cannon and digital communications links, the conference report would authorize $636 million, as Clinton requested, rejecting the Senate's $20 million increase. But to the $309 million the administration requested to modernize early-model Bradley troop carriers, the conference report would authorize another $72 million to add improved night-vision equipment and other upgrades for older Bradleys assigned to National Guard units.

At the same time, following the lead of the House, the conference report would authorize an additional $12 million beyond the $65 million requested to develop a future combat vehicle that would weigh much less than the 70-ton M-1 tank. That is intended to make it much easier to quickly deploy U.S. forces to distant trouble spots. The conferees ordered the Pentagon to come up with a plan for such a radically new combat vehicle that would be ready to go into development by 2007.

Helicopters. Additions to the Clinton budget request for the Army's current and future armed helicopters, included in both the House and Senate bills, were retained in the conference report. To the $765 million requested to equip tank-hunting Apache heli-

copters with Longbow ground-target radar, the final version of the bill would authorize an additional $45 million to replace obsolete electronic components. It would authorize $56 million more than the $427 million Clinton requested to accelerate development of the Comanche scout helicopter.

Crusader cannon. The conferees approved the $283 million Clinton requested to develop the Crusader mobile cannon, criticized by some for its 70-ton bulk.

But they also added $31 million to accelerate development of a much lighter artillery rocket launcher that could be deployed in the Air Force's hundreds of C-130 cargo planes.

Small arms. The conference report would authorize $43 million more than the $31 million requested for three types of small arms. The House bill had authorized additional funds for two types of machine guns built by FN Manufacturing in Columbia, S.C., which is represented both by House Armed Services Committee Chairman Floyd D. Spence and Strom Thurmond, a senior member of the Senate Armed Services Committee. Both are Republicans.

The Senate bill added an authorization for grenade launchers built by Saco Defense, in Saco, Maine. The city

is represented by Senate Armed Services member Olympia J. Snowe, a Republican, and House Armed Services member Tom Allen, a Democrat.

Air Combat

The Air Force request for $1.9 billion in production funds for the F-22 fighter was not an issue in the authorization conference, since both the House and Senate approved production and $1.2 billion to continue developing the plane.

The authorizers did not include the purchase of additional F-15 fighters, something included in both House and Senate versions of the defense appropriations bill. The House Appropriations Committee said the F-15 is a cheaper alternative to the F-22.

The conferees approved without change the administration requests for $253 million to buy 10 F-16 fighters for the Air Force and $2.7 billion to buy 36 F/A-18 E/F jets for the Navy. The conference report would authorize $30 million above the $477 million requested to continue developing the Joint Strike Fighter, slated to enter service in about 2007 as a lower-cost complement to the F-22.

The conference report would authorize adding $112 million to the $202 million requested to develop improvements to the B-2 stealth bomber. It would also authorize $15 million more than the $32 million requested to develop improvements in the 1960s-vintage B-52 fleet, which the Air Force expects to soldier on for nearly four more decades.

The conferees approved less than one-tenth of the $524 million the House version of the bill added to the budget request for three types of precision-guided bombs and missiles, which had accounted for most of the U.S. weaponry used against Yugoslavia earlier this year. The conference report would add $50 million to the $161 million requested for satellite-guided bombs, whereas the House had added $114 million. The final version would also authorize $235 million for glider bombs and $51 million for Tomahawk ship-launched cruise missiles, in both cases the amount requested. The House had authorized $110 million for glider bombs and $300 million for Tomahawks, including $90 million to restart Raytheon Corp.'s Tomahawk production line in Tucson, Ariz.

The conference report would authorize the $145 million requested to develop a cheaper version of the Tomahawk and the $166 million requested to develop a stealthy air-launched missile with a range of a few hundred miles. It would also require the Pentagon to explain how it plans to replace its diminishing supply of air-launched cruise missiles, which fly farther and carry a much larger warhead than the new, stealthy missile.

To upgrade the aging fleet of Prowler radar-jamming planes, the conferees would authorize $25 million more than the $161 million requested. The conference report would also authorize $5 million to begin designing a replacement for the Vietnam War-era Prowler.

The J-STARS ground-surveillance plane, a converted jetliner with radar that can track ground vehicles more than 100 miles away, also got a considerable boost from the conferees. In addition to endorsing the $282 million requested for the 14th of the big planes, they approved $46 million for components to be used in a 15th plane, to be funded in fiscal 2001. They also authorized adding $48 million to the $131 million requested to improve the J-STARS radar and $25 million more than the $82 million requested for mobile terminals on which

ground commanders could view J-STARS data.

Naval Combat

Neither version of the authorization bill made significant changes to the budget request for combat vessels. Nor did the conference report, which approved, as requested:

● $2.7 billion for three Aegis destroyers.
● $748 million for components to be used in new submarines, to be funded in future years.
● $752 million for components to be used in a nuclear-powered aircraft carrier, most of the funds for which will be included in the fiscal 2001 budget.

The conferees approved the amounts requested to continue designing two new classes of warships: $195 million for a carrier, the first of which would be funded in fiscal 2006, and $270 million for a new destroyer intended to save money by using a crew of fewer than 100, about one-third the number aboard current destroyers.

The new destroyers, the first of which is slated for funding in fiscal 2004, are intended to strike land targets up to 150 miles away with guided missiles and rocket-boosted cannon shells that use Global Positioning Satellite signals to steer to their targets. The conference report would authorize $15 million more than the $102 million requested to develop these land-attack weapons.

The conference report incorporates a Senate initiative that would add $13 million to plan for equipping four large missile-launching submarines to carry 132 Tomahawk missiles apiece instead of the 24 nuclear-armed Trident missiles they currently carry.

Sea and Air Transport

The conferees followed the Senate's lead in approving $375 million for components to be used in a helicopter carrier designed to carry up to 2,000 Marines. The ship would be built by Litton Industries in Pascagoula, Miss., the home of Senate Majority Leader Trent Lott, a Republican. The authorization would leave about $1.1 billion of the ship's cost to be covered by future budgets. The Pentagon had planned to begin funding the ship in fiscal 2004. But an earlier start was avidly desired by the Marines, the Mississippi congressional delegation and Litton, which said the faster timetable would cut $780 million from the ship's

projected $2.3 billion price tag.

The conferees also agreed to authorize $80 million, which Clinton had not requested, to begin work on a high-speed cargo ship.

The conference report would authorize $1.5 billion for two transport ships to carry Marine landing forces.

Like the House and Senate bills, the final version would authorize adding $26 million to the $95 million requested to develop an amphibious troop carrier that could haul Marines ashore at 30 mph, four times as fast as the Marines' current vehicle.

The budget included no funds for Lockheed Martin C-130s, but the conferees added $252 million for four of the planes equipped to refuel Marine aircraft in midflight.

For a dozen V-22 Osprey tilt-rotor aircraft, which the Marines will use to carry troops ashore from transport ships, the conferees approved $919 million, adding two aircraft and $123 million to the Clinton request.

To the $511 million requested for 28 H-60 helicopters built by United Technologies' Sikorsky division in Stratford, Conn., the conferees approved an additional $157 million for 12 additional aircraft.

The report would authorize $127 million, $56 million more than was requested, to modernize the Army's fleet of Chinook cargo helicopters, an increase that was one of the Army's top priorities. The upgrade project is run jointly by Boeing's helicopter division in Philadelphia and by Allied Signal in Phoenix.

The conferees also authorized adding $12 million to buy two of the three Cessna Citation executive jets that were a top Marine Corps priority. They would also authorize two Boeing 737 passenger jets at $49 million apiece, rather than the one plane requested. The Navy uses the 737s chiefly to shuttle reservists to and from training sites.

Russia and China

The conference report would authorize $476 million, the amount requested, for Cooperative Threat Reduction. This is the Pentagon's portion of the so-called Nunn-Lugar program intended to help Russia and other former Soviet republics dispose of nuclear, chemical and biological weapons. (*Background, 1999 CQ Weekly, p. 839*)

Nevertheless, the conferees chal-

Conferees' History Homework

The defense authorization conference report (H Rept 106-301) would freeze for two years any action on the emotional issue of whether the United States should give back to the Philippines a pair of church bells seized from an island village in 1901 after an attack on U.S. troops.

The "Bells of Balangiga" are part of a veterans memorial at F. E. Warren Air Force Base near Cheyenne, Wyo. Philippine President Fidel Ramos has been asking for at least one of the bells back.

The bells commemorate a particularly grisly episode in the U.S. Army's war with Philippine independence fighters. The conflict began shortly after the United States won the Pacific island group from Spain in 1898 and is estimated to have cost the lives of more than 200,000 Filipinos by the time it ended in 1902.

On Sept. 28, 1901, the bells of Balangiga, on the island of Samar, rang as a signal for a surprise attack on the U.S. infantry company garrisoned in the village. Some of the Americans were hacked to death with machetes smuggled into town in a child's coffin carried by Filipino soldiers disguised as women. More than half the U.S. soldiers were killed.

U.S. forces reoccupied the town a few days later under orders from Brig. Gen. Jacob "Hell Roaring Jake" Smith to kill every male Filipino on the island over the age of 10. Smith was cashiered from the Army for the resulting brutality, which was investigated by Congress. The number of people killed specifically as a result of his order is disputed, though estimates are more than 5,000.

The town's bells were taken back to Wyoming by an Army unit, where they stayed in relative obscurity until 1990, when Ramos, not yet president, first asked for their return. Eventually, the Philippine government, the Clinton administration and the Wyoming Legislature rallied around a compromise under which replicas of the two bells would be cast and each country would get one original bell and one duplicate.

But veterans organizations, backed by the Wyoming congressional delegation, denounced any tampering with the monument as a desecration. The Senate added to its version of the defense bill (S 1059) an amendment by Wyoming Republicans Craig Thomas and Michael B. Enzi barring the return of any veterans memorial object to a foreign country unless authorized by law. The conference version would apply that limitation only during fiscal 2000 and 2001.

On other issues of history, the conferees dropped a Senate provision that would have posthumously reinstated Rear Adm. Husband E. Kimmel and Maj. Gen. Walter C. Short to the ranks they held in command on Hawaii when Japan attacked Pearl Harbor in 1941. Both were fired and forced to retire at a lower rank. The Senate provision, which would have exonerated the two of charges of dereliction of duty, was sponsored by William V. Roth Jr., R-Del., one of whose constituents is Kimmel's son.

The conference report also would authorize:
● A presidential unit citation for the crew of the cruiser USS *Indianapolis*, sunk by a Japanese submarine in 1945 after it delivered the atomic bomb to an airfield on Tinian Island.
● Up to $5 million for military participation in a ceremony marking the U.S. victory in the Cold War.
● Turning over to a private foundation the site of Fort Des Moines in Iowa, where the first training center for African-American Army officers was created in 1917.
● A commission to study whether a national military museum should be built in the Washington, D.C., area. On the other hand, the conferees expressly barred the use of funds authorized by the bill for relocating the National Atomic Museum in Albuquerque, N.M.

lenged an important aspect of the program by barring the use of Nunn-Lugar funds for construction of a storage facility in Russia to hold chemical weapons. The $130 million requested for the storage site would be allocated to other projects. (*Background, 1999 CQ Weekly, p. 1671*)

As requested, $145 million was approved for the Energy Department's Nunn-Lugar initiatives aimed at helping former Soviet states secure their stockpiles of nuclear material from theft. But the conferees agreed to authorize only $40 million of the $60 million requested for two other Energy Department programs aimed at getting Russia's nuclear weapons workers employed in commercial activities.

In addition to the Energy Department reorganization issue that could prompt an administration veto, the conference report included other provisions triggered by allegations that China had tried to obtain militarily useful information. Among these were provisions that would:
● Prohibit U.S.-Chinese military exchanges that would "inappropriately" expose certain U.S. military capabilities.
● Require an annual report on the transfer of militarily significant U.S. technology to China, Russia or terrorist states.
● Require the president to notify Congress of any alleged violation of export control laws by U.S. companies having their satellites launched from China.

Other Provisions

Among the hundreds of other items in the conference report were provisions that would:
● Expand Arlington National Cemetery, which is projected to fill its current burial plots by 2025, by adding 44 acres of adjacent Defense Department property.
● Require the armed services to provide, on request, at least a two-person honor guard for a veteran's funeral.
● Give top Pentagon officials the final say over whether the Defense Department would be required to surrender to other users portions of the radio-frequency spectrum currently reserved for defense use.

The conference report also includes a House provision that would require the Pentagon's inspector general to review whether the Defense Department is buying dumbbells and barbells that are American-made only. ◆

Lawmakers hope international convocation revives interest among colleagues, public

Approach of World Conference Re-Energizes Free-Trade Debate

It has not been an easy year to be a trade advocate in Congress. Many priorities, such as forging new trade agreements and renewing fast-track trade negotiating authority for the president, have been largely ignored, while such matters as the surging trade deficit and calls for quotas on steel imports have captured attention.

But with the United States scheduled to host its largest international trade event ever from Nov. 30 through Dec. 3, free traders are heartened to see Washington, and Congress, again alive with debate on how best to structure the trading system to achieve goals.

The tone of the discussions is not always upbeat, however. Several lawmakers have said they are concerned that the United States will be put at a disadvantage by other countries' resolve to retain trade barriers and by the president's lack of fast-track authority, which assures other nations that Congress cannot amend trade pacts to which the president has agreed.

When delegates from the 134 member nations of the World Trade Organization (WTO) meet in Seattle, they will set parameters for the next round of multilateral trade negotiations, a system previously known as the General Agreement on Tariffs and Trade (GATT). The decisions they make about which subjects to open for discussion will start intense negotiations that the Clinton administration hopes will be complete in three years. Among possibilities for discussion are agriculture, financial services, manufacturing and government procurement. (GATT, 1994 Almanac, p. 123)

Though Congress is not likely to take any votes until final agreements are reached in three years, several members are actively planning for the Seattle event, aiming to help key industries in their districts and states broaden their market access or stave off challenges from foreign producers. Most involved so far have been members from agricultural districts, who have established a bicameral, bipartisan group of 37 members called the WTO Trade Caucus for Farmers and Ranchers.

"One of the best remedies for our agriculture situation here is increased markets," said Sen. Craig Thomas, R-Wyo., a member of

Trade Deficit

The U.S. trade deficit has more than tripled since January 1996. It jumped $9 billion from January to July this year, setting a record dollar amount of $25.2 billion as imports continued to outpace exports. The trade deficit is close to 2.8 percent of gross domestic product (GDP). Some economists see the deficit as a threat to the dollar and a drag on the U.S. economy, but others say it shows that the United States is open to trade.

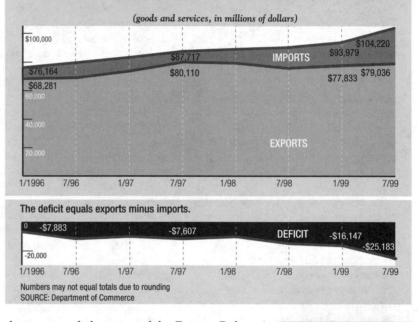

(goods and services, in millions of dollars)

$100,000 · $76,164 · $68,281 · $87,717 · $80,110 · IMPORTS · $93,979 · $104,220 · $77,833 · $79,036 · EXPORTS · 60,000 · 40,000 · 20,000

1/1996 7/96 1/97 7/97 1/98 7/98 1/99 7/99

The deficit equals exports minus imports.

0 · -$7,883 · -$7,607 · DEFICIT · -$16,147 · -$25,183 · -20,000

1/1996 7/96 1/97 7/97 1/98 7/98 1/99 7/99

Numbers may not equal totals due to rounding
SOURCE: Department of Commerce

the group and chairman of the Foreign Relations Subcommittee on East Asian and Pacific Affairs.

In addition to formulating trade goals for the U.S. trade representative, as the agriculture group is doing, some members, such as Rep. Philip M. Crane, R-Ill., chairman of the Ways and Means Subcommittee on Trade, are putting together delegations to attend the Seattle event.

Many lawmakers are concentrating on parochial interests, but a few members and many academics are focusing on how to change the system to regain a confidence in free trade that many feel has been lost among lawmakers and their constituents.

That point was acknowledged by senators from both parties and high-level administration officials at a Finance Committee hearing Sept. 29.

Panel Chairman William V. Roth Jr., R-Del., expressed concern to U.S. Trade Representative Charlene Barshefsky about the need to open agricultural markets, particularly in the European Union, "if we're going to

Quick Contents

Congress is not likely to vote on multilateral trade agreements until the next round of talks is complete in about three years. But members are planning for the World Trade Organization meeting in Seattle, where they aim to help industries broaden access to markets or stave off challenges from foreign producers.

maintain the kind of support [for free trade] we need in this country."

But the panel's ranking Democrat, Daniel Patrick Moynihan of New York, told Roth that "maintain" was the wrong word. "The problem is we have to 'regain,' " Moynihan said. "We have lost support for trade liberalization in this country." Roth responded: "I stand corrected. I wholeheartedly agree." (*Free trade and protectionism*, 1999 CQ *Weekly*, p. 431)

Barshefsky disagreed that trade liberalization was dead but said the greatest threat to the fledgling WTO, created in 1995, a year after the last round of GATT negotiations "is the lack of public support for trade policies. . . . The WTO will not survive as a business-only institution."

Commerce Secretary William M. Daley, who along with Agriculture Secretary Dan Glickman joined Barshefsky at the Sept. 29 hearing, said one reason that much of the public does not believe in world trade is that "people have felt that this is a club; that this is where business goes to cut deals. . . . People that care about issues deeply have to feel that they're in this process."

Left Out of the Club

Among those most often feeling left out of the club Daley mentioned are labor unions and environmentalists. The issues of concern to them — such as jobs and pollution — are not often priorities for trade negotiators focused on industry, but trade officials and members of Congress appear increasingly eager to find ways to satisfy the groups.

Because of opposition from the two groups, as well as a general malaise about free trade, most of the legislative trade agenda put forth in the past few Congresses has failed to reach the president's desk. And with an election year approaching, U.S. officials, particularly Vice President Al Gore and other Democrats, want to shore up support from politically powerful labor unions.

At the Finance Committee hearing, Barshefsky and Daley said they were committed to bringing up issues the groups care about. Barshefsky said she would work to cut fishing subsidies that have contributed to depleting marine life, and she said the WTO should consider a closer relationship with the International Labour Organization, a group of 174 member nations who set labor standards — for which compliance is often voluntary.

But labor and environmental organizations, at least at this early stage, are of two minds on how to approach the WTO meeting.

While they plan to take part in some of the numerous protests and other events organized by certain labor, environmental and consumer groups, some of the more mainstream organizations, such as the AFL-CIO, do not necessarily want to be associated with efforts to kill the WTO. (*Protests*, 1999 CQ *Weekly*, p. 2272)

Instead, they want a seat at the table and are pushing for a spot on the official U.S. delegation attending the meeting, a union official said.

Looking for Other Fixes

Labor unions and environmental groups are not the only ones who want a seat at the negotiating table. More than 30 countries are in various stages of discussions with WTO member nations about joining the trade regulating body. Many of these countries are communist or former communist nations seeking to embrace more of a market economy.

Some experts say that admitting such countries, particularly China, to the WTO runs the risk of undermining confidence in the organization because many of those nations do not have the same kind of legal systems or "transparency" (open government) that Western nations prize.

"The WTO is really less about trade than it is about law," said Sylvia Ostry, a former Canadian trade negotiator and now a research fellow at the University of Toronto.

The WTO seeks to resolve trade disputes through its regulatory arm, based in Geneva. Member countries are obliged to adhere to the panelists' decisions, though some countries are slower than others to adopt the necessary remedies. The United States, for instance, is still insisting that the European Union comply with WTO rulings to open its market to bananas and hormone-treated beef sold by U.S. companies.

If the WTO is required to negotiate disputes between countries with different political and legal systems, it could easily become overextended, said Ernest H. Preeg, a former U.S. ambassador to Haiti and now an analyst in international business at the Center for Strategic and International Studies, a Washington think tank.

If U.S. and European negotiators reach a deal for China's accession to the WTO, a goal they hope to complete before the meeting in Seattle, Preeg says the next major country that will want to be included is Russia.

"At some stage in the next couple of years, there's going to have to be a reassessment" of the WTO's structure to deal with the new member countries, Preeg said at a forum of the American Enterprise Institute, a business-oriented Washington think tank, at which he and Ostry spoke Sept. 27. "I think it's going to become a lot more unwieldy."

But China's accession to the WTO, much less Russia's, does not appear to be imminent. A team of Chinese negotiators flew to Washington for accession talks Sept. 27, but they left the next day with little to show for their trip, in part, U.S. officials said, because the lead negotiator had not come with the group.

Though U.S. and Chinese negotiators reached some agreements in April on opening Chinese agriculture markets, U.S. trade negotiators have said they need to make headway in other sectors, such as financial services, before they could agree to China's accession. The European Union also is continuing to negotiate with China on its WTO entry.

In a recent book, "Tiger by the Tail: China and the World Trade Organization," Mark A. Groombridge of the Cato Institute, a libertarian economic think tank, and Claude E. Barfield of the American Enterprise Institute said trade negotiators should focus more on making sure China's political and legal systems could work within the WTO than on ensuring access to specific sectors of its market.

At a Sept. 27 American Enterprise Institute symposium, Groombridge said negotiators were "losing sight of sort of the grand picture" and were "devoting too much attention to market access issues" instead of to setting up institutions in China that could help free trade survive there. ◆

Conferees, White House grind out agreement to overturn Depression-era law

Financial Services Bill In the Final Stretch

Quick Contents

Two committee chairmen and a united financial services industry have brought Congress to the brink of historic legislation to tear down the barriers among banks, brokerages and insurance companies.

A historic measure that would radically alter the financial services world is ready for approval by Congress and President Clinton because of two committee chairmen with strong personal reasons for wanting a

bill, as well as a powerhouse lobby united to an unprecedented degree and determined that this year's opportunity would not slip away.

As a result, the deal reached in the early morning hours of Oct. 22 eluded a number of pitfalls that doomed previous efforts. The path was not easy. Conference negotiations, both public and private, were lengthy and often contentious. But one by one, negotiators reached agreements that cleared the way for congressional approval of a bill likely to win Clinton's signature.

The chief strategists were Rep. Jim Leach, R-Iowa, and Sen. Phil Gramm, R-Texas, who chair their chambers' respective Banking committees. Leach has watched in frustration as previous overhaul plans evaporated despite his painstaking efforts to craft bipartisan agreements. Under House rules, he will have to relinquish his chairmanship

at the end of the 106th Congress, and this year's bill represented his last shot at passing the most sweeping financial services legislation in decades.

For Gramm, a primary player in bringing down last session's overhaul in the Senate, taking the helm of the Banking, Housing and Urban Affairs Committee imposed a new set of responsibilities. Instead of playing spoiler over pet issues, Gramm found himself under heavy pressure from the GOP leadership to get a bill passed.

And although he stuck to his guns and won some of what he wanted on a controversial anti-redlining provision, Gramm ended up agreeing to a finished product that was far different from the legislation he set before his committee early this year.

Republican leaders were pushed by the financial services lobby, which was unwilling to let this year's effort get away, particularly

Gramm and Leach talk Oct. 18 before a conference session. Gramm had his own 'lines in the sand' on some key provisions, but found a measure of flexibility under pressure from the GOP leadership.

after the legislation reached the conference stage for the first time ever. Banks, brokerages and insurance interests largely put aside their differences to get a bill, and they presented a united front, applying heat several times when conference negotiations seemed to be falling apart.

Long Road

Negotiators painstakingly cleared away land mines to merge the House and Senate versions of the bill (S 900), announcing at 2 a.m. on Oct. 22 that a deal was at hand. The bill would undo restrictions on cross-ownership among banks, brokerages and insurance companies.

The road had been a treacherous one.

First the Federal Reserve and the Treasury Department had to resolve a long-running feud over the structure and regulation of financial conglomerates by agreeing on a compromise. Negotiators then worked out language on the privacy of customer financial records, which left some consumer groups and Democrats unhappy but drew an approving nod from the White House. Negotiators also agreed to prohibit thrifts from merging with commercial businesses, eliminating another potential veto point.

But one sticking point lingered. Gramm was butting heads with the White House over the Community Reinvestment Act (CRA), a 1977 anti-redlining law (PL 95-128) aimed at forcing banks to make loans in poor neighborhoods. Gramm said the law was excessively coercive and a heavy regulatory burden for small banks, and he insisted on what he described as modest changes. The White House — backed by civil rights leaders such as the Rev. Jesse Jackson — drew a line in the sand, saying any retreat on community reinvestment was unacceptable.

Conferees resolved the issue in the early morning hours Oct. 22 in a bipartisan agreement that sent a euphoric cheer through the financial industry representatives who have been fighting for the measure for decades.

Cory N. Strupp, head of government relations for J.P. Morgan & Co., said the overhaul was the biggest financial industry bill ever passed by Congress, including the landmark Depression-era legislation it would overturn. "The scope of this bill is broader

Many of the lobbyists flooding the hallway prior to the conference represented a new unity of purpose in the financial services industry, which was determined not to let another overhaul movement die.

Financial Services Accord

Issue	Agreement
Privacy	The conference agreement generally would follow the House provisions. It calls for banks to develop written privacy policies and disclose them conspicuously to customers, and to give consumers the right to opt out of information-sharing with unaffiliated third parties. In one exception, the measure would not require banks to let customers opt out of joint marketing agreements with other financial institutions. Small banks requested the exception, arguing that without it they would be at a competitive disadvantage because large banks were more likely to have in-house affiliates to participate in cross-marketing projects. Republicans thwarted Democratic-led attempts to pass stronger privacy measures, including an amendment that would have allowed customers to opt out of information-sharing with affiliates as well as third parties. The bill would also make a crime of "pretext" calling, the practice of gathering personal information from a bank about a customer by using false information or deceptive tactics. The provision contains exceptions for law enforcement activities and for attempts to collect child support payments.
Community Reinvestment Act	The Community Reinvestment Act (PL 95-128) is an anti-redlining law that requires banks to document efforts to invest in all segments of their communities. The conference agreement would require fewer reinvestment reviews by federal regulators for most banks with less than $250 million in assets unless they sought to merge, establish a new branch or relocate. Banks wishing to expand the scope of their businesses into insurance or securities activities would have to have satisfactory reinvestment ratings to do so. The agreement also includes a "sunshine" requirement that is similar to a provision in the Senate bill. It would require banks and community groups to disclose deals in which grants or loans were offered by a bank to a community group in exchange for the group's support of the bank's reinvestment activities. Critics of reinvestment requirements said the confidential agreements allowed community groups to abuse the law by making deals with banks eager to avoid public opposition to their expansion plans.
Title insurance	The agreement would allow federal bank subsidiaries to sell title insurance. The measure would also override any state laws prohibiting such sales by national bank themselves if state banks were allowed to sell title insurance.

than anything that's been done before," Strupp said.

In an Oct. 22 statement praising conferees, the American Bankers Association, which represents many of the nation's largest banks, said outdated laws were crippling financial institutions' ability to compete. "For more than 20 years, banks and other financial institutions have been seeking the kind of legal reform that is contained in legislation now on the verge of enactment."

The administration is awaiting the drafting of final language before giving their final approval, but Treasury Secretary Lawrence H. Summers all but gave the administration's endorsement of the bill, clearing the way for likely floor approval and Clinton's signature

before Congress adjourns for the year. "Nothing is done until the language is fully reviewed," Summers said in a handwritten statement distributed to reporters in the wee hours of Oct. 22. However, Summers said that "significant improvements" were made to the reinvestment provisions and that the administration was "very pleased" with some key elements.

Conference committee Democrats also were optimistic but awaited the final language before giving their assent. In a telephone interview Oct. 22, Paul S. Sarbanes of Maryland, the top Democrat on the Senate Banking Committee, called the agreement a "major accomplishment."

The Senate originally passed its version of the bill with only one Democrat

joining Republicans in favor of it. Sarbanes said he expected the conference agreement to draw much more Democratic support because of the changes made in conference. "This bill is much better than the bill that passed the Senate," he said.

The agreement with its new language will be circulated among conferees for their signatures, said House Banking and Financial Services Committee spokesman David Runkel, so the report can be filed the week of Oct. 25.

Gramm a Key Player

Leach has been working on an overhaul bill for years, but it was Gramm who emerged as the key player in the debate. He was the focus of the White

Issue	Agreement
Structure and regulatory oversight	Negotiators adopted a compromise on the structure of new financial conglomerates worked out by the Federal Reserve and the Treasury Department, which share jurisdiction in bank regulation. The Fed had argued that financial conglomerates should be required to keep non-bank affiliates at arms' length by organizing them as affiliates under a holding company. The White House insisted that banks be allowed to organize non-banking financial activities as subsidiaries. Treasury now oversees banks and subsidiaries that are not part of a holding company, and the Fed regulates holding companies. Under the deal, banks generally would be allowed to operate most financial services, except insurance underwriting and real estate development, as subsidiaries. However, the total assets of a bank's subsidiaries could not exceed $50 billion or 45 percent of the bank's assets, whichever was less.
Regulation of insurance and securities	The agreement, which hews more closely to the House bill, would require that insurance and securities activities be overseen by their respective state and federal regulators, even if the activities were conducted by a bank affiliate or subsidiary. Exceptions would be made for some traditional bank activities, such as trust management, which would continue to be overseen by bank regulators. The Senate bill would have placed more securities functions under the review of bank regulators, rather than the Securities and Exchange Commission.
Automated teller machine fees	The agreement would require that automated teller machines give notice of transaction fees and allow customers to cancel transactions before any fees were imposed.
Thrifts	The agreement follows the Senate version, which would forbid new and existing thrifts from affiliating with commercial firms. Opponents of affiliation argued that mixing banking and commerce places the financial industry at risk, and that it could be anti-competitive if thrifts refused to grant loans to potential competitors of their commercial affiliates. Banks also complained that existing thrifts have an unfair advantage because they are currently allowed to affiliate with commercial firms, and banks are not.
Wholesale financial institutions	The agreement would allow the creation of a new type of bank called a wholesale financial institution, nicknamed a "woofie" because of the WFI acronym. These institutions would not be as heavily regulated as regular banks, and their deposits would not be federally insured. They would require a minimum deposit of $100,000 and would be geared toward the needs of institutional and large individual investors. These institutions could not be affiliated with federally insured banks, and the reinvestment act would not apply to them.

House's attention, and the bane of community groups opposed to his efforts to scale back reinvestment provisions.

Gramm thwarted Democrats in several areas, including consumer protection measures he considered unworkable and onerous for business, but he also lost on at least two big points. He had insisted that he would rather deal with consumer privacy in separate legislation, and he also opposed a provision preventing thrifts from affiliating with commercial firms. Winning some concessions on reinvestment appeared to be his line in the sand. In an Oct. 22 statement, Gramm said he was pleased with the final product, which he predicted would "pass both houses of Congress by large margins and . . . be signed by the president."

In relation to the bill's gigantic scope, the proposed reinvestment changes seemed relatively minor, but both sides dug in firmly on the issue for most of the week of Oct. 18, saying to compromise would be to sacrifice principles.

The law is intended to encourage banks to make loans in low-income neighborhoods, and it allows regulators to block banks' applications for mergers, expansions or acquisitions if they do not have satisfactory reinvestment ratings.

Leach, Gramm, and Rep. Thomas J. Bliley Jr. of Virginia, the three GOP committee chairmen who initially merged the House and Senate versions of the overhaul, unveiled their backroom handiwork Oct. 12.

Their bill sought to reduce the frequency of reinvestment regulatory ex-

ams for many small banks. It also contained a "sunshine" provision that would prohibit banks and community groups from striking confidential deals intended to keep community groups from protesting a bank's reinvestment activities in exchange for loans or grants. Those provisions were altered somewhat Oct. 22, but remained essentially intact in the final product.

Democrats warned that even though the GOP draft dropped a controversial provision to exempt small, rural banks from reinvestment compliance, the remaining provisions were still unacceptable to the White House. Community groups also objected.

Gramm's opponents accused him of trying to gut the 1977 law's effectiveness and take the first steps toward eliminating it. House Banking panel ranking Democrat John J. LaFalce of New York sought to undo the changes in the conference draft, but House conferees rejected his amendment.

With negotiations bogged down over community reinvestment, Summers paid a surprise late-night visit to Capitol Hill on Oct. 18. It appeared that Republicans were ready to push ahead with reinvestment provisions that the White House strongly opposed. Committee chairmen and ranking Democrats met with Summers for about two hours.

Over the next two days, fearing that the White House could be softening its stand on the reinvestment law and ceding ground to Republicans, supporters of the law swung into action. On Oct. 20, Democrats Maxine Waters of California, Melvin Watt of North Carolina, Stephanie Tubbs Jones of Ohio and Edward J. Markey of Massachusetts held a news conference to denounce the GOP's proposed reinvestment provisions. Watt said he was concerned about what the administration might be giving up in private negotiations with Gramm. "A group of men have retired into a back room to discuss the communities' business," Watt said. "I'm not happy about that."

Watt added that his discussion with administration officials had not satisfied his concerns.

Marathon talks among Gramm, Summers and other White House officials continued through Oct. 20, when Summers left Gramm's office late in the evening apparently believing he had reached a deal acceptable to the administration. But the White House rejected it, according to several industry sources and a Senate staff aide.

Gramm insisted he had compromised repeatedly on the community lending law, first by dropping a provision exempting small, rural banks from compliance, which he had done in the closed-door negotiations with Leach and Bliley. In his discussions with White House officials, Gramm said, he made further concessions.

Gramm said he had altered the sunshine provision and modified the regulatory relief provisions, among other changes, to move the bill toward the White House position.

In a somber news conference at 1 p.m. Oct. 21, Gramm said negotiations had failed to produce an agreement, but that the conference would push ahead on the bill anyway in hopes that the concessions he had made would be enough to avoid a veto.

In a conference session later that day, conferees discussed the reinvestment law but made little headway. Several Senate Democrats who were enthusiastic about passing an overhaul bill, including Christopher J. Dodd of Connecticut, Charles E. Schumer of New York and John Kerry of Massachusetts, urged Gramm to delay further proceedings in hopes that more talks could avoid a veto.

Kenneth A. Guenther, executive vice president of the Independent Community Bankers of America, a group of mostly small banks, said a large segment of the financial services industry wanted the bill, and it mobilized that day to urge conferees to hold off if Gramm and the administration could not reach a deal.

"There's a large group of people, financial services industry people, who do not want this bill going down over CRA for a second year running, and we are together conveying that message at the highest levels of the House and Senate leadership," he said.

But Republican leaders pushed ahead with the conference.

Break in Action Produces Deal

On the evening of Oct. 21, the conference session broke up for a series of House floor votes. As members drifted back to the conference room, impromptu backroom discussions among committee Democrats and Republicans appeared to be making headway. Leach recessed the conference so talks could continue.

Administration officials were present, but it was the Senate Democrats who had pushed for more time to get a deal who were instrumental in getting constructive talks going, Senate Banking Committee spokeswoman Christi Harlan said. "The White House had already pooh-poohed the proposal that Treasury was OK with on Wednesday [Oct. 20] night," Harlan said.

Again sensing that a key moment could be at hand, backers of the 1977 law restated their demands. At about 10 p.m., the Congressional Black Caucus distributed a copy of a letter sent to Clinton urging him "to maintain your strong support" of the law. The letter said, "Unless we maintain strong Community Reinvestment Act provisions, the ongoing consolidation of the bank-

ing industry will adversely affect disadvantaged low- and moderate-income communities."

At around 2 a.m. Oct. 22, conference Chairman Leach emerged to say negotiators had reached a deal. One key to the White House's support was a provision requiring that banks have a satisfactory reinvestment rating before expanding into securities or insurance activities.

Some members and consumer groups expressed their displeasure with the legislation later Oct. 22. In addition to their concerns about administration concessions on reinvestment, consumer groups were unhappy with the White House on another score — its endorsement of the privacy provisions adopted earlier in the week.

After wrangling for hours over privacy amendments, conferees settled Oct. 18 on provisions similar to those passed in the House.

The measure calls for banks to develop written privacy policies and disclose them conspicuously to customers, and to give consumers the right to opt out of information sharing with unaffiliated third parties. In one exception, banks would not be required to let customers opt out of joint marketing agreements with other financial institutions.

Republicans turned back several attempts by Democrats, some of them with some GOP support, to pass stronger privacy measures.

Privacy Provisions Endorsed

The White House quickly endorsed the privacy provisions, and Democrats who fought for stronger measures said they felt abandoned by an administration that previously had said it wanted strong provisions. They complained that even though conference negotiations were ongoing, the administration's public endorsement ended the debate. "In effect, they've cut our legs off," complained Sen. Richard H. Bryan, D-Nev.

Republicans had opposed an amendment by Markey that would have allowed customers to opt out of information sharing with affiliates as well as third parties, a position Markey said the administration supported in earlier statements. Markey encouraged the White House to veto the bill over privacy provisions.

Republicans who substituted weaker privacy language for Markey's amendment said his provision would have prevented companies from offering consumers a broad array of services.

Rep. W.J. "Billy" Tauzin, R-La., said provisions in Republican-backed privacy language offered by Michael G. Oxley, R-Ohio, would provide sufficient protections by requiring companies to disclose their information-sharing policies, allowing consumers to take their business to companies with privacy policies they could accept.

The amendment by Oxley closely followed language in the House bill, requiring companies to let customers opt out of information-sharing with third parties. The Oxley amendment also

there were numerous potential problems with banks selling title insurance, including conflicts of interest because bank title insurance subsidiaries would be eager to clear potentially suspect titles so that their parent banks' loans would go through.

Gramm opposed the amendment, saying it would allow states to prohibit national banks from selling title insurance. He argued that such a move would undermine the bill's central purpose, which is to tear down barriers among the three industries.

"It makes absolutely no sense,"

on states' rights depending on the position most favorable for business.

Gramm said his position on title insurance was a matter of prohibiting states from discriminating against banks, which would happen if banks were denied the right to sell certain kinds of insurance while insurers could engage in banking.

One-Stop Shopping

Industry representatives who support the legislation see it as a boon for consumers and financial services companies. They say consumers will benefit from one-stop shopping for financial services, lower-cost financial products, special package deals, and increased competition as a growing number of financial conglomerates jump into new service areas and vie for customers. (*New world, 1999 CQ Weekly, p. 2504*)

But consumer advocates worry that consolidation will reduce competition and customer choice. They also have complained that the legislation fails to protect individuals from an assault on their privacy. They see a world where faceless financial conglomerates compile detailed digital files containing personal information, and then sell it to the highest bidder.

California Rep. Lucille Roybal-Allard, at microphone, and members of the Hispanic and black caucuses defend the Community Reinvestment Act at a June news conference.

contained a provision not in the House bill, which would exempt joint marketing agreements from the opt-out requirement. Some Democrats called the exception a huge loophole rendering the entire provision nearly meaningless.

House conferees approved the Oxley substitute, 20-10. After a few small amendments were also accepted, Senate conferees approved the privacy measure by voice vote, and the House conferees adopted it, 22-7, with one abstention.

Title Insurance

The bill would allow bank subsidiaries to sell title insurance to home buyers.

Conferees rejected an amendment by Rep. Spencer Bachus, R-Ala., that would have expanded states' ability to regulate the sale of title insurance by national bank subsidiaries. Bachus said

Gramm said of the Bachus amendment. House conferees approved the measure by voice vote, but Senate conferees defeated it, 7-10.

Conferees rejected an amendment by LaFalce that would have stripped a provision from the bill allowing states to pre-empt federal consumer protection standards on insurance sales and set lower standards. LaFalce said federal consumer insurance protections should be a floor that states could exceed but not go below. Gramm said states should be trusted to set their own standards. "I think it is possible that we don't know everything," Gramm said.

Rep. Barney Frank, D-Mass., citing Gramm's positions on prohibiting state intervention in the sale of title insurance but supporting the right of states to reduce consumer protection standards, accused Gramm of switching positions

Industry supporters and consumer groups agree on at least two things though — the changes in the financial industry will be profound, and nobody is exactly sure how they will go.

With the help of favorable decisions by courts and regulators, the financial services industries have already been consolidating. Industry representatives said the legislation would not have an immediate, jarring impact on the evolution of the financial world. Instead, it would probably accelerate changes that have already been going on for years.

Some industry players will likely move aggressively to expand their reach, particularly large banks moving deeper into insurance and securities, but some financial sectors may have little interest in branching out into new areas of business.

The financial markets appeared to be pleased with the deal, although the reaction was subdued. Financial sector stocks generally rose during trading Oct. 22, but much of that rise could be attributed to a good day across the board for most stocks, said Raphael Soifer, a financial services analyst for Brown Brothers Harriman & Co. in New York. ◆

Financial services overhaul will have profound — perhaps surprising — effects

Who Wins if Barriers Between Financial Services Industries Fall?

The financial services overhaul is expected to prompt more handshakes like this one in 1998 between NationsBank CEO Hugh McColl Jr., left, and BankAmerica CEO David Coulter.

Consumers who write checks, buy insurance and invest in stocks may not have one-stop shopping at the local bank on the top of their wish lists, but Congress is ready to give them just that.

Assuming the financial services overhaul bill (S 900) about to make it through Congress becomes law, consumers will be able to buy insurance policies at their banks or open checking accounts at their insurance agencies. They will be able to invest their bank accounts in stocks and bonds more easily. And their stockbroker may be a banker as well. But large commercial companies such as Wal-Mart Stores will not be allowed into the banking business.

For many consumers, this will not seem like anything new. Banks already offer many investment services through associations with other businesses, and banks in some states and small towns can sell insurance.

But the bill would make it much easier for financial services companies to offer consumers such products. It would allow banks, securities firms and insurance companies to own each other, tearing down the Glass-Steagall Act of 1933 (PL 73-66) and subsequent laws that put barriers between the three industries in an effort to prevent a recurrence of Depression-era financial failures. (*Conference, 1999 CQ Weekly, p. 2498*)

Some industry officials and analysts say removing those barriers will foster competition, and lead to reduced fees and new financial products. But beyond any consumer benefit, they are frank that the bill would be a boon to many companies' stock prices and would, over the years, greatly increase their bottom lines.

Those whose stock would rise most would be buy-out targets, mostly banks and insurance businesses plus a few companies from the already highly consolidated securities industry. "This is going to fuel a significant merger and acquisition wave," said Kenneth Guenther, executive vice president of the Independent Community Bankers of America, a group of mostly small banks.

But others are not so sure. "Predicting this market is very risky," said Leigh Ann Pusey, senior vice president for federal af-

fairs at the American Insurance Association, a group of insurance companies. "You don't know where this will go."

Several industry officials and consumer advocates say they are not sure that life immediately after Glass-Steagall will be much different than it is now, but most believe the change will have lasting, long-term effects, for better or for worse.

Wave of Mergers

For most of the affected industry groups, there is little doubt that the bill would be a substantial improvement over current law.

Many in the industry now try to offer a variety of financial instruments and such "hybrid" products as annuities, but they can generally do so only in ways that are labor- or technology-intensive and that do not encourage new product development.

The bill would let each company own banking, securities and insurance businesses and cross-market its products. Potential home buyers shopping for financing, for instance, could be offered a discount under certain circumstances if they purchased homeowner's insurance from the same company, though under existing law they could not be denied a mortgage for refusing to buy a policy.

Such economies of scale are attractive to financial services companies, which often compete with German, French and Japanese behemoths that do not face legal barriers to dealing in all financial products. Many in the industry believe that the desire to compete on an international level will drive companies to buy each other.

"At least over the short term, there will be concentration within the financial services industry, and we will have some of the biggest kids on the block internationally," said Robert A. Rusbuldt, executive vice president of the Independent Insurance Agents of America. But Rusbuldt does not think U.S. financial companies will merge as much as Canadian companies did when their government removed barriers among banks, brokerages, insurance companies and

Decades of Efforts To Change The Glass-Steagall Act

In response to thousands of bank failures and a deepening Depression, Congress enacted the Glass-Steagall Act in 1933 to separate the commercial and savings bank industries from investment banking.

The 1933 law (PL 73-66), named after Sen. Carter Glass, D-Va. (1920-46), and Rep. Henry Steagall, D-Ala. (1915-43), prohibited banks from underwriting or selling securities.

After enactment, support grew for regulation of bank holding companies to prevent bank monopolies. President Franklin D. Roosevelt requested legislation in 1938, and bills to regulate holding companies were introduced in nearly every Congress until the Bank Holding Company Act (PL 84-511) became law in 1956.

The law defined holding companies as those with at least a 25 percent share of two or more banks. It limited their activity to the ownership and management of banks and prevented them from controlling assets in non-banking enterprises. Certain companies, however, were exempt, including one-bank holding companies, some long-term investment trusts and certain registered investment companies. Those entities could own as many banks as they wanted and could also engage in non-banking businesses.

1965-66
The House passed legislation in 1965 that sought to eliminate virtually all exemptions from the 1956 law, including its exemption for one-bank holding companies. President Lyndon B. Johnson signed the bill (PL 89-485) in 1966. But by then it included Senate-passed provisions to restore many exemptions, including the one for one-bank holding companies.

1969-70
President Richard M. Nixon promised legislation to extend the 1956 law to one-bank holding companies. The House passed such a bill in 1969. The Senate cleared it in 1970, and Nixon signed it (PL 91-607).

1978
Amendments to the 1956 law to allow bank holding companies to engage in limited insurance activities were included in a 1978 omnibus financial services bill. But the House failed to complete work on the holding company provisions before the bill became law (PL 95-630).

1980
The House passed a bill to restrict certain bank holding companies from acting as insurance agents. Similar legislation never reached the Senate floor.

1983
President Ronald Reagan proposed to permit banks to engage in securities, real estate and insurance activities. But legislators had little incentive to act, as there was general agreement that a repeal of Glass-Steagall would adversely affect constituents in every district.

1984
House legislation was introduced to close loopholes in the 1956 law, including requiring banks to divest themselves of their non-banking activities within two years. It never saw floor action. The Senate passed legislation to allow bank holding companies to form subsidiaries to underwrite mortgage-backed securities and municipal bonds.

1987
A law to bail out the Federal Savings and Loan Insurance Corporation (PL 100-86) also amended the 1956 law to close loopholes on non-banking activities, through which some retailers and financial houses had opened limited banking operations.

1988
The Senate passed a bill to repeal portions of the Glass-Steagall Act to allow banks to participate in securities activities while restricting their insurance activities. Two House committees approved a similar bill but could not compromise on jurisdictional issues. (*1988 Almanac, p. 230*)

1991
The House rejected a bill to repeal parts of Glass-Steagall and to allow banks to open branch offices nationwide. The Senate passed a bill overhauling the deposit insurance system only after the Glass-Steagall language was stripped on the floor. (*1991 Almanac, p. 75*)

1995
A bill to deregulate the financial services industry, including Glass-Steagall changes, failed to reach the House floor after opposition from banks and others persuaded leaders to shelve it. (*1995 Almanac, p. 2-78*)

1996
The 1995 bill was redrafted several times, but banks opposed it because it included restrictions on selling insurance. Bill sponsors lost hope after it became clear that House leaders would not allow floor action. (*1996 Almanac, p. 2-51*)

1997
House leaders were again unable to bring a bill to repeal the Glass-Steagall Act to the floor because of disagreements between the banking and insurance industries. (*1997 Almanac, p. 2-73*)

1998
The House passed the bill by one vote. It sought to repeal the 1933 law and other laws separating the banking, securities and insurance industries. The bill stalled in the Senate because of disagreements over community reinvestment and operating subsidiaries. (*1998 Almanac, p. 5-3*)

trust companies in the late 1980s and early 1990s. Fewer than a dozen major financial services companies now exist there. (*1998 CQ Weekly, p. 729*)

Others are not so sure that mergers will be the immediate result. Many of the largest banks have already grown through recent mergers, as have securities firms. Insurance agencies and companies have also merged, with foreign companies such as Allianz of Germany acquiring stateside insurance businesses.

Some say they are not interested in quick mergers. Of banks, said Jack Dolan, a spokesman for the American Council of Life Insurance: "We don't have any grand plans to get into their business." But others are convinced that cross-sector mergers are inevitable and that they will add to the increasingly corporate character of U.S. business.

Consumer Concerns

"This bill creates one-stop financial supermarkets," said Ed Mierzwinski, consumer program director for the U.S. Public Interest Research Group, which advocates consumer and environmental causes. "They're going to get bigger and there are going to be fewer of them. That means less competition, less shopping around and higher prices."

Though small banks, most of which are represented by the Independent Community Bankers of America, have signed on to the bill, they are also concerned that the measure may change their business radically. "There are going to be a relatively small handful of dominant big players," said Guenther, the group's director. "I do think that life is going to be tougher for your smaller players, and I think the consumer, particularly the consumer with less [money], is going to face less service at a higher price."

Consumer groups are not just concerned that customers will be charged more for banking services. They fear that companies will profit from selling information on consumers' health and financial records, data they would glean from applications for banking, investment and insurance services.

The bill contains a provision that would require banks to disclose their policies on data privacy and would allow customers to withhold information from data sharing, but many consumer advocates say the measure is confusing and does not go far enough.

"Consumers are going to be captive customers subject to the most sophisti-

cated database profiling ever and as a result targeted aggressively with overpriced products," Mierzwinski said.

Frances B. Smith, executive director of Consumer Alert, an organization with a more pro-business bent than other consumer groups, said she did not share Mierzwinski's concern that privacy provisions were too lax. But she worried that the paperwork that banks would be required to give consumers on privacy policies might be too complicated and could lead to needless litigation. "Is this going to be information overload for consumers?" she asked. "Is it something they really want? Or do consumers seek out those institutions that have the types of privacy provisions they want?"

Rusbuldt, of the Independent Insurance Agents, said bill critics were underestimating the ability of small, niche banks and other companies to thrive and meet the needs of customers who want to avoid a corporate financial services setting. "There's always going to be a demand for that retail, hands-on, face-to-face service people want," he said, adding that insurance agents will now be able to provide much of it.

But Rusbuldt does liken the changes in the bill to "putting a fire hose to the mouth of consumers. . . . You can't absorb it all," he said, adding that it will likely "increase demand for professionals who can advise and counsel."

Mierzwinski is concerned that the bill would allow Treasury Department bank regulators from the Office of the Comptroller of the Currency to overrule state laws, including consumer laws.

But Smith said she believes that consumers will likely see fewer changes than many are predicting. "I don't think consumers are going to see immediate differences in the services offered because right now you can get just about any service almost anywhere," she said. "Principally, it's going to make it easier for firms to offer those services."

Banding Together

Evidence that the bill would benefit financial services companies is reflected in its support from all major industry groups, large and small, and from their sometimes feuding regulators. In past years, bill sponsors lost bankers' support if they won approval from the insurance agents or antagonized the Treasury Department if they pleased the Federal Reserve. Now every group is on board, although America's Community Bankers, a group that represents thrifts, opposes

some provisions.

Thrifts oppose portions of the bill for the same reason that small banks, led by Guenther's group, have come to support it: It would generally prevent commercial companies from owning thrifts in the future. Because regulations on thrifts, which offer services similar to banks, are looser than on banks, many commercial companies — including such giants as General Electric Co. — have purchased thrifts in recent years.

The bill would prohibit the creation of thrifts after March 4, 1999, and prevent commercial companies from buying them after that time unless the Federal Reserve approved. The Fed has traditionally opposed ownership of thrifts by commercial businesses.

The bill's March 4 deadline for forming a thrift would preclude the nation's largest retailer, Wal-Mart, from buying an Oklahoma thrift as planned. Wal-Mart's intentions were not announced until June.

Wal-Mart's missing the retroactive deadline, one banker said, was no accident. Small banks, which have watched Wal-Mart put many a Main Street company out of business, were not eager to go the same way. If Wal-Mart owned a thrift, it would be able to offer banking services nationwide.

Senate Banking, Housing and Urban Affairs Chairman Phil Gramm, R-Texas, whose state is home to many small banks, said at a House-Senate conference committee meeting Oct. 21: "Wal-Mart will be doing banking within a month if this bill is vetoed."

It is unclear if that would be bad for consumers — Wal-Mart has made its money by drastically cutting prices — but it would be trying for small banks and would bring to Middle America the kind of fierce competition already taking place in larger banking centers.

Because Congress has been slow to repeal Depression-era laws, many financial services companies — such as Citigroup, a combination of Citibank and Travelers Group — have taken matters into their own hands, stretching the law to the limit to keep ahead.

Much of S 900 is codifying changes that have already taken place, industry officials say, but the bill would undoubtedly push the envelope further. Said Rusbuldt: "I keep telling people that there's a radical component to this bill that people are not focusing on. It's going to have an effect . . . not just on Wall Street but on Main Street." ◆

Appendix

The Legislative Process in Brief

Note: Parliamentary terms used below are defined in the glossary.

Introduction of Bills

A House member (including the resident commissioner of Puerto Rico and non-voting delegates of the District of Columbia, Guam, the Virgin Islands and American Samoa) may introduce any one of several types of bills and resolutions by handing it to the clerk of the House or placing it in a box called the hopper. A senator first gains recognition of the presiding officer to announce the introduction of a bill. If objection is offered by any senator, the introduction of the bill is postponed until the following day.

As the next step in either the House or Senate, the bill is numbered, referred to the appropriate committee, labeled with the sponsor's name and sent to the Government Printing Office so that copies can be made for subsequent study and action. Senate bills may be jointly sponsored and carry several senators' names. Until 1978, the House limited the number of members who could cosponsor any one bill; the ceiling was eliminated at the beginning of the 96th Congress. A bill written in the executive branch and proposed as an administration measure usually is introduced by the chairman of the congressional committee that has jurisdiction.

Bills — Prefixed with HR in the House, S in the Senate, followed by a number. Used as the form for most legislation, whether general or special, public or private.

Joint Resolutions — Designated H J Res or S J Res. Subject to the same procedure as bills, with the exception of a joint resolution proposing an amendment to the Constitution. The latter must be approved by two-thirds of both houses and is thereupon sent directly to the administrator of general services for submission to the states for ratification instead of being presented to the president for his approval.

Concurrent Resolutions — Designated H Con Res or S Con Res. Used for matters affecting the operations of both houses. These resolutions do not become law.

Resolutions — Designated H Res or S Res. Used for a matter concerning the operation of either house alone and adopted only by the chamber in which it originates.

Committee Action

With few exceptions, bills are referred to the appropriate standing committees. The job of referral formally is the responsibility of the Speaker of the House and the presiding officer of the Senate, but this task usually is carried out on their behalf by the parliamentarians of the House and Senate. Precedent, statute and the jurisdictional mandates of the committees as set forth in the rules of the House and Senate determine which committees receive what kinds of bills. An exception is the referral of private bills, which are sent to whatever committee is designated by their sponsors. Bills are technically considered "read for the first time" when referred to House committees.

When a bill reaches a committee it is placed on the committee's calendar. At that time the bill comes under the sharpest congressional focus. Its chances for passage are quickly determined — and the great majority of bills falls by the legislative roadside. Failure of a committee to act on a bill is equivalent to killing it; the measure can be withdrawn from the committee's purview only by a discharge petition signed by a majority of the House membership on House bills, or by adoption of a special resolution in the Senate. Discharge attempts rarely succeed.

The first committee action taken on a bill usually is a request for comment on it by interested agencies of the government. The committee chairman may assign the bill to a subcommittee for study and hearings, or it may be considered by the full committee. Hearings may be public, closed (executive session) or both. A subcommittee, after considering a bill, reports to the full committee its recommendations for action and any proposed amendments.

The full committee then votes on its recommendation to the House or Senate. This procedure is called "ordering a bill reported." Occasionally a committee may order a bill reported unfavorably; most of the time a report, submitted by the chairman of the committee to the House or Senate, calls for favorable action on the measure since the committee can effectively "kill" a bill by simply failing to take any action.

After the bill is reported, the committee chairman instructs the staff to prepare a written report. The report describes the purposes and scope of the bill, explains the committee revisions, notes proposed changes in existing law and, usually, includes the views of the executive branch agencies consulted. Often committee members opposing a measure issue dissenting minority statements that are included in the report.

Usually, the committee "marks up" or proposes amendments to the bill. If they are substantial and the measure is complicated, the committee may order a "clean bill" introduced, which will embody the proposed amendments. The original bill then is put aside and the clean bill, with a new number, is reported to the floor.

The chamber must approve, alter or reject the committee amendments before the bill itself can be put to a vote.

Floor Action

After a bill is reported back to the house where it originated, it is placed on the calendar.

There are five legislative calendars in the House, issued in one cumulative calendar titled *Calendars of the United States House of Representatives and History of Legislation*. The House

This graphic shows the most typical way in which proposed legislation is enacted into law. There are more complicated, as well as simpler, routes, and most bills never become law. The process is illustrated with two hypothetical bills, House bill No. 1 (HR 1) and

Senate bill No. 2 (S 2). Bills must be passed by both houses in identical form before they can be sent to the president. The path of HR 1 is traced by a gray line, that of S 2 by a black line. In practice, most bills begin as similar proposals in both houses.

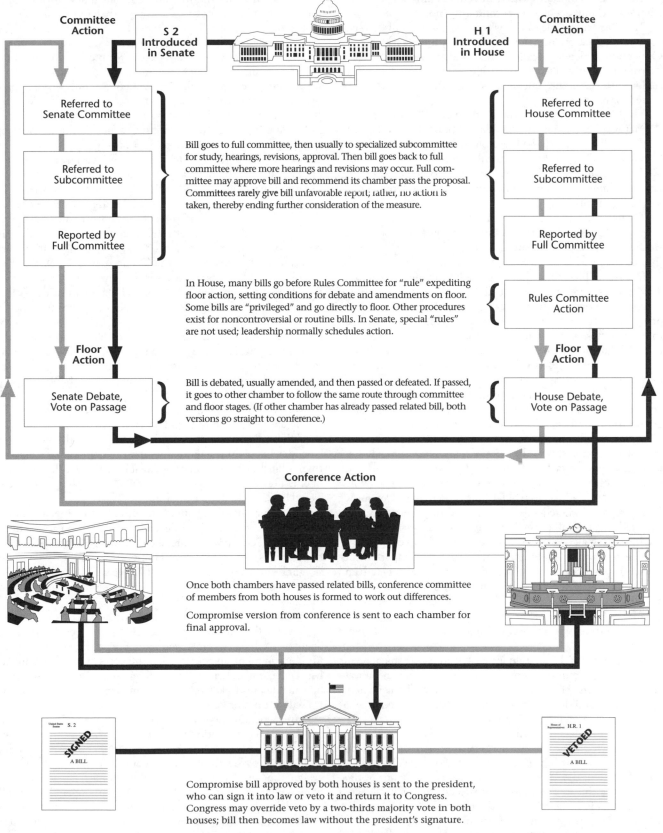

Committee Action

S 2 Introduced in Senate

H 1 Introduced in House

Committee Action

Referred to Senate Committee

Referred to Subcommittee

Reported by Full Committee

Bill goes to full committee, then usually to specialized subcommittee for study, hearings, revisions, approval. Then bill goes back to full committee where more hearings and revisions may occur. Full committee may approve bill and recommend its chamber pass the proposal. Committees rarely give bill unfavorable report; rather, no action is taken, thereby ending further consideration of the measure.

Referred to House Committee

Referred to Subcommittee

Reported by Full Committee

In House, many bills go before Rules Committee for "rule" expediting floor action, setting conditions for debate and amendments on floor. Some bills are "privileged" and go directly to floor. Other procedures exist for noncontroversial or routine bills. In Senate, special "rules" are not used; leadership normally schedules action.

Rules Committee Action

Floor Action

Floor Action

Senate Debate, Vote on Passage

Bill is debated, usually amended, and then passed or defeated. If passed, it goes to other chamber to follow the same route through committee and floor stages. (If other chamber has already passed related bill, both versions go straight to conference.)

House Debate, Vote on Passage

Conference Action

Once both chambers have passed related bills, conference committee of members from both houses is formed to work out differences.

Compromise version from conference is sent to each chamber for final approval.

S. 2 — SIGNED — A BILL

H.R. 1 — VETOED — A BILL

Compromise bill approved by both houses is sent to the president, who can sign it into law or veto it and return it to Congress. Congress may override veto by a two-thirds majority vote in both houses; bill then becomes law without the president's signature.

calendars are:

The Union Calendar to which are referred bills raising revenues, general appropriations bills and any measures directly or indirectly appropriating money or property. It is the Calendar of the Committee of the Whole House on the State of the Union.

The House Calendar to which are referred bills of public character not raising revenue or appropriating money.

The Corrections Calendar to which are referred bills to repeal rules and regulations deemed excessive or unnecessary when the Corrections Calendar is called the second and fourth Tuesday of each month. (Instituted in the 104th Congress to replace the seldom-used Consent Calendar.) A three-fifths majority is required for passage.

The Private Calendar to which are referred bills for relief in the nature of claims against the United States or private immigration bills that are passed without debate when the Private Calendar is called the first and third Tuesdays of each month.

The Discharge Calendar to which are referred motions to discharge committees when the necessary signatures are signed to a discharge petition.

There is only one legislative calendar in the Senate and one "executive calendar" for treaties and nominations submitted to the Senate. When the Senate Calendar is called, each senator is limited to five minutes' debate on each bill.

Debate. A bill is brought to debate by varying procedures. If a routine measure, it may await the call of the calendar. If it is urgent or important, it can be taken up in the Senate either by unanimous consent or by a majority vote. The majority leader, in consultation with the minority leader and others, schedules the bills that will be taken up for debate.

In the House, precedence is granted if a special rule is obtained from the Rules Committee. A request for a special rule usually is made by the chairman of the committee that favorably reported the bill, supported by the bill's sponsor and other committee members. The request, considered by the Rules Committee in the same fashion that other committees consider legislative measures, is in the form of a resolution providing for immediate consideration of the bill. The Rules Committee reports the resolution to the House where it is debated and voted on in the same fashion as regular bills. If the Rules Committee fails to report a rule requested by a committee, there are several ways to bring the bill to the House floor — under suspension of the rules, on Calendar Wednesday or by a discharge motion.

The resolutions providing special rules are important because they specify how long the bill may be debated and whether it may be amended from the floor. If floor amendments are banned, the bill is considered under a "closed rule," which permits only members of the committee that first reported the measure to the House to alter its language, subject to chamber acceptance.

When a bill is debated under an "open rule," amendments may be offered from the floor. Committee amendments always are taken up first but may be changed, as may all amendments up to the second degree; that is, an amendment to an amendment to an amendment is not in order.

Duration of debate in the House depends on whether the bill is under discussion by the House proper or before the House when it is sitting as the Committee of the Whole House on the State of the Union. In the former, the amount of time for debate either is determined by special rule or is allocated with an hour for each member if the measure is under consideration without a rule. In the Committee of the Whole the amount of time agreed on for general debate is equally divided between proponents and opponents. At the end of general discussion, the bill is read section by section for amendment. Debate on an amendment is limited to five minutes for each side; this is called the "five-minute rule." In practice, amendments regularly are debated more than ten minutes, with members gaining the floor by offering pro forma amendments or obtaining unanimous consent to speak longer than five minutes.

Senate debate usually is unlimited. It can be halted only by unanimous consent by "cloture," which requires a three-fifths majority of the entire Senate except for proposed changes in the Senate rules. The latter requires a two-thirds vote.

The House considers almost all important bills within a parliamentary framework known as the Committee of the Whole. It is not a committee as the word usually is understood; it is the full House meeting under another name for the purpose of speeding action on legislation. Technically, the House sits as the Committee of the Whole when it considers any tax measure or bill dealing with public appropriations. It also can resolve itself into the Committee of the Whole if a member moves to do so and the motion is carried. The Speaker appoints a member to serve as the chairman. The rules of the House permit the Committee of the Whole to meet when a quorum of 100 members is present on the floor and to amend and act on bills, within certain time limitations. When the Committee of the Whole has acted, it "rises," the Speaker returns as the presiding officer of the House and the member appointed chairman of the Committee of the Whole reports the action of the committee and its recommendations. The Committee of the Whole cannot pass a bill; instead it reports the measure to the full House with whatever changes it has approved. The full House then may pass or reject the bill — or, on occasion, recommit the bill to committee. Amendments adopted in the Committee of the Whole may be put to a second vote in the full House.

Votes. Voting on bills may occur repeatedly before they are finally approved or rejected. The House votes on the rule for the bill and on various amendments to the bill. Voting on amendments often is a more illuminating test of a bill's support than is the final tally. Sometimes members approve final passage of bills after vigorously supporting amendments that, if adopted, would have scuttled the legislation.

The Senate has three different methods of voting: an untabulated voice vote, a standing vote (called a division) and a recorded roll call to which members answer "yea" or "nay" when their names are called. The House also employs voice and standing votes, but since January 1973 yeas and nays have been recorded by an electronic voting device, eliminating the need for time-consuming roll calls.

Another method of voting, used in the House only, is the teller vote. Traditionally, members filed up the center aisle past counters; only vote totals were announced. Since 1971, one-fifth of a quorum can demand that the votes of individual members be recorded, thereby forcing them to take a public position on amendments to key bills. Electronic voting now is commonly used for this purpose.

After amendments to a bill have been voted upon, a vote may be taken on a motion to recommit the bill to committee. If carried, this vote removes the bill from the chamber's calendar and is usually a death blow to the bill. If the motion is unsuccessful, the bill then is "read for the third time." An actual reading usually is dispensed with. Until 1965, an opponent of a bill could delay this move by objecting and asking for a full reading of an engrossed (certified in final form) copy of the bill. After the "third reading," the vote on final passage is taken.

Examples of Legislative Documents

The final vote may be followed by a motion to reconsider, and this motion may be followed by a move to lay the motion on the table. Usually, those voting for the bill's passage vote for the tabling motion, thus safeguarding the final passage action. With that, the bill has been formally passed by the chamber. While a motion to reconsider a Senate vote is pending on a bill, the measure cannot be sent to the House.

Action in Second House

After a bill is passed it is sent to the other chamber. This body may then take one of several steps. It may pass the bill as is — accepting the other chamber's language. It may send the bill to committee for scrutiny or alteration, or reject the entire bill, advising the other house of its actions. Or it simply may ignore the bill submitted while it continues work on its own version of the proposed legislation. Frequently, one chamber may approve a version of a bill that is greatly at variance with the version already passed by the other house, and then substitute its contents for the language of the other, retaining only the latter's bill number.

A provision of the Legislative Reorganization Act of 1970 permits a separate House vote on any non-germane amendment added by the Senate to a House-passed bill and requires a majority vote to retain the amendment. Previously the House was forced to act on the bill as a whole; the only way to defeat the non-germane amendment was to reject the entire bill.

Often the second chamber makes only minor changes. If these are readily agreed to by the other house, the bill then is routed to the president. However, if the opposite chamber significantly alters the bill submitted to it, the measure usually is "sent to conference." The chamber that has possession of the "papers" (engrossed bill, engrossed amendments, messages of transmittal) requests a conference and the other chamber must agree to it. If the second house does not agree, the bill dies.

Conference, Final Action

Conference. A conference works out conflicting House and Senate versions of a legislative bill. The conferees usually are senior members appointed by the presiding officers of the two houses, from the committees that managed the bills. Under this arrangement the conferees of one house have the duty of trying to maintain their chamber's position in the face of amending actions by the conferees (also referred to as "managers") of the other house.

The number of conferees from each chamber may vary, the range usually being from three to nine members in each group, depending upon the length or complexity of the bill involved. There may be five representatives and three senators on the conference committee, or the reverse. But a majority vote controls the action of each group so that a large representation does not give one chamber a voting advantage over the other chamber's conferees.

Theoretically, conferees are not allowed to write new legislation in reconciling the two versions before them, but this curb sometimes is bypassed. Many bills have been put into acceptable compromise form only after new language was provided by the conferees. The 1970 Reorganization Act attempted to tighten restrictions on conferees by forbidding them to introduce any language on a topic that neither chamber sent to conference or to modify any topic beyond the scope of the different House and Senate versions.

Frequently the ironing out of difficulties takes days or even weeks. Conferences on involved appropriations bills sometimes are particularly drawn out.

As a conference proceeds, conferees reconcile differences between the versions, but generally they grant concessions only insofar as they remain sure that the chamber they represent will accept the compromises. Occasionally, uncertainty over how either house will react, or the positive refusal of a chamber to back down on a disputed amendment, results in an impasse, and the bills die in conference even though each was approved by its sponsoring chamber.

Conferees sometimes go back to their respective chambers for further instructions, when they report certain portions in disagreement. Then the chamber concerned can either "recede and concur" in the amendment of the other house or "insist on its amendment."

When the conferees have reached agreement, they prepare a conference report embodying their recommendations (compromises). The report, in document form, must be submitted to each house.

The conference report must be approved by each house. Consequently, approval of the report is approval of the compromise bill. In the order of voting on conference reports, the chamber which asked for a conference yields to the other chamber the opportunity to vote first.

Final Steps. After a bill has been passed by both the House and Senate in identical form, all of the original papers are sent to the enrolling clerk of the chamber in which the bill originated. He then prepares an enrolled bill, which is printed on parchment paper. When this bill has been certified as correct by the secretary of the Senate or the clerk of the House, depending on which chamber originated the bill, it is signed first (no matter whether it originated in the Senate or House) by the Speaker of the House and then by the president of the Senate. It is next sent to the White House to await action.

If the president approves the bill, he signs it, dates it and usually writes the word "approved" on the document. If he does not sign it within 10 days (Sundays excepted) and Congress is in session, the bill becomes law without his signature.

However, should Congress adjourn before the 10 days expire, and the president has failed to sign the measure, it does not become law. This procedure is called the pocket veto.

A president vetoes a bill by refusing to sign it and, before the 10-day period expires, returning it to Congress with a message stating his reasons. The message is sent to the chamber that originated the bill. If no action is taken on the message, the bill dies. Congress, however, can attempt to override the president's veto and enact the bill, "the objections of the president to the contrary notwithstanding." Overriding a veto requires a two-thirds vote of those present, who must number a quorum and vote by roll call.

Debate can precede this vote, with motions permitted to lay the message on the table, postpone action on it or refer it to committee. If the president's veto is overridden by a two-thirds vote in both houses, the bill becomes law. Otherwise it is dead.

When bills are passed finally and signed, or passed over a veto, they are given law numbers in numerical order as they become law. There are two series of numbers, one for public and one for private laws, starting at the number "1" for each two-year term of Congress. They are then identified by law number and by Congress — for example, Private Law 21, 97th Congress; Public Law 250, 97th Congress (or PL 97–250).

The Budget Process in Brief

Through the budget process, the president and Congress decide how much to spend and tax during the upcoming fiscal year. More specifically, they decide how much to spend on each activity, ensure that the government spends no more and spends it only for that activity, and report on that spending at the end of each budget cycle.

The President's Budget

The law requires that, by the first Monday in February, the president submit to Congress his proposed federal budget for the next fiscal year, which begins on October 1. In order to accomplish this, the president establishes general budget and fiscal policy guidelines. Based on these guidelines, executive branch agencies make requests for funds and submit them to the White House's Office of Management and Budget (OMB) nearly a year prior to the start of a new fiscal year. The OMB, receiving direction from the president and administration official, reviews the agencies' requests and develops a detailed budget by December. From December to January the OMB prepares the budget documents, so that the president can deliver it to Congress in February.

The president's budget is the executive branch's plan for the next year — but it is just a proposal. After receiving it, Congress has its own budget process to follow from February to October. Only after Congress passes the required spending bills — and the president signs them — has the government created its actual budget.

Action in Congress

Congress first must pass a "budget resolution" — a framework within which the members of Congress will make their decisions about spending and taxes. It includes targets for total spending, total revenues, and the deficit, and allocations within the spending target for the two types of spending — discretionary and mandatory.

Discretionary spending, which currently accounts for about 33 percent of all federal spending, is what the president and Congress must decide to spend for the next year through the thirteen annual appropriations bills. It includes money for such activities as the FBI and the Coast Guard, for housing and education, for NASA and highway and bridge construction, and for defense and foreign aid.

Mandatory spending, which currently accounts for 67 percent of all spending, is authorized by laws that have already been passed. It includes entitlement spending — such as for Social Security, Medicare, veterans' benefits, and food stamps — through which individuals receive benefits because they are eligible based on their age, income, or other criteria. It also includes interest on the national debt, which the government pays to individuals and institutions that hold Treasury bonds and other government securities. The only way the president

and Congress can change the spending on entitlement and other mandatory programs is if they change the laws that authorized the programs.

Currently, the law imposes a limit or "cap" through 1998 on total annual discretionary spending. Within the cap, however, the president and Congress can, and often do, change the spending levels from year to year for the thousands of individual federal programs.

In addition, the law requires that legislation that would raise mandatory spending or lower revenues — compared to existing law — be offset by spending cuts or revenue increases. This requirement, called "pay-as-you-go" is designed to prevent new legislation from increasing the deficit.

Once Congress passes the budget resolution, it turns its attention to passing the thirteen annual appropriations bills and, if it chooses, "authorizing" bills to change the laws governing mandatory spending and revenues.

Congress begins by examining the president's budget in detail. Scores of committees and subcommittees hold hearings on proposals under their jurisdiction. The House and Senate Armed Services Authorizing Committees, and the Defense and Military Construction Subcommittees of the Appropriations Committees, for instance, hold hearings on the president's defense budget. The White House budget director, cabinet officers, and other administration officials work with Congress as it accepts some of the president's proposals, rejects others, and changes still others. Congress can change funding levels, eliminate programs, or add programs not requested by the president. It can add or eliminate taxes and other sources of revenue, or make other changes that affect the amount of revenue collected. Congressional rules require that these committees and subcommittees take actions that reflect the congressional budget resolution.

The president's budget, the budget resolution, and the appropriations or authorizing bills measure spending in two ways — "budget authority" and "outlays." Budget authority is what the law authorizes the federal government to spend for certain programs, projects, or activities. What the government actually spends in a particular year, however, is an outlay. For example, when the government decides to build a space exploration system, the president and Congress may agree to appropriate $1 billion in budget authority. But the space system may take ten years to build. Thus, the government may spend $100 million in outlays in the first year to begin construction and the remaining $900 million during the next nine years as the construction continues.

Congress must provide budget authority before the federal agencies can obligate the government to make outlays. When Congress fails to complete action on one or more of the regular annual appropriations bills before the fiscal year begins on October 1, budget authority may be made on a temporary basis through continuing resolutions. Continuing resolutions make budget authority available for limited periods of time, generally at rates related through some formula to the rate provided in the previous year's appropriation.

Monitoring the Budget

Once Congress passes and the president signs the federal appropriations bills or authorizing laws for the fiscal year, the government monitors the budget through (1) agency program managers and budget officials, including the Inspectors General, who report only to the agency head; (2) the Office of Management and Budget; (3) congressional committees; and (4) the General Accounting Office, an auditing arm of Congress.

This oversight is designed to (1) ensure that agencies comply with legal limits on spending, and that they use budget authority only for the purposes intended; (2) see that programs are operating consistently with legal requirements and existing policy; and (3) ensure that programs are well managed and achieving the intended results.

The president may withhold appropriated amounts from obligation only under certain limited circumstances — to provide for contingencies, to achieve savings made possible through changes in requirements or greater efficiency of operations, or as otherwise provided by law. The Impoundment Control Act of 1974 specifies the procedures that must be followed if funds are withheld. Congress can also cancel previous authorized budget authority by passing a rescissions bill — but it also must be signed by the president.

Glossary of Congressional Terms

Absolute Majority—A vote requiring approval by a majority of all members of a house rather than a majority of members present and voting. Also referred to as constitutional majority.

Act—(1) A bill passed in identical form by both houses of Congress and signed into law by the president or enacted over his veto. A bill also becomes an act without the president's signature if he does not return it to Congress within 10 days (Sundays excepted) and if Congress has not adjourned within that period. (2) Also, the technical term for a bill passed by at least one house and engrossed.

Adjourn for More Than Three Days—Under Article I, Section 5, of the Constitution, neither house may adjourn for more than three days without the approval of the other. The necessary approval is given in a concurrent resolution and agreed to by both houses, which may permit one or both to take such an adjournment.

Adjournment Sine Die—Final adjournment of an annual or two-year session of Congress; literally, adjournment without a day. The two houses must agree to a privileged concurrent resolution for such an adjournment. A sine die adjournment precludes Congress from meeting again until the next constitutionally fixed date of a session (January 3 of the following year) unless Congress determines otherwise by law or the president calls it into special session. Article II, Section 3, of the Constitution authorizes the president to adjourn both houses until such time as he thinks proper when the two houses cannot agree to a time of adjournment, but no president has ever exercised this authority.

Adjournment to a Day (and Time) Certain—An adjournment that fixes the next date and time of meeting for one or both houses. It does not end an annual session of Congress.

Advice and Consent—The Senate's constitutional role in consenting to or rejecting the president's nominations to executive branch and judicial offices and the treaties he submits. Confirmation of nominees requires a simple majority vote of the senators present and voting. Treaties must be approved by a two-thirds majority of senators present and voting.

Amendment—A formal proposal to alter the text of a bill, resolution, amendment, motion, treaty, or some other text. Technically, it is a motion. An amendment may strike out (eliminate) part of a text, insert new text, or strike out and insert—that is, replace all or part of the text with new text. The texts of amendments considered on the floor are printed in full in the *Congressional Record*.

Amendment in the Nature of a Substitute—Usually, an amendment to replace the entire text of a measure. It strikes out everything after the enacting clause and inserts a version that may be somewhat, substantially, or entirely different. When a committee adopts extensive amendments to a measure, it often incorporates them into such an amendment. Occasionally, the term is applied to an amendment that replaces a major portion of a measure's text.

Annual Authorization—Legislation that authorizes appropriations for a single fiscal year and usually for a specific amount. Under the rules of the authorization-appropriation process, an annually authorized agency or program must be reauthorized each year if it is to receive appropriations for that year. Sometimes Congress fails to enact the reauthorization but nevertheless provides appropriations to continue the program, circumventing the rules by one means or another.

Appeal—A member's formal challenge of a ruling or decision by the presiding officer. On appeal, a house or a committee may overturn the ruling by majority vote. The right of appeal ensures the body against arbitrary control by the chair. Appeals are rarely made in the House and are even more rarely successful. Rulings are more frequently appealed in the Senate and occasionally overturned, in part because its presiding officer is not the majority party's leader, as in the House.

Apportionment—The action, after each decennial census, of allocating the number of members in the House of Representatives to each state. By law, the total number of House members (not counting delegates and a resident commissioner) is fixed at 435. The number allotted to each state is based approximately on its proportion of the nation's total population. Since the Constitution guarantees each state one representative no matter how small its population, exact proportional distribution is virtually impossible. The mathematical formula currently used to determine the apportionment is called the Method of Equal Proportions. (*See Method of Equal Proportions.*)

Appropriation—(1) Legislative language that permits a federal agency to incur obligations and make payments from the Treasury for specified purposes, usually during a specified period of time. (2) The specific amount of money made available by such language. The Constitution prohibits payments from the Treasury except "in Consequence of Appropriations made by Law." With some exceptions, the rules of both houses forbid consideration of appropriations for purposes that are unauthorized in law or of appropriation amounts larger than those authorized in law. The House of Representatives claims the exclusive right to originate appropriation bills—a claim the Senate denies in theory but accepts in practice.

Authorization—(1) A statutory provision that establishes or continues a federal agency, activity or program for a fixed or indefinite period of time. It may also establish policies and restrictions and deal with organizational and administrative matters. (2) A statutory provision that authorizes appropriations for an agency, activity, or program. The appropriations may be authorized for one year, several years, or an indefinite period of time, and the authorization may be for a specific amount of money or an indefinite amount ("such sums as may be necessary"). Authorizations of specific amounts are construed as ceilings on the amounts that subsequently may be appropriated in an appropriation bill, but not as minimums; either house may appropriate lesser amounts or nothing at all.

Backdoor Spending Authority—Authority to incur obligations that evades the normal congressional appropriations process because it is provided in legislation other than appropriation acts. The most common forms are borrowing authority, contract authority, and entitlement authority.

Baseline—A projection of the levels of federal spending, revenues, and the resulting budgetary surpluses or deficits for the upcoming and subsequent fiscal years, taking into account laws enacted to date and assuming no new policy decisions. It provides a benchmark for measuring the budgetary effects of proposed changes in federal revenues or spending, assuming certain economic conditions.

Bill—The term for the chief vehicle Congress uses for enacting laws. Bills that originate in the House of Representatives are designated as H.R., those in the Senate as S., followed by a number assigned in the order in which they are introduced during a two-year Congress. A bill becomes a law if passed in identical language by both houses and signed by the president, or passed over his veto, or if the president fails to sign it within 10 days after he has received it while Congress is in session.

Bills and Resolutions Introduced—Members formally present measures to their respective houses by delivering them to a clerk in the chamber when their house is in session. Both houses permit any number of members to join in introducing a bill or resolution. The first member listed on the measure is the sponsor; the other members listed are its cosponsors.

Bills and Resolutions Referred—After a bill or resolution is introduced, it is normally sent to one or more committees that have jurisdiction over its subject, as defined by House and Senate rules and precedents. A Senate measure is usually referred to the committee with jurisdiction over the predominant subject of its text, but it may be sent to two or more committees by unanimous consent or on a motion offered jointly by the majority and minority leaders. In the House, a rule requires the Speaker to refer a measure to the committee that has primary jurisdiction. The Speaker is also authorized to refer measures sequentially to additional committees.

Borrowing Authority—Statutory authority permitting a federal agency, such as the Export-Import Bank, to borrow money from the public or the Treasury to finance its operations. It is a form of backdoor spending. To bring such spending under the control of the congressional appropriation process, the Congressional Budget Act requires that new borrowing authori-

ty shall be effective only to the extent and in such amounts as are provided in appropriations acts.

Budget—A detailed statement of actual or anticipated revenues and expenditures during an accounting period. For the national government, the period is the federal fiscal year (October 1–September 30). The budget usually refers to the president's budget submission to Congress early each calendar year. The president's budget estimates federal government income and spending for the upcoming fiscal year and contains detailed recommendations for appropriation, revenue, and other legislation. Congress is not required to accept or even vote directly on the president's proposals, and it often revises the president's budget extensively. (*See Fiscal Year.*)

Budget Act—Common name for the Congressional Budget and Impoundment Control Act of 1974, which established the basic procedures of the current congressional budget process; created the House and Senate Budget committees; and enacted procedures for reconciliation, deferrals, and rescissions. (*See Budget Process, Deferral, Impoundment, Reconciliation, Rescission. See also Gramm-Rudman-Hollings Act of 1985.*)

Budget and Accounting Act of 1921—The law that, for the first time, authorized the president to submit to Congress an annual budget for the entire federal government. Prior to the act, most federal agencies sent their budget requests to the appropriate congressional committees without review by the president.

Budget Authority—Generally, the amount of money that may be spent or obligated by a government agency or for a government program or activity. Technically, it is statutory authority to enter into obligations that normally result in outlays. The main forms of budget authority are appropriations, borrowing authority, and contract authority. It also includes authority to obligate and expend the proceeds of offsetting receipts and collections. Congress may make budget authority available for only one year, several years, or an indefinite period, and it may specify definite or indefinite amounts.

Budget Process—(1) In Congress, the procedural system it uses (a) to approve an annual concurrent resolution on the budget that sets goals for aggregate and functional categories of federal expenditures, revenues, and the surplus or deficit for an upcoming fiscal year; and (b) to implement those goals in spending, revenue, and, if necessary, reconciliation and debt-limit legislation. (2) In the executive branch, the process of formulating the president's annual budget, submitting it to Congress, defending it before congressional committees, implementing subsequent budget-related legislation, impounding or sequestering expenditures as permitted by law, auditing and evaluating programs, and compiling final budget data. The Budget and Accounting Act of 1921 and the Congressional Budget and Impoundment Control Act of 1974 established the basic elements of the current budget process. Major revisions were enacted in the Gramm-Rudman-Hollings Act of 1985 and the Budget Enforcement Act of 1990.

Budget Resolution—A concurrent resolution in which Congress establishes or revises its version of the federal budget's broad financial features for the upcoming fiscal year and several additional fiscal years. Like other concurrent resolutions, it does not have the force of law, but it provides the framework within which Congress subsequently considers revenue, spending, and other budget-implementing legislation. The framework consists of two basic elements: (1) aggregate budget amounts (total revenues, new budget authority, outlays, loan obligations and loan guarantee commitments, deficit or surplus, and debt limit); and (2) subdivisions of the relevant aggregate amounts among the functional categories of the budget. Although it does not allocate funds to specific programs or accounts, the budget committees' reports accompanying the resolution often discuss the major program assumptions underlying its functional amounts. Unlike those amounts, however, the assumptions are not binding on Congress.

By Request—A designation indicating that a member has introduced a measure on behalf of the president, an executive agency, or a private individual or organization. Members often introduce such measures as a courtesy because neither the president nor any person other than a member of Congress can do so. The term, which appears next to the sponsor's name, implies that the member who introduced the measure does not necessarily endorse it. A House rule dealing with by-request introductions dates from 1888, but the practice goes back to the earliest history of Congress.

Calendar—A list of measures or other matters (most of them favorably reported by committees) that are eligible for floor consideration. The House has five calendars; the Senate has two. A place on a calendar does not guarantee consideration. Each house decides which measures and matters it will take up, when, and in what order, in accordance with its rules and practices.

Calendar Wednesday—A House procedure that on Wednesdays permits its committees to bring up for floor consideration nonprivileged measures they have reported. The procedure is so cumbersome and susceptible to dilatory tactics, however, that committees rarely use it.

Call of the Calendar—Senate bills that are not brought up for debate by a motion, unanimous consent, or a unanimous consent agreement are brought before the Senate for action when the calendar listing them is "called." Bills must be called in the order listed. Measures considered by this method usually are noncontroversial, and debate on the bill and any proposed amendments is limited to a total of five minutes for each senator.

Caucus—(1) A common term for the official organization of each party in each house. (2) The official title of the organization of House Democrats. House and Senate Republicans and Senate Democrats call their organizations "conferences." (3) A term for an informal group of members who share legislative interests, such as the Black Caucus, Hispanic Caucus, and Children's Caucus.

Censure—The strongest formal condemnation of a member for misconduct short of expulsion. A house usually adopts a resolution of censure to express its condemnation, after which the presiding officer reads its rebuke aloud to the member in the presence of his colleagues.

Chamber—The Capitol room in which a house of Congress normally holds its sessions. The chamber of the House of Representatives, officially called the Hall of the House, is consider-

ably larger than that of the Senate because it must accommodate 435 representatives, four delegates, and one resident commissioner. Unlike the Senate chamber, members have no desks or assigned seats. In both chambers, the floor slopes downward to the well in front of the presiding officer's raised desk. A chamber is often referred to as "the floor," as when members are said to be on or going to the floor. Those expressions usually imply that the member's house is in session.

Christmas Tree Bill—Jargon for a bill adorned with amendments, many of them unrelated to the bill's subject, that provide benefits for interest groups, specific states, congressional districts, companies, and individuals.

Classes of Senators—A class consists of the 33 or 34 senators elected to a six-year term in the same general election. Since the terms of approximately one-third of the senators expire every two years, there are three classes.

Clean Bill—After a House committee extensively amends a bill, it often assembles its amendments and what is left of the bill into a new measure that one or more of its members introduces as a "clean bill." The revised measure is assigned a new number.

Clerk of the House—An officer of the House of Representatives responsible principally for administrative support of the legislative process in the House. The clerk is invariably the candidate of the majority party.

Cloture—A Senate procedure that limits further consideration of a pending proposal to 30 hours in order to end a filibuster. Sixteen senators must first sign and submit a cloture motion to the presiding officer. One hour after the Senate meets on the second calendar day thereafter, the chair puts the motion to a yea-and-nay vote following a live quorum call. If three-fifths of all senators (60 if there are no vacancies) vote for the motion, the Senate must take final action on the cloture proposal by the end of the 30 hours of consideration and may consider no other business until it takes that action. Cloture on a proposal to amend the Senate's standing rules requires approval by two-thirds of the senators present and voting.

Code of Official Conduct—A House rule that bans certain actions by House members, officers, and employees; requires them to conduct themselves in ways that "reflect creditably" on the House; and orders them to adhere to the spirit and the letter of House rules and those of its committees. The code's provisions govern the receipt of outside compensation, gifts, and honoraria, and the use of campaign funds; prohibit members from using their clerk-hire allowance to pay anyone who does not perform duties commensurate with that pay; forbids discrimination in members' hiring or treatment of employees on the grounds of race, color, religion, sex, handicap, age, or national origin; orders members convicted of a crime who might be punished by imprisonment of two or more years not to participate in committee business or vote on the floor until exonerated or reelected; and restricts employees' contact with federal agencies on matters in which they have a significant financial interest. The Senate's rules contain some similar prohibitions.

College of Cardinals—A popular term for the subcommittee chairmen of the appropriations committees, reflecting their influence over appropriation measures. The chairmen of the full appropriations committees are sometimes referred to as popes.

Committee—A panel of members elected or appointed to perform some service or function for its parent body. Congress has four types of committees: standing, special or select, joint, and, in the House, a Committee of the Whole.

Committees conduct investigations, make studies, issue reports and recommendations, and, in the case of standing committees, review and prepare measures on their assigned subjects for action by their respective houses. Most committees divide their work among several subcommittees. With rare exceptions, the majority party in a house holds a majority of the seats on its committees, and their chairmen are also from that party.

Committee of the Whole—Common name of the Committee of the Whole House on the State of the Union, a committee consisting of all members of the House of Representatives. Measures from the union calendar must be considered in the Committee of the Whole before the House officially completes action on them; the committee often considers other major bills as well. A quorum of the committee is 100, and it meets in the House chamber under a chairman appointed by the Speaker. Procedures in the Committee of the Whole expedite consideration of legislation because of its smaller quorum requirement, its ban on certain motions, and its five-minute rule for debate on amendments. Those procedures usually permit more members to offer amendments and participate in the debate on a measure than is normally possible. The Senate no longer uses a Committee of the Whole.

Committee Veto—A procedure that requires an executive department or agency to submit certain proposed policies, programs, or action to designated committees for review before implementing them. Before 1983, when the Supreme Court declared that a legislative veto is unconstitutional, these provisions permitted committees to veto the proposals. They no longer do so, and the term is now something of a misnomer. Nevertheless, agencies usually take the pragmatic approach of trying to reach a consensus with the committees before carrying out their proposals, especially when an appropriations committee is involved.

Concurrent Resolution—A resolution that requires approval by both houses but is not sent to the president for his signature and therefore cannot have the force of law. Concurrent resolutions deal with the prerogatives or internal affairs of Congress as a whole. Designated H. Con. Res. in the House and S. Con. Res. in the Senate, they are numbered consecutively in each house in their order of introduction during a two-year Congress.

Conference—(1) A formal meeting or series of meetings between members representing each house to reconcile House and Senate differences on a measure (occasionally several measures). Since one house cannot require the other to agree to its proposals, the conference usually reaches agreement by compromise. When a conference completes action on a measure, or as much action as appears possible, it sends its recommendations to both houses in the form of a conference report, accompanied by an explanatory statement. (2) The official title of the organization of all Democrats or Republicans in the Senate and of all Republicans in the House of Representatives. (*See Party Caucus.*)

Confirmations—(*See Nomination.*)

Congress—(1) The national legislature of the United States, consisting of the House of Representatives and the Senate. (2) The national legislature in office during a two-year period. Congresses are numbered sequentially; thus, the 1st Congress of 1789–1791 and the 102d Congress of 1991–1993. Before 1935, the two-year period began on the first Monday in December of odd-numbered years. Since then it has extended from January of an odd-numbered year through noon on January 3 of the next odd-numbered year. A Congress usually holds two annual sessions, but some have had three sessions and the 67th Congress had four. When a Congress expires, measures die if they have not yet been enacted.

Congressional Record—The daily, printed, and substantially verbatim account of proceedings in both the House and Senate chambers. Extraneous materials submitted by members appear in a section titled "Extensions of Remarks." A "Daily Digest" appendix contains highlights of the day's floor and committee action plus a list of committee meetings and floor agendas for the next day's session.

Although the official reporters of each house take down every word spoken during the proceedings, members are permitted to edit and "revise and extend" their remarks before they are printed. In the Senate section, all speeches, articles, and other material submitted by senators but not actually spoken or read on the floor are set off by large black dots, called bullets. However, bullets do not appear when a senator reads part of a speech and inserts the rest. In the House section, undelivered speeches and materials are printed in a distinctive typeface. The term "permanent *Record*" refers to the bound volumes of the daily *Records* of an entire session of Congress.

Congressional Terms of Office—A term normally begins on January 3 of the year following a general election and runs two years for representatives and six years for senators. A representative chosen in a special election to fill a vacancy is sworn in for the remainder of his predecessor's term. An individual appointed to fill a Senate vacancy usually serves until the next general election or until the end of the predecessor's term, whichever comes first. Some states, however, require their governors to call a special election to fill a Senate vacancy shortly after an appointment has been made.

Continuing Resolution (CR)—A joint resolution that provides funds to continue the operation of federal agencies and programs at the beginning of a new fiscal year if their annual appropriation bills have not yet been enacted; also called continuing appropriations.

Contract Authority—Statutory authority permitting an agency to enter into contracts or incur other obligations even though it has not received an appropriation to pay for them. Congress must eventually fund them because the government is legally liable for such payments. The Congressional Budget Act of 1974 requires that new contract authority may not be used unless provided for in advance by an appropriation act, but it permits a few exceptions.

Controllable Expenditures—Federal spending that is permitted but not mandated by existing authorization law and therefore may be adjusted by congressional action in appropriation bills. (*See Appropriation.*)

Correcting Recorded Votes—The rules of both houses prohibit members from changing their votes after a vote result has been announced. Nevertheless, the Senate permits its members to withdraw or change their votes, by unanimous consent, immediately after the announcement. In rare instances, senators have been granted unanimous consent to change their votes several days or weeks after the announcement.

Votes tallied by the electronic voting system in the House may not be changed. But when a vote actually given is not recorded during an oral call of the roll, a member may demand a correction as a matter of right. On all other alleged errors in a recorded vote, the Speaker determines whether the circumstances justify a change. Occasionally, members merely announce that they were incorrectly recorded; announcements can occur hours, days, or even months after the vote and appear in the *Congressional Record*.

Corrections Calendar—Members of the House may place on this calendar bills reported favorably from committee that repeal rules and regulations considered excessive or unnecessary. Bills on the Corrections Calendar normally are called on the second and fourth Tuesday of each month at the discretion of the Speaker in consultation with the minority leader. A bill must be on the calendar for at least three legislative days before it can be brought up for floor consideration. Once on the floor, a bill is subject to one hour of debate equally divided between the chairman and ranking member of the committee of jurisdiction. A vote may be called on whether to recommit the bill to committee with or without instructions. To pass, a three-fifths majority, or 261 votes if all House members vote, is required.

Cosponsor—A member who has joined one or more other members to sponsor a measure. (*See Bills and Resolutions Introduced.*)

Current Services Estimates—Executive branch estimates of the anticipated costs of federal programs and operations for the next and future fiscal years at existing levels of service and assuming no new initiatives or changes in existing law. The president submits these estimates to Congress with his annual budget and includes an explanation of the underlying economic and policy assumptions on which they are based, such as anticipated rates of inflation, real economic growth, and unemployment, plus program caseloads and pay increases.

Custody of the Papers—Possession of an engrossed measure and certain related basic documents that the two houses produce as they try to resolve their differences over the measure.

Dance of the Swans and the Ducks—A whimsical description of the gestures some members use in connection with a request for a recorded vote, especially in the House. When a member wants his colleagues to stand in support of the request, he moves his hands and arms in a gentle upward motion resembling the beginning flight of a graceful swan. When he wants his colleagues to remain seated in order to avoid such a vote, he moves his hands and arms in a vigorous downward motion resembling a diving duck.

Dean—Within a state's delegation in the House of Representatives, the member with the longest continuous service.

Debt Limit—The maximum amount of outstanding federal public debt permitted by law. The limit (or ceiling) covers virtually all debt incurred by the government except agency debt. Each congressional budget resolution sets forth the new debt limit that may be required under its provisions.

Deferral—An impoundment of funds for a specific period of time that may not extend beyond the fiscal year in which it is proposed. Under the Impoundment Control Act of 1974, the president must notify Congress that he is deferring the spending or obligation of funds provided by law for a project or activity. Congress can disapprove the deferral by legislation.

Deficit—The amount by which the government's outlays exceed its budget receipts for a given fiscal year. Both the president's budget and the annual congressional budget resolution provide estimates of the deficit or surplus for the upcoming and several future fiscal years.

Degrees of Amendment—Designations that indicate the relationships of amendments to the text of a measure and to each other. In general, an amendment offered directly to the text of a measure is an amendment in the first degree, and an amendment to that amendment is an amendment in the second degree. Both houses normally prohibit amendments in the third degree—that is, an amendment to an amendment to an amendment.

Dilatory Tactics—Procedural actions intended to delay or prevent action by a house or a committee. They include, among others, offering numerous motions, demanding quorum calls and recorded votes at every opportunity, making numerous points of order and parliamentary inquiries, and speaking as long as the applicable rules permit. The Senate's rules permit a battery of dilatory tactics, especially lengthy speeches, except under cloture. In the House, possible dilatory tactics are more limited. Speeches are always subject to time limits and debate-ending motions. Moreover, a House rule instructs the Speaker not to entertain dilatory motions and lets the Speaker decide whether a motion is dilatory. However, the Speaker may not override the constitutional right of a member to demand the yeas and nays, and in practice usually waits for a point of order before exercising that authority. (*See Cloture.*)

Discharge a Committee—Remove a measure from a committee to which it has been referred in order to make it available for floor consideration. Noncontroversial measures are often discharged by unanimous consent. However, because congressional committees have no obligation to report measures referred to them, each house has procedures to extract controversial measures from recalcitrant committees. Six discharge procedures are available in the House of Representatives. The Senate uses a motion to discharge, which is usually converted into a discharge resolution.

Discharge Calendar—The House calendar to which motions to discharge committees are referred when they have the required number of signatures (218) and are awaiting floor action.

Discharge Petition—(*See Discharge a Committee.*)

Discharge Resolution—In the Senate, a special motion that any senator may introduce to relieve a committee from consideration of a bill before it. The resolution can be called up for Senate approval or disapproval in the same manner as any other Senate business. (*House procedure, see Discharge a Committee.*)

Division Vote—A vote in which the chair first counts those in favor of a proposition and then those opposed to it, with no record made of how each member votes. In the Senate, the chair may count raised hands or ask senators to stand, whereas the House requires members to stand; hence, often called a standing vote. Committees in both houses ordinarily use a show of hands. A division usually occurs after a voice vote and may be demanded by any member or ordered by the chair if there is any doubt about the outcome of the voice vote. The demand for a division can also come before a voice vote. In the Senate, the demand must come before the result of a voice vote is announced. It may be made after a voice vote announcement in the House, but only if no intervening business has transpired and only if the member was standing and seeking recognition at the time of the announcement. A demand for the yeas and nays or, in the House, for a recorded vote, takes precedence over a division vote.

Enacting Clause—The opening language of each bill, beginning "Be it enacted by the Senate and House of Representatives of the United States of America in Congress assembled..." This language gives legal force to measures approved by Congress and signed by the president or enacted over his veto. A successful motion to strike it from a bill kills the entire measure.

Engrossed Bill—The official copy of a bill or joint resolution as passed by one chamber, including the text as amended by floor action, and certified by the clerk of the House or the secretary of the Senate (as appropriate). Amendments by one house to a measure or amendments of the other also are engrossed. House engrossed documents are printed on blue paper; the Senate's are printed on white paper.

Enrolled Bill—The final official copy of a bill or joint resolution passed in identical form by both houses. An enrolled bill is printed on parchment. After it is certified by the chief officer of the house in which it originated and signed by the House Speaker and the Senate president pro tempore, the measure is sent to the president for his signature.

Entitlement Program—A federal program under which individuals, businesses, or units of government that meet the requirements or qualifications established by law are entitled to receive certain payments if they seek such payments. Major examples include Social Security, Medicare, Medicaid, unemployment insurance, and military and federal civilian pensions. Congress cannot control their expenditures by refusing to appropriate the sums necessary to fund them because the government is legally obligated to pay eligible recipients the amounts to which the law entitles them.

Executive Calendar—The Senate's calendar for committee reports on its executive business, namely treaties and nominations. The calendar numbers indicate the order in which items were referred to the calendar but have no bearing on when or if the Senate will consider them. The Senate, by motion or unanimous consent, resolves itself into executive session to consider them.

Executive Document—A document, usually a treaty, sent by the president to the Senate for approval. It is referred to a committee in the same manner as other measures. Resolutions to ratify treaties have their own "treaty document" numbers. For example, the first treaty submitted in the 106th Congress would be "Treaty Doc 106-1."

Executive Order—A unilateral proclamation by the president that has a policy-making or legislative impact. Members of Congress have challenged some executive orders on the grounds that they usurped the authority of the legislative branch. Although the Supreme Court has ruled that a particular order exceeded the president's authority, it has upheld others as falling within the president's general constitutional powers.

Executive Privilege—The assertion that presidents have the right to withhold certain information from Congress. Presidents have based their claim on: (1) the constitutional separation of powers; (2) the need for secrecy in military and diplomatic affairs; (3) the need to protect individuals from unfavorable publicity; (4) the need to safeguard the confidential exchange of ideas in the executive branch; and (5) the need to protect individuals who provide confidential advice to the president.

Executive Session—A meeting of a Senate or House committee (or occasionally of either chamber) that only its members may attend. Witnesses regularly appear at committee meetings in executive session — for example, Defense Department officials during presentations of classified defense information. Other members of Congress may be invited, but the public and press are not to attend.

Expenditures—The actual spending of money as distinguished from the appropriation of funds. Expenditures are made by the disbursing officers of the administration; appropriations are made only by Congress. The two are rarely identical in any fiscal year. In addition to some current budget authority, expenditures may represent budget authority made available one, two, or more years earlier.

Expulsion—A member's removal from office by a two-thirds vote of his house; the super majority is required by the Constitution. It is the most severe and most rarely used sanction a house can invoke against a member. Although the Constitution provides no explicit grounds for expulsion, the courts have ruled that it may be applied only for misconduct during a member's term of office, not for conduct before the member's election. Generally, neither house will consider expulsion of a member convicted of a crime until the judicial processes have been exhausted. At that stage, members sometimes resign rather than face expulsion. In 1977 the House adopted a rule urging members convicted of certain crimes to voluntarily abstain from voting or participating in other legislative business.

Federal Debt—The total amount of monies borrowed and not yet repaid by the federal government. Federal debt consists of public debt and agency debt. Public debt is the portion of the federal debt borrowed by the Treasury or the Federal Financing Bank directly from the public or from another federal fund or account. For example, the Treasury regularly borrows money from the Social Security trust fund. Public debt accounts for about 99 percent of the federal debt. Agency debt refers to the debt incurred by federal agencies like the Export-Import Bank, but excluding the Treasury and the Federal Financing Bank, which are authorized by law to borrow funds from the public or from another government fund or account.

Filibuster—The use of obstructive and time-consuming parliamentary tactics by one member or a minority of members to delay, modify, or defeat proposed legislation or rules changes. Filibusters are also sometimes used to delay urgently needed measures in order to force the body to accept other legislation. The Senate's rules permitting unlimited debate and the extraordinary majority it requires to impose cloture make filibustering particularly effective in that chamber. Under the stricter rules of the House, filibusters in that body are short-lived and therefore ineffective and rarely attempted

Fiscal Year—The federal government's annual accounting period. It begins October 1 and ends on the following September 30. A fiscal year is designated by the calendar year in which it ends and is often referred to as FY. Thus, fiscal year 1999 began October 1, 1998, ended September 30, 1999, and is called FY99. In theory, Congress is supposed to complete action on all budgetary measures applying to a fiscal year before that year begins. It rarely does so.

Five-Minute Rule—In its most common usage, a House rule that limits debate on an amendment offered in Committee of the Whole to five minutes for its sponsor and five minutes for an opponent. In practice, the committee routinely permits longer debate by two devices: the offering of pro forma amendments, each debatable for five minutes, and unanimous consent for a member to speak longer than five minutes. Also a House rule that limits a committee member to five minutes when questioning a witness at a hearing until each member has had an opportunity to question that witness.

Floor Manager—A majority party member responsible for guiding a measure through its floor consideration in a house and for devising the political and procedural strategies that might be required to get the measure passed. The presiding officer gives the floor manager priority recognition to debate, offer amendments, oppose amendments, and make crucial procedural motions.

Frank—Informally, a member's legal right to send official mail postage free under his or her signature; often called the franking privilege. Technically, it is the autographic or facsimile signature used on envelopes instead of stamps that permits members and certain congressional officers to send their official mail free of charge. The franking privilege has been authorized by law since the first Congress, except for a few months in 1873. Congress reimburses the U.S. Postal Service for the franked mail it handles.

Function or Functional Category—A broad category of national need and spending of budgetary significance. A category provides an accounting method for allocating and keeping track of budgetary resources and expenditures for that function because it includes all budget accounts related to the functions subject or purpose such as agriculture, administration of justice, commerce and housing and energy. Functions do not necessarily correspond with appropriations acts or with the budgets of individual agencies.

Germane—Basically, on the same subject as the matter under consideration. A House rule requires that all amendments be germane. In the Senate, only amendments proposed to general appropriation bills and budget resolutions or under cloture must be germane. Germaneness rules can be evaded by suspension of the rules in both houses, by unanimous consent agreements in the Senate, and by special rules from the Rules Committee in the House.

Gerrymandering—The manipulation of legislative district boundaries to benefit a particular party, politician, or minority group. The term originated in 1812 when the Massachusetts legislature redrew the lines of state legislative districts to favor the party of Gov. Elbridge Gerry, and some critics said one district looked like a salamander.

Gramm-Rudman-Hollings Act of 1985—Common name for the Balanced Budget and Emergency Deficit Control Act of 1985, which established new budget procedures intended to balance the federal budget by fiscal year 1991. The timetable subsequently was extended and then deleted. The act's chief sponsors were senators Phil Gramm (R-Texas), Warren Rudman (R-N.H.), and Ernest Hollings (D-S.C.).

Grandfather Clause—A provision in a measure, law, or rule that exempts an individual, entity, or a defined category of individuals or entities from complying with a new policy or restriction. For example, a bill that would raise taxes on persons who reach the age of 65 after a certain date inherently grandfathers out those who are 65 before that date. Similarly, a Senate rule limiting senators to two major committee assignments also grandfathers some senators who were sitting on a third major committee prior to a specified date.

Grants-in-Aid—Payments by the federal government to state and local governments to help provide for assistance programs or public services.

Hearing—Committee or subcommittee meetings to receive testimony from witnesses on proposed legislation during investigations or for oversight purposes. Relatively few bills are important enough to justify formal hearings. Witnesses often include experts, government officials, spokespersons for interested groups, officials of the General Accounting Office, and members of Congress. Also, the printed transcripts of hearings.

Hold—A senator's request that his or her party leaders delay floor consideration of certain legislation or presidential nominations. The majority leader usually honors a hold for a reasonable period of time, especially if its purpose is to assure the senator that the matter will not be called up during his or her absence or to give the senator time to gather necessary information.

Hold-Harmless Clause—In legislation providing a new formula for allocating federal funds, a clause to ensure that recipients of those funds do not receive less in a future year than they did in the current year if the new formula would result in a reduction for them. Similar to a grandfather clause, it has been used most frequently to soften the impact of sudden reductions in federal grants. (*See Grandfather Clause.*)

Hopper—A box on the clerk's desk in the House chamber into which members deposit bills and resolutions to introduce them. In House jargon, to drop a bill in the hopper is to introduce it.

Hour Rule—(1) A House rule that permits members, when recognized, to hold the floor in debate for no more than one hour each. The majority party member customarily yields one-half the time to a minority member. Although the hour rule applies to general debate in Committee of the Whole as well as in the House, special rules routinely vary the length of time for such debate and its control to fit the circumstances of particular measures.

House—The House of Representatives, as distinct from the Senate, although each body is a "house" of Congress.

House as in Committee of the Whole—A hybrid combination of procedures from the general rules of the House and from the rules of the Committee of the Whole, sometimes used to expedite consideration of a measure on the floor.

House Calendar—The calendar reserved for all public bills and resolutions that do not raise revenue or directly or indirectly appropriate money or property when they are favorably reported by House committees.

House Manual—A commonly used title for the handbook of the rules of the House of Representatives, published in each Congress. Its official title is *Constitution, Jefferson's Manual, and Rules of the House of Representatives*.

House of Representatives—The house of Congress in which states are represented roughly in proportion to their populations, but every state is guaranteed at least one representative. By law, the number of voting representatives is fixed at 435. Four delegates and one resident commissioner also serve in the House; they may vote in their committees but not on the House floor. Although the House and Senate have equal legislative power, the Constitution gives the House sole authority to originate revenue measures. The House also claims the right to originate appropriation measures, a claim the Senate disputes in theory but concedes in practice. The House has the sole power to impeach, and it elects the president when no candidate has received a majority of the electoral votes. It is sometimes referred to as the lower body.

Immunity—(1) Members' constitutional protection from lawsuits and arrest in connection with their legislative duties. They may not be tried for libel or slander for anything they say on the floor of a house or in committee. Nor may they be arrested while attending sessions of their houses or when traveling to or from sessions of Congress, except when charged with treason, a felony, or a breach of the peace. (2) In the case of a witness before a committee, a grant of protection from prosecution based on that person's testimony to the committee. It is used to compel witnesses to testify who would otherwise refuse to do so on the constitutional ground of possible self-incrimination. Under such a grant, none of a witness testimony may be used against him or her in a court proceeding except in a prosecution for perjury or for giving a false statement to Congress.

Impeachment—The first step to remove the president, vice president, or other federal civil officers from office and to disqualify them from any future federal office "of honor, Trust or Profit." An impeachment is a formal charge of treason, bribery, or "other high Crimes and Misdemeanors." The House has the sole power of impeachment and the Senate the sole power of trying the charges and convicting. The House impeaches by a simple majority vote; conviction requires a two-thirds vote of all senators present.

Impoundment—An executive branch action or inaction that delays or withholds the expenditure or obligation of budget authority provided by law. The Impoundment Control Act of 1974 classifies impoundments as either deferrals or rescissions, requires the president to notify Congress about all such actions, and gives Congress authority to approve or reject them. The Constitution is unclear on whether a president may refuse to spend appropriated money, but Congress usually expects the president to spend at least enough to achieve the purposes for which the money was provided whether or not he agrees with those purposes.

Joint Committee—A committee composed of members selected from each house. The functions of most joint committees involve investigation, research, or oversight of agencies closely related to Congress. Permanent joint committees, created by statute, are sometimes called standing joint committees. Once quite numerous, only four joint committees remained as of 1997: Joint Economic, Joint Taxation, Joint Library, and Joint Printing. No joint committee has authority to report legislation.

Joint Resolution—A legislative measure that Congress uses for purposes other than general legislation. Like a bill, it has the force of law when passed by both houses and either approved by the president or passed over the president's veto. Unlike a bill, a joint resolution enacted into law is not called an act; it retains its original title.

Most often, joint resolutions deal with such relatively limited matters as the correction of errors in existing law, continuing appropriations, a single appropriation, or the establishment of permanent joint committees. Unlike bills, however, joint resolutions also are used to propose constitutional amendments; these do not require the president's signature and become effective only when ratified by three-fourths of the states. The House designates joint resolutions as H.J. Res., the Senate as S.J. Res. Each house numbers its joint resolutions consecutively in the order of introduction during a two-year Congress.

Journal—The official record of House or Senate actions, including every motion offered, every vote cast, amendments agreed to, quorum calls, and so forth. Unlike the *Congressional Record*, it does not provide reports of speeches, debates, statements, and the like. The Constitution requires each house to maintain a *Journal* and to publish it periodically.

King of the Mountain (or Hill) Rule—(*See Queen of the Hill Rule.*)

Lame Duck—Jargon for a member who has not been reelected, or did not seek reelection, and is serving the balance of his or her term.

Lame Duck Session—A session of a Congress held after the election for the succeeding Congress, so-called after the lame duck members still serving.

Law—An act of Congress that has been signed by the president, passed over the president's veto, or allowed to become law without the president's signature.

Legislative Day—The day that begins when a house meets after an adjournment and ends when it next adjourns. Because the House of Representatives normally adjourns at the end of a daily session, its legislative and calendar days usually coincide. The Senate, however, frequently recesses at the end of a daily session, and its legislative day may extend over several calendar days, weeks, or months. Among other uses, this technicality permits the Senate to save time by circumventing its morning hour, a procedure required at the beginning of every legislative day

Legislative Veto—A procedure, declared unconstitutional in 1983, that allowed Congress or one of its houses to nullify certain actions of the president, executive branch agencies, or independent agencies. Sometimes called congressional vetoes or congressional disapprovals. Following the Supreme Court's 1983 decision, Congress amended several legislative veto statutes to require enactment of joint resolutions, which are subject to presidential veto, for nullifying executive branch actions.

Live Pair—A voluntary and informal agreement between two members on opposite sides of an issue under which the member who is present for a recorded vote withholds or withdraws his or her vote because the other member is absent.

Loan Guarantee—A statutory commitment by the federal government to pay part or all of a loans principal and interest to a lender or the holder of a security in case the borrower defaults.

Lobby—To try to persuade members of Congress to propose, pass, modify, or defeat proposed legislation or to change or repeal existing laws. A lobbyist attempts to promote his or her own preferences or those of a group, organization, or industry. Originally the term referred to persons frequenting the lobbies or corridors of legislative chambers in order to speak to lawmakers. In a general sense, lobbying includes not only direct contact with members but also indirect attempts to influence them, such as writing to them or persuading others to write or visit them, attempting to mold public opinion toward a desired legislative goal by various means, and contributing or arranging for contributions to members election campaigns. The right to lobby stems from the First Amendment to the Constitution, which bans laws that abridge the right of the people to petition the government for a redress of grievances.

Logrolling—Jargon for a legislative tactic or bargaining strategy in which members try to build support for their legislation by promising to support legislation desired by other members or by accepting amendments they hope will induce their colleagues to vote for their bill.

Mace—The symbol of the office of the House sergeant at arms. Under the direction of the Speaker, the sergeant at arms is responsible for preserving order on the House floor by holding up the mace in front of an unruly member, or by carrying the mace up and down the aisles to quell boisterous behavior. When the House is in session, the mace sits on a pedestal at the Speaker's right; when the House is in Committee of the Whole, it is moved to a lower pedestal. The mace is 46 inches high and consists of 13 ebony rods bound in silver and topped by a silver globe with a silver eagle, wings outstretched, perched on it.

Majority Leader—The majority party's chief floor spokesman, elected by that party's caucus—sometimes called floor leader. In the Senate, the majority leader also develops the party's political and procedural strategy, usually in collaboration with other party officials and committee chairmen. He negotiates the Senates agenda and committee ratios with the minority leader and usually calls up measures for floor action. The chamber traditionally concedes to the majority leader the right to determine the days on which it will meet and the hours at which it will convene and adjourn. In the House, the majority leader is the Speaker's deputy and heir apparent. He helps plan the floor agenda and the party's legislative strategy and often speaks for the party leadership in debate.

Majority Whip—In effect, the assistant majority leader, in either the House or Senate. His job is to help marshal majority forces in support of party strategy and legislation.

Manual—The official handbook in each house prescribing in detail its organization, procedures, and operations.

Marking Up a Bill—Going through the contents of a piece of legislation in committee or subcommittee to, for example, consider its provisions in large and small portions, act on amendments to provisions and proposed revisions to the language, and insert new sections and phraseology. If the bill is extensively amended, the committee's version may be introduced as a separate bill, with a new number, before being considered by the full House or Senate. (*See Clean Bill.*)

Method of Equal Proportions—The mathematical formula used since 1950 to determine how the 435 seats in the House of Representatives should be distributed among the 50 states in the apportionment following each decennial census. It minimizes as much as possible the proportional difference between the average district population in any two states. Because the Constitution guarantees each state at least one representative, 50 seats are automatically apportioned. The formula calculates priority numbers for each state, assigns the first of the 385 remaining seats to the state with the highest priority number, the second to the state with the next highest number, and so on until all seats are distributed. (*See Apportionment.*)

Midterm Election—The general election for members of Congress that occurs in November of the second year in a presidential term.

Minority Leader—The minority party's leader and chief floor spokesman, elected by the party caucus; sometimes called minority floor leader. With the assistance of other party officials and the ranking minority members of committees, the minority leader devises the party's political and procedural strategy.

Minority Whip—Performs duties of whip for the minority party. (*See also Majority Whip.*)

Minority Staff—Employees who assist the minority party members of a committee. Most committees hire separate majority and minority party staffs, but they also may hire nonpartisan staff.

Motion—A formal proposal for a procedural action, such as to consider, to amend, to lay on the table, to reconsider, to recess, or to adjourn. It has been estimated that at least 85 motions are possible under various circumstances in the House of Representatives, somewhat fewer in the Senate. Not all motions are created equal; some are privileged or preferential and enjoy priority over others. And some motions are debatable, amendable or divisible, while others are not.

Nomination—A proposed presidential appointment to a federal office submitted to the Senate for confirmation. Approval is by majority vote. The Constitution explicitly requires confirmation for ambassadors, consuls, public Ministers (department heads), and Supreme Court justices. By law, other federal judges, all military promotions of officers, and many high-level civilian officials must be confirmed.

Oath of Office—Upon taking office, members of Congress must swear or affirm that they will "support and defend the Constitution . . . against all enemies, foreign and domestic," that they will "bear true faith and allegiance" to the Constitution, that they take the obligation "freely, without any mental reservation or purpose of evasion," and that they will "well and faithfully discharge the duties" of their office. The oath is required by the Constitution; the wording is prescribed by a statute. All House members must take the oath at the beginning of each new Congress.

Obligations—Orders placed, contracts awarded, services received, and similar transactions during a given period that will require payments during the same or future period. Such amounts include outlays for which obligations had not been previously recorded and reflect adjustments for differences between obligations previously recorded and actual outlays to liquidate those obligations.

Omnibus Bill—A measure that combines the provisions of several disparate subjects into a single and often lengthy bill.

One-Minute Speeches—Addresses by House members at the beginning of a legislative day. The speeches may cover any subject but are limited to one minute's duration.

Order of Business (House)—The sequence of events during the meeting of the House on a new legislative day prescribed by a House rule; also called the general order of business. The sequence consists of (1) the chaplain's prayer; (2) approval of the *Journal*; (3) pledge of allegiance (4) correction of the reference of public bills; (5) disposal of business on the Speaker's table; (6) unfinished business; (7) the morning hour call of committees and consideration of their bills (largely obsolete); (8) motions to go into Committee of the Whole; and (9) orders of the day (also obsolete). In practice, on days specified in the rules, the items of business that follow approval of the *Journal* are supplanted in part by the special order of business (for example, the corrections, discharge, or private calendars or motions to suspend the rules) and on any day by other privileged business (for example, general appropriation bills and special rules)

or measures made in order by special rules. By this combination of an order of business with privileged interruptions, the House gives precedence to certain categories of important legislation, brings to the floor other major legislation from its calendars in any order it chooses, and provides expeditious processing for minor and noncontroversial measures.

Order of Business (Senate)—The sequence of events at the beginning of a new legislative day prescribed by Senate rules. The sequence consists of (1) the chaplain's prayer; (2) *Journal* reading and correction; (3) morning business in the morning hour; (4) call of the calendar during the morning hour; and (5) unfinished business.

Outlays—Amounts of government spending. They consist of payments, usually by check or in cash, to liquidate obligations incurred in prior fiscal years as well as in the current year, including the net lending of funds under budget authority. In federal budget accounting, net outlays are calculated by subtracting the amounts of refunds and various kinds of reimbursements to the government from actual spending.

Override a Veto—Congressional enactment of a measure over the president's veto. A veto override requires a recorded two-thirds vote of those voting in each house, a quorum being present. Because the president must return the vetoed measure to its house of origin, that house votes first, but neither house is required to attempt an override, whether immediately or at all. If an override attempt fails in the house of origin, the veto stands and the measure dies.

Oversight—Congressional review of the way in which federal agencies implement laws to ensure that they are carrying out the intent of Congress and to inquire into the efficiency of the implementation and the effectiveness of the law. The Legislative Reorganization Act of 1946 defined oversight as the function of exercising continuous watchfulness over the execution of the laws by the executive branch.

Pairing—A procedure that permits two or three members to enter into voluntary arrangements that offset their votes so that one or more of the members can be absent without changing the result. The names of paired members and their positions on the vote (except on general pairs) appear in the *Congressional Record*. Members can be paired on one vote or on a series of votes.

Parliamentarian—The official advisor to the presiding officer in each house on questions of procedure. The parliamentarian and his assistants also answer procedural questions from members and congressional staff, refer measures to committees on behalf of the presiding officer, and maintain compilations of the precedents. The House parliamentarian revises the House Manual at the beginning of every Congress and usually reviews special rules before the Rules Committee reports them to the House. Either a parliamentarian or an assistant is always present and near the podium during sessions of each house.

Party Caucus—Generic term for each party's official organization in each house. Only House Democrats officially call their organization a caucus. House and Senate Republicans and Senate Democrats call their organizations conferences. The party caucuses elect their leaders, approve committee assignments and chairmanships (or ranking minority members, if the party is in the minority), establish party committees and study groups, and discuss party and legislative policies. On rare occasions, they have stripped members of committee seniority or expelled them from the caucus for party disloyalty.

Petition—A request or plea sent to one or both chambers from an organization or private citizens' group asking support of particular legislation or favorable consideration of a matter not yet receiving congressional attention. Petitions are referred to appropriate committees.

Pocket Veto—The indirect veto of a bill as a result of the president withholding approval of it until after Congress has adjourned sine die. A bill the president does not sign, but does not formally veto while Congress is in session, automatically becomes a law 10 days (excluding Sundays) after it is received. But if Congress adjourns its annual session during that 10-day period, the measure dies even if the president does not formally veto it.

Point of Order—A parliamentary term used in committee and on the floor to object to an alleged violation of a rule and to demand that the chair enforce the rule. The point of order immediately halts the proceedings until the chair decides whether the contention is valid.

Pork or Pork Barrel Legislation—Pejorative terms for federal appropriations, bills, or policies that provide funds to benefit a legislator's district or state, with the implication that the legislator presses for enactment of such benefits to ingratiate himself or herself with constituents rather than on the basis of an impartial, objective assessment of need or merit.

The terms are often applied to such benefits as new parks, post offices, dams, canals, bridges, roads, water projects, sewage treatment plants, and public works of any kind, as well as demonstration projects, research grants, and relocation of government facilities. Funds released by the president for various kinds of benefits or government contracts approved by him allegedly for political purposes are also sometimes referred to as pork.

Postcloture Filibuster—A filibuster conducted after the Senate invokes cloture. It employs an array of procedural tactics rather than lengthy speeches to delay final action. The Senate curtailed the postcloture filibusters effectiveness by closing a variety of loopholes in the cloture rule in 1979 and 1986.

President of the Senate—The vice president of the United States in his constitutional role as presiding officer of the Senate. The Constitution permits the vice president to cast a vote in the Senate only to break a tie, but he is not required to do so.

President Pro Tempore—Under the Constitution, an officer elected by the Senate to preside over it during the absence of the vice president of the United States. Often referred to as the "pro tem," he is usually the majority party senator with the longest continuous service in the chamber and also, by virtue of his seniority, a committee chairman. When attending to committee and other duties, the president pro tempore appoints other senators to preside.

Previous Question—A nondebatable motion which, when agreed to by majority vote, usually cuts off further debate, prevents the offering of additional amendments, and brings the pending matter to an immediate vote. It is a major debate-limiting device in the House; it is not permitted in Committee of the Whole or in the Senate.

Printed Amendment—A House rule guarantees five minutes of floor debate in support and five minutes in opposition, and no other debate time, on amendments printed in the Congressional Record at least one day prior to the amendment's consideration in the Committee of the Whole. In the Senate, although amendments may be submitted for printing, they have no parliamentary standing or status. An amendment submitted for printing in the Senate, however, may be called up by any senator.

Private Bill—A bill that applies to one or more specified persons, corporations, institutions, or other entities, usually to grant relief when no other legal remedy is available to them. Many private bills deal with claims against the federal government, immigration and naturalization cases, and land titles.

Private Calendar—Commonly used title for a calendar in the House reserved for private bills and resolutions favorably reported by committees. The private calendar is officially called the Calendar of the Committee of the Whole House.

Privilege—An attribute of a motion, measure, report, question, or proposition that gives it priority status for consideration. Privileged motions and motions to bring up privileged questions are not debatable.

Privileged Questions—The order in which bills, motions, and other legislative measures are considered by Congress is governed by strict priorities. A motion to table, for instance, is more privileged than a motion to recommit. Thus, a motion to recommit can be superseded by a motion to table, and a vote would be forced on the latter motion only. A motion to adjourn, however, takes precedence over a tabling motion and thus is considered of the "highest privilege." (*See also Questions of Privilege.*)

Pro Forma Amendment—In the House, an amendment that ostensibly proposes to change a measure or another amendment by moving "to strike the last word" or "to strike the requisite number of words." A member offers it not to make any actual change in the measure or amendment but only to obtain time for debate.

Proxy Voting—The practice of permitting a member to cast the vote of an absent colleague in addition to his own vote. Proxy voting is prohibited on the floors of the House and Senate, but the Senate permits its committees to authorize proxy voting, and most do. In 1995, House rules were changed to prohibit proxy voting in committee.

Public Law—A public bill or joint resolution enacted into law. It is cited by the letters P.L. followed by a hyphenated number. The digits before the hyphen indicate the number of the Congress in which it was enacted; the digits after the hyphen indicate its position in the numerical sequence of public measures that became law during that Congress. For example, the

Budget Enforcement Act of 1990 became P.L. 101-508 because it was the 508th measure in that sequence for the 101st Congress. (*See also Private Bill.*)

Queen of the Hill Rule—A special rule from the House Rules Committee that permits votes on a series of amendments, especially complete substitutes for a measure, in a specified order, but directs that the amendment receiving the greatest number of votes shall be the winning one. This kind of rule permits the House to vote directly on a variety of alternatives to a measure. In doing so, it sets aside the precedent that once an amendment has been adopted, no further amendments may be offered to the text it has amended. Under an earlier practice, the Rules Committee reported "king of the hill" rules under which there also could be votes on a series of amendments, again in a specified order. If more than one of the amendments was adopted under this kind of rule, it was the last amendment to receive a majority vote that was considered as having been finally adopted, whether or not it had received the greatest number of votes.

Questions of Privilege—These are matters affecting members of Congress individually or collectively. Matters affecting the rights, safety, dignity, and integrity of proceedings of the House or Senate as a whole are questions of privilege in both chambers.

Questions involving individual members are called questions of "personal privilege." A member rising to ask a question of personal privilege is given precedence over almost all other proceedings. An annotation in the House rules points out that the privilege rests primarily on the Constitution, which gives a member a conditional immunity from arrest and an unconditional freedom to speak in the House. (*See also Privileged Questions.*)

Quorum—The minimum number of members required to be present for the transaction of business. Under the Constitution, a quorum in each house is a majority of its members: 218 in the House and 51 in the Senate when there are no vacancies. By House rule, a quorum in Committee of the Whole is 100. In practice, both houses usually assume a quorum is present even if it is not, unless a member makes a point of no quorum in the House or suggests the absence of a quorum in the Senate. Consequently, each house transacts much of its business, and even passes bills, when only a few members are present.

For House and Senate committees, chamber rules allow a minimum quorum of one-third of a committee's members to conduct most types of business.

Ramseyer Rule—A House rule that requires a committee's report on a bill or joint resolution to show the changes the measure, and any committee amendments to it, would make in existing law.

Readings of Bills—Traditional parliamentary procedure required bills to be read three times before they were passed. This custom is of little modern significance. Normally a bill is considered to have its first reading when it is introduced and printed, by title, in the *Congressional Record*. In the House, its second reading comes when floor consideration begins. (This is the most likely point at which there is an actual reading of the bill, if there is any.) The second reading in the Senate is supposed to occur on the legislative day after the measure is introduced, but before it is referred to committee. The third reading (again, usually by title) takes place when floor action has been completed on amendments.

Reapportionment—(*See Apportionment.*)

Recess—(1) A temporary interruption or suspension of a meeting of a chamber or committee. Unlike an adjournment, a recess does not end a legislative day. Because the Senate often recesses from one calendar day to another, its legislative day may extend over several calendar days, weeks, or even months. (2) A period of adjournment for more than three days to a day certain, especially over a holiday or in August during odd-numbered years.

Recognition—The power of recognition of a member is lodged in the Speaker of the House and the presiding officer of the Senate. The presiding officer names the member who will speak first when two or more members simultaneously request recognition.

Recommit—To send a measure back to the committee that reported it; sometimes called a straight motion to recommit to distinguish it from a motion to recommit with instructions. A successful motion to recommit kills the measure unless it is accompanied by instructions.

Reconciliation—A procedure for changing existing revenue and spending laws to bring total federal revenues and spending within the limits established in a budget resolution. Congress has applied reconciliation chiefly to revenues and mandatory spending programs, especially entitlements. Discretionary spending is controlled through annual appropriation bills.

Reconsider a Vote—A motion to reconsider the vote by which an action was taken has, until it is disposed of, the effect of putting the action in abeyance. In the Senate, the motion can be made only by a member who voted on the prevailing side of the original question or by a member who did not vote at all. In the House, it can be made only by a member on the prevailing side.

A common practice in the Senate after close votes on an issue is a motion to reconsider, followed by a motion to table the motion to reconsider. On this motion to table, senators vote as they voted on the original question, which allows the motion to table to prevail, assuming there are no switches. The matter then is finally closed and further motions to reconsider are not entertained. In the House, as a routine precaution, a motion to reconsider usually is made every time a measure is passed. Such a motion almost always is tabled immediately, thus shutting off the possibility of future reconsideration, except by unanimous consent.

Motions to reconsider must be entered in the Senate within the next two days of actual session after the original vote has been taken. In the House they must be entered either on the same day or on the next succeeding day the House is in session.

Recorded Vote—(1) Generally, any vote in which members are recorded by name for or against a measure; also called a record vote or roll-call vote. The only recorded vote in the Senate is a vote by the yeas and nays and is commonly called a roll-call vote. (2) Technically, a recorded vote is one demanded in the House of Representatives and supported by at least one-fifth of a quorum (44 members) in the House sitting as the House or at least 25 members in Committee of the Whole.

Report—(1) As a verb, a committee is said to report when it submits a measure or other document to its parent chamber. (2) A clerk is said to report when he or she reads a measure's title, text, or the text of an amendment to the body at the direction of the chair. (3) As a noun, a committee document that accompanies a reported measure. It describes the measure, the committee's views on it, its costs, and the changes it proposes to make in existing law; it also includes certain impact statements. (4) A committee document submitted to its parent chamber that describes the results of an investigation or other study or provides information the committee is required to provide by rule or law.

Reprimand—A formal condemnation of a member for misbehavior, considered a milder reproof than censure. The House of Representatives first used it in 1976. The Senate first used it in 1991. (*See also Censure, Code of Official Conduct, Expulsion.*)

Rescission—A provision of law that repeals previously enacted budget authority in whole or in part. Under the Impoundment Control Act of 1974, the president can impound such funds by sending a message to Congress requesting one or more rescissions and the reasons for doing so. If Congress does not pass a rescission bill for the programs requested by the president within 45 days of continuous session after receiving the message, the president must make the funds available for obligation and expenditure. If the president does not, the comptroller general of the United States is authorized to bring suit to compel the release of those funds. A rescission bill may rescind all, part, or none of an amount proposed by the president, and may rescind funds the president has not impounded.

Resolution—(1) A simple resolution; that is, a nonlegislative measure effective only in the house in which it is proposed and not requiring concurrence by the other chamber or approval by the president. Simple resolutions are designated H. Res. in the House and S. Res. in the Senate. Simple resolutions express nonbinding opinions on policies or issues or deal with the internal affairs or prerogatives of a house. (2) Any type of resolution: simple, concurrent, or joint. (*See Concurrent Resolution, Joint Resolution.*)

Revise and Extend One's Remarks—A unanimous consent request to publish in the *Congressional Record* a statement a member did not deliver on the floor, a longer statement than the one made on the floor, or miscellaneous extraneous material.

Rider—Congressional slang for an amendment unrelated or extraneous to the subject matter of the measure to which it is attached. Riders often contain proposals that are less likely to become law on their own merits as separate bills, either because of opposition in the committee of jurisdiction, resistance in the other house, or the probability of a presidential veto. Riders are more common in the Senate.

Rule—(1) A permanent regulation that a house adopts to govern its conduct of business, its procedures, its internal organization, behavior of its members, regulation of its facilities, duties of an officer, or some other subject it chooses to govern in that form. (2) In the House, a privileged simple resolution reported by the Rules Committee that provides methods and conditions for floor consideration of a measure or, rarely, several measures.

Secretary of the Senate—The chief administrative and budgetary officer of the Senate. The secretary manages a wide range of functions that support the operation of the Senate as an organization as well as those functions necessary to its legislative process, including recordkeeping, document management, certifications, housekeeping services, administration of oaths, and lobbyist registrations.

Select or Special Committee—A committee established by a resolution in either house for a special purpose and, usually, for a limited time. Most select and special committees are assigned specific investigations or studies, but are not authorized to report measures to their chambers.

Senate—The house of Congress in which each state is represented by two senators; each senator has one vote. Article V of the Constitution declares that "No State, without its Consent, shall be deprived of its equal Suffrage in the Senate." The Constitution also gives the Senate equal legislative power with the House of Representatives. Although the Senate is prohibited from originating revenue measures, and as a matter of practice it does not originate appropriation measures, it can amend both. Only the Senate can give or withhold consent to treaties and nominations from the president. It also acts as a court to try impeachments by the House and elects the vice president when no candidate receives a majority of the electoral votes. It is often referred to as "the upper body," but not by members of the House.

Senate Manual—The handbook of the Senate's standing rules and orders and the laws and other regulations that apply to the Senate, usually published once each Congress.

Senatorial Courtesy—The Senate's practice of declining to confirm a presidential nominee for an office in the state of a senator of the president's party unless that senator approves.

Sequestration—A procedure for canceling budgetary resources that is, money available for obligation or spending to enforce budget limitations established in law. Sequestered funds are no longer available for obligation or expenditure.

Sine Die—(*See Adjournment Sine Die.*)

Slip Law—The first official publication of a measure that has become law. It is published separately in unbound, single-sheet form or pamphlet form. A slip law usually is available two or three days after the date of the law's enactment.

Speaker—The presiding officer of the House of Representatives and the leader of its majority party. The Speaker is selected by the majority party and formally elected by the House at the beginning of each Congress. Although the Constitution does not require the Speaker to be a member of the House, in fact, all Speakers have been members.

Special Session—A session of Congress convened by the president, under his constitutional authority, after Congress has adjourned sine die at the end of a regular session. (*See Adjournment Sine Die.*)

Spending Authority—The technical term for backdoor spending. The Congressional Budget Act of 1974 defines it as borrowing authority, contract authority, and entitlement authority for which appropriation acts do not provide budget authority in advance. Under the Budget Act, legislation that provides new spending authority may not be considered unless it provides that the authority shall be effective only to the extent or in such amounts as provided in an appropriation act.

Sponsor—The principal proponent and introducer of a measure or an amendment.

Standing Committee—A permanent committee established by a House or Senate standing rule or standing order. The rule also describes the subject areas on which the committee may report bills and resolutions and conduct oversight. Most introduced measures must be referred to one or more standing committees according to their jurisdictions.

Standing Vote—An alternative and informal term for a division vote, during which members in favor of a proposal and then members opposed stand and are counted by the chair. (*See Division Vote.*)

Star Print—A reprint of a bill, resolution, amendment, or committee report correcting technical or substantive errors in a previous printing; so called because of the small black star that appears on the front page or cover.

Statutes at Large—A chronological arrangement of the laws enacted in each session of Congress. Though indexed, the laws are not arranged by subject matter nor is there an indication of how they affect or change previously enacted laws. The volumes are numbered by Congress, and the laws are cited by their volume and page number. The Gramm-Rudman-Hollings Act, for example, appears as 99 Stat. 1037.

Strike from the *Record*—Expunge objectionable remarks from the *Congressional Record*, after a member's words have been taken down on a point of order.

Strike Out the Last Word—A motion whereby a House member is entitled to speak for five minutes on an amendment then being debated by the chamber. A member gains recognition from the chair by moving to "strike out the last word" of the amendment or section of the bill under consideration. The motion is proforma, requires no vote, and does not change the amendment being debated.

Substitute—A motion, amendment, or entire bill introduced in place of the pending legislative business. Passage of a substitute measure kills the original measure by supplanting it. The substitute also may be amended. (*See also Amendment in the Nature of a Substitute.*)

Sunshine Rules—Rules requiring open committee hearings and business meetings, including markup sessions, in both houses, and also open conference committee meetings. However, all may be closed under certain circumstances and using certain procedures required by the rules.

Super Majority—A term sometimes used for a vote on a matter that requires approval by more than a simple majority of those members present and voting; also referred to as extraordinary majority.

Supplemental Appropriation Bill—A measure providing appropriations for use in the current fiscal year, in addition to those already provided in annual general appropriation bills. Supplemental appropriations are often for unforeseen emergencies.

Suspension of the Rules (House)—An expeditious procedure for passing relatively noncontroversial or emergency measures by a two-thirds vote of those members voting, a quorum being present.

Suspension of the Rules (Senate)—A procedure to set aside one or more of the Senate's rules; it is used infrequently, and then most often to suspend the rule banning legislative amendments to appropriation bills.

Table a Bill—Motions to table, or to "lay on the table," are used to block or kill amendments or other parliamentary questions. When approved, a tabling motion is considered the final disposition of that issue. One of the most widely used parliamentary procedures, the motion to table is not debatable, and adoption requires a simple majority vote.

In the Senate, however, different language sometimes is used. The motion may be worded to let a bill "lie on the table," perhaps for subsequent "picking up." This motion is more flexible, keeping the bill pending for later action, if desired. Tabling motions on amendments are effective debate-ending devices in the Senate.

Teller Vote—A voting procedure, formerly used in the House, in which members cast their votes by passing through the center aisle to be counted, but not recorded by name, by a member from each party appointed by the chair. The House deleted the procedure from its rules in 1993, but during floor discussion of the deletion a leading member stated that a teller vote would still be available in the event of a breakdown of the electronic voting system.

Treaty—A formal document containing an agreement between two or more sovereign nations. The Constitution authorizes the president to make treaties, but he must submit them to the Senate for its approval by a two-thirds vote of the senators present. Under the Senate's rules, that vote actually occurs on a resolution of ratification. Although the Constitution does not give the House a direct role in approving treaties, that body has sometimes insisted that a revenue treaty is an invasion of its prerogatives. In any case, the House may significantly affect the application of a treaty by its equal role in enacting legislation to implement the treaty.

Trust Funds—Special accounts in the Treasury that receive earmarked taxes or other kinds of revenue collections, such as user fees, and from which payments are made for special purposes or to recipients who meet the requirements of the trust funds as established by law. Of the more than 150 federal government trust funds, several finance major entitlement programs, such as Social Security, Medicare, and retired federal employees' pensions. Others fund infrastructure construction and improvements, such as highways and airports.

Unanimous Consent—Without an objection by any member. A unanimous consent request asks permission, explicitly or implicitly, to set aside one or more rules. Both houses and their committees frequently use such requests to expedite their proceedings.

Unanimous Consent Agreement—A device used in the Senate to expedite legislation. Much of the Senate's legislative business, dealing with both minor and controversial issues, is conducted through unanimous consent or unanimous consent agreements. On major legislation, such agreements usually are printed and transmitted to all senators in advance of floor debate. Once agreed to, they are binding on all members unless the Senate, by unanimous consent, agrees to modify them. An agreement may list the order in which various bills are to be considered, specify the length of time bills and contested amendments are to be debated and when they are to be voted upon, and, frequently, require that all amendments introduced be germane to the bill under consideration. In this regard, unanimous consent agreements are similar to the "rules" issued by the House Rules Committee for bills pending in the House.

Unfunded Mandate—Generally, any provision in federal law or regulation that imposes a duty or obligation on a state or local government or private sector entity without providing the necessary funds to comply. The Unfunded Mandates Reform Act of 1995 amended the Congressional Budget Act of 1974 to provide a mechanism for the control of new unfunded mandates.

Union Calendar—A calendar of the House of Representatives for bills and resolutions favorably reported by committees that raise revenue or directly or indirectly appropriate money or property. In addition to appropriation bills, measures that authorize expenditures are also placed on this calendar. The calendar's full title is the Calendar of the Committee of the Whole House on the State of the Union.

U.S. Code—Popular title for the *United States Code: Containing the General and Permanent Laws of the United States in Force on . . . .* It is a consolidation and partial codification of the general and permanent laws of the United States arranged by subject under 50 titles. The first six titles deal with general or political subjects, the other 44 with subjects ranging from agriculture to war, alphabetically arranged. A supplement is published after each session of Congress, and the entire Code is revised every six years.

Veto—The president's disapproval of a legislative measure passed by Congress. He returns the measure to the house in which it originated without his signature but with a veto message stating his objections to it. When Congress is in session, the president must veto a bill within 10 days, excluding Sundays, after he has received it; otherwise it becomes law without his signature. The 10-day clock begins to run at midnight following his receipt of the bill. (*See also Committee Veto, Item Veto, Override a Veto, Pocket Veto.*)

Voice Vote—A method of voting in which members who favor a question answer aye in chorus, after which those opposed answer no in chorus, and the chair decides which position prevails.

War Powers Resolution of 1973—An act that requires the president "in every possible instance" to consult Congress before he commits U.S. forces to ongoing or imminent hostilities. If he commits them to a combat situation without congressional consultation, he must notify Congress within 48 hours. Unless Congress declares war or otherwise authorizes the operation to continue, the forces must be withdrawn within 60 or 90 days, depending on certain conditions. No president has ever acknowledged the constitutionality of the resolution.

Whip—The majority or minority party member in each house who acts as assistant leader, helps plan and marshal support for party strategies, encourages party discipline, and advises his leader on how his colleagues intend to vote on the floor. In the Senate, the Republican whip's official title is assistant leader.

Without Objection—Used in lieu of a vote on noncontroversial motions, amendments, or bills that may be passed in either the House or Senate if no member voices an objection.

Yeas and Nays—A vote in which members usually respond "aye" or "no" (despite the official title of the vote) on a question when their names are called in alphabetical order. The Constitution requires the yeas and nays when a demand for it is supported by one-fifth of the members present, and it also requires an automatic yea-and-nay vote on overriding a veto. Senate precedents require the support of at least one-fifth of a quorum, a minimum of 11 members with the present membership of 100.

Yielding—When a member has been recognized to speak, no other member may speak unless he or she obtains permission from the member recognized. This permission is called yielding and usually is requested in the form, "Will the gentleman yield to me?" While this activity occasionally is seen in the Senate, the Senate has no rule or practice to parcel out time.

Constitution of the United States

We the People of the United States, in Order to form a more perfect Union, establish Justice, insure domestic Tranquility, provide for the common defence, promote the general Welfare, and secure the Blessings of Liberty to ourselves and our Posterity, do ordain and establish this Constitution for the United States of America.

ARTICLE I

Section 1. All legislative Powers herein granted shall be vested in a Congress of the United States, which shall consist of a Senate and House of Representatives.

Section 2. The House of Representatives shall be composed of Members chosen every second Year by the People of the several States, and the Electors in each State shall have the Qualifications requisite for Electors of the most numerous Branch of the State Legislature.

No Person shall be a Representative who shall not have attained to the age of twenty five Years, and been seven Years a Citizen of the United States, and who shall not, when elected, be an Inhabitant of that State in which he shall be chosen.

[Representatives and direct Taxes shall be apportioned among the several States which may be included within this Union, according to their respective Numbers, which shall be determined by adding to the whole Number of free Persons, including those bound to Service for a Term of Years, and excluding Indians not taxed, three fifths of all other Persons.] The actual Enumeration shall be made within three Years after the first Meeting of the Congress of the United States, and within every subsequent Term of ten Years, in such Manner as they shall by Law direct. The Number of Representatives shall not exceed one for every thirty Thousand, but each State shall have at Least one Representative; and until such enumeration shall be made, the State of New Hampshire shall be entitled to chuse three, Massachusetts eight, Rhode-Island and Providence Plantations one, Connecticut five, New-York six, New Jersey four, Pennsylvania eight, Delaware one, Maryland six, Virginia ten, North Carolina five, South Carolina five, and Georgia three.

When vacancies happen in the Representation from any State, the Executive Authority thereof shall issue Writs of Election to fill such Vacancies.

The House of Representatives shall chuse their Speaker and other Officers; and shall have the sole Power of Impeachment.

Section 3. The Senate of the United States shall be composed of two Senators from each State, [chosen by the Legislature thereof,] for six Years; and each Senator shall have one Vote.

Immediately after they shall be assembled in Consequence of the first Election, they shall be divided as equally as may be into three Classes. The Seats of the Senators of the first Class shall be vacated at the Expiration of the second Year, of the second Class at the Expiration of the fourth Year, and of the third Class at the Expiration of the sixth Year, so that one third may be chosen every second Year; [and if Vacancies happen by Resignation, or otherwise, during the Recess of the Legislature of any State, the Executive thereof may make temporary Appointments until the next Meeting of the Legislature, which shall then fill such Vacancies.]

No Person shall be a Senator who shall not have attained to the Age of thirty Years, and been nine Years a Citizen of the United States, and who shall not, when elected, be an Inhabitant of that State for which he shall be chosen.

The Vice President of the United States shall be President of the Senate, but shall have no Vote, unless they be equally divided.

The Senate shall chuse their other Officers, and also a President pro tempore, in the Absence of the Vice President, or when he shall exercise the Office of President of the United States.

The Senate shall have the sole Power to try all Impeachments. When sitting for that Purpose, they shall be on Oath or Affirmation. When the President of the United States is tried, the Chief Justice shall preside: And no Person shall be convicted without the Concurrence of two thirds of the Members present.

Judgment in Cases of Impeachment shall not extend further than to removal from Office, and disqualification to hold and enjoy any Office of honor, Trust or Profit under the United States: but the Party convicted shall nevertheless be liable and subject to Indictment, Trial, Judgment and Punishment, according to Law.

Section 4. The Times, Places and Manner of holding Elections for Senators and Representatives, shall be prescribed in each State by the Legislature thereof; but the Congress may at any time by Law make or alter such Regulations, except as to the Places of chusing Senators.

The Congress shall assemble at least once in every Year, and such Meeting shall [be on the first Monday in December], unless they shall by Law appoint a different Day.

Section 5. Each House shall be the Judge of the Elections, Returns and Qualifications of its own Members, and a Majority of each shall constitute a Quorum to do Business; but a smaller Number may adjourn from day to day, and may be authorized to compel the Attendance of absent Members, in such Manner, and under such Penalties as each House may provide.

Each House may determine the Rules of its Proceedings, punish its Members for disorderly Behaviour, and, with the Concurrence of two thirds, expel a Member.

Each House shall keep a Journal of its Proceedings, and from time to time publish the same, excepting such Parts as may in their Judgment require Secrecy; and the Yeas and Nays of the Members of either House on any question shall, at the Desire of one fifth of those Present, be entered on the Journal.

Section 10. No State shall enter into any Treaty, Alliance, or Confederation; grant Letters of Marque and Reprisal; coin Money; emit Bills of Credit; make any Thing but gold and silver Coin a Tender in Payment of Debts; pass any Bill of Attainder, ex post facto Law, or Law impairing the Obligation of Contracts, or grant any Title of Nobility.

No State shall, without the Consent of the Congress, **lay** any Imposts or Duties on Imports or Exports, except what may be absolutely necessary for executing it's inspection Laws: and the net Produce of all Duties and Imposts, laid by any State on Imports or Exports, shall be for the Use of the Treasury of the United States; and all such Laws shall be subject to the Revision and Controul of the Congress.

No State shall, without the Consent of Congress, lay any Duty of Tonnage, keep Troops, or Ships of War in time of Peace, enter into any Agreement or Compact with another State, or with a foreign Power, or engage in War, unless actually invaded, or in such imminent Danger as will not admit of delay.

ARTICLE II

Section 1. The executive Power shall be vested in a President of the United States of America. He shall hold his Office during the Term of four Years, and, together with the Vice President, chosen for the same Term, be elected, as follows

Each State shall appoint, in such Manner as the Legislature thereof may direct, a Number of Electors, equal to the whole Number of Senators and Representatives to which the State may be entitled in the Congress: but no Senator or Representative, or Person holding an Office of Trust or Profit under the United States, shall be appointed an Elector.

[The Electors shall meet in their respective States, and vote by Ballot for two Persons, of whom one at least shall not be an Inhabitant of the same State with themselves. And they shall make a List of all the Persons voted for, and of the Number of Votes for each; which List they shall sign and certify, and transmit sealed to the Seat of the Government of the United States, directed to the President of the Senate. The President of the Senate shall, in the Presence of the Senate and House of Representatives, open all the Certificates, and the Votes shall then be counted. The Person having the greatest Number of Votes shall be the President, if such Number be a Majority of the whole Number of Electors appointed; and if there be more than one who have such Majority, and have an equal Number of Votes, then the House of Representatives shall immediately chuse by Ballot one of them for President; and if no Person have a Majority, then from the five highest on the list the said House shall in like Manner chuse the President. But in chusing the President, the Votes shall be taken by States, the Representation from each State having one Vote; A quorum for this Purpose shall consist of a Member or Members from two thirds of the States, and a Majority of all the States shall be necessary to a Choice. In every Case, after the Choice of the President, the Person having the greatest Number of Votes of the Electors shall be the Vice President. But if there should remain two or more who have equal Votes, the Senate shall chuse from them by Ballot the Vice President.][6]

The Congress may determine the Time of chusing the Electors, and the Day on which they shall give their Votes; which Day shall be the same throughout the United States.

No Person except a natural born Citizen, or a Citizen of the United States, at the time of the Adoption of this Constitution, shall be eligible to the Office of President; neither shall any Person be eligible to that Office who shall not have attained to the Age of thirty five Years, and been fourteen Years a Resident within the United States.

In Case of the Removal of the President from Office, or of his Death, Resignation, or Inability to discharge the Powers and Duties of the said Office,[7] the Same shall devolve on the Vice President, and the Congress may by Law provide for the Case of Removal, Death, Resignation or Inability, both of the President and Vice President, declaring what Officer shall then act as President, and such Officer shall act accordingly, until the Disability be removed, or a President shall be elected.

The President shall, at stated Times, receive for his Services, a Compensation, which shall neither be encreased nor diminished during the Period for which he shall have been elected, and he shall not receive within that Period any other Emolument from the United States, or any of them.

Before he enter on the Execution of his Office, he shall take the following Oath or Affirmation: — "I do solemnly swear (or affirm) that I will faithfully execute the Office of President of the United States, and will to the best of my Ability, preserve, protect and defend the Constitution of the United States."

Section 2. The President shall be Commander in Chief of the Army and Navy of the United States, and of the Militia of the several States, when called into the actual Service of the United States; he may require the Opinion, in writing, of the principal Officer in each of the executive Departments, upon any Subject relating to the Duties of their respective Offices, and he shall have Power to grant Reprieves and Pardons for Offences against the United States, except in Cases of Impeachment.

He shall have Power, by and with the Advice and Consent of the Senate, to make Treaties, provided two thirds of the Senators present concur; and he shall nominate, and by and with the Advice and Consent of the Senate, shall appoint Ambassadors, other public Ministers and Consuls, Judges of the supreme Court, and all other Officers of the United States, whose Appointments are not herein otherwise provided for, and which shall be established by Law: but the Congress may by Law vest the Appointment of such inferior Officers, as they think proper, in the President alone, in the Courts of Law, or in the Heads of Departments.

The President shall have Power to fill up all Vacancies that may happen during the Recess of the Senate, by granting Commissions which shall expire at the End of their next Session.

Section 3. He shall from time to time give to the Congress Information of the State of the Union, and recommend to their Consideration such Measures as he shall judge necessary and expedient; he may, on extraordinary Occasions, convene both Houses, or either of them, and in Case of Disagreement between them, with Respect to the Time of Adjournment, he may adjourn them to such Time as he shall think proper; he shall receive Ambassadors and other public Ministers; he shall take Care that the Laws be faithfully executed, and shall Commission all the Officers of the United States.

Section 4. The President, Vice President and all civil Officers of the United States, shall be removed from Office on Impeachment for, and Conviction of, Treason, Bribery, or other high Crimes and Misdemeanors.

ARTICLE III

Section 1. The judicial Power of the United States, shall be vested in one supreme Court, and in such inferior Courts as the Congress may from time to time ordain and establish. The Judges, both of the supreme and inferior Courts, shall hold their

Neither House, during the Session of Congress, shall, without the Consent of the other, adjourn for more than three days, nor to any other Place than that in which the two Houses shall be sitting.

Section 6. The Senators and Representatives shall receive a Compensation for their Services, to be ascertained by Law, and paid out of the Treasury of the United States. They shall in all Cases, except Treason, Felony and Breach of the Peace, be privileged from Arrest during their Attendance at the Session of their respective Houses, and in going to and returning from the same; and for any Speech or Debate in either House, they shall not be questioned in any other Place.

No Senator or Representative shall, during the Time for which he was elected, be appointed to any civil Office under the Authority of the United States, which shall have been created, or the Emoluments whereof shall have been encreased during such time; and no Person holding any Office under the United States, shall be a Member of either House during his Continuance in Office.

Section 7. All Bills for raising Revenue shall originate in the House of Representatives; but the Senate may propose or concur with Amendments as on other Bills.

Every Bill which shall have passed the House of Representatives and the Senate, shall, before it become a Law, be presented to the President of the United States; If he approve he shall sign it, but if not he shall return it, with his Objections to that House in which it shall have originated, who shall enter the Objections at large on their Journal, and proceed to reconsider it. If after such Reconsideration two thirds of that House shall agree to pass the Bill, it shall be sent, together with the Objections, to the other House, by which it shall likewise be reconsidered, and if approved by two thirds of that House, it shall become a Law. But in all such Cases the Votes of both Houses shall be determined by yeas and Nays, and the Names of the Persons voting for and against the Bill shall be entered on the Journal of each House respectively. If any Bill shall not be returned by the President within ten Days (Sundays excepted) after it shall have been presented to him, the Same shall be a Law, in like Manner as if he had signed it, unless the Congress by their Adjournment prevent its Return, in which Case it shall not be a Law.

Every Order, Resolution, or Vote to which the Concurrence of the Senate and House of Representatives may be necessary (except on a question of Adjournment) shall be presented to the President of the United States; and before the Same shall take Effect, shall be approved by him, or being disapproved by him, shall be repassed by two thirds of the Senate and House of Representatives, according to the Rules and Limitations prescribed in the Case of a Bill.

Section 8. The Congress shall have Power To lay and collect Taxes, Duties, Imposts and Excises, to pay the Debts and provide for the common Defence and general Welfare of the United States; but all Duties, Imposts and Excises shall be uniform throughout the United States;

To borrow Money on the credit of the United States;

To regulate Commerce with foreign Nations, and among the several States, and with the Indian Tribes;

To establish an uniform Rule of Naturalization, and uniform Laws on the subject of Bankruptcies throughout the United States;

To coin Money, regulate the Value thereof, and of foreign Coin, and fix the Standard of Weights and Measures;

To provide for the Punishment of counterfeiting the Securities and current Coin of the United States;

To establish Post Offices and post Roads;

To promote the Progress of Science and useful Arts, by securing for limited Times to Authors and Inventors the exclusive Right to their respective Writings and Discoveries;

To constitute Tribunals inferior to the supreme Court;

To define and punish Piracies and Felonies committed on the high Seas, and Offences against the Law of Nations;

To declare War, grant Letters of Marque and Reprisal, and make Rules concerning Captures on Land and Water;

To raise and support Armies, but no Appropriation of Money to that Use shall be for a longer Term than two Years;

To provide and maintain a Navy;

To make Rules for the Government and Regulation of the land and naval Forces;

To provide for calling forth the Militia to execute the Laws of the Union, suppress Insurrections and repel Invasions;

To provide for organizing, arming, and disciplining, the Militia, and for governing such Part of them as may be employed in the Service of the United States, reserving to the States respectively, the Appointment of the Officers, and the Authority of training the Militia according to the discipline prescribed by Congress;

To exercise exclusive Legislation in all Cases whatsoever, over such District (not exceeding ten Miles square) as may, by Cession of particular States, and the Acceptance of Congress, become the Seat of the Government of the United States, and to exercise like Authority over all Places purchased by the Consent of the Legislature of the State in which the Same shall be, for the Erection of Forts, Magazines, Arsenals, dock-Yards, and other needful Buildings; — And

To make all Laws which shall be necessary and proper for carrying into Execution the foregoing Powers, and all other Powers vested by this Constitution in the Government of the United States, or in any Department or Officer thereof.

Section 9. The Migration or Importation of such Persons as any of the States now existing shall think proper to admit, shall not be prohibited by the Congress prior to the Year one thousand eight hundred and eight, but a Tax or duty may be imposed on such Importation, not exceeding ten dollars for each Person.

The Privilege of the Writ of Habeas Corpus shall not be suspended, unless when in Cases of Rebellion or Invasion the public Safety may require it.

No Bill of Attainder or ex post facto Law shall be passed.

No Capitation, or other direct, Tax shall be laid, unless in Proportion to the Census or Enumeration herein before directed to be taken.[5]

No Tax or Duty shall be laid on Articles exported from any State.

No Preference shall be given by any Regulation of Commerce or Revenue to the Ports of one State over those of another; nor shall Vessels bound to, or from, one State, be obliged to enter, clear, or pay Duties in another.

No Money shall be drawn from the Treasury, but in Consequence of Appropriations made by Law; and a regular Statement and Account of the Receipts and Expenditures of all public Money shall be published from time to time.

No Title of Nobility shall be granted by the United States: And no Person holding any Office of Profit or Trust under them, shall, without the Consent of the Congress, accept of any present, Emolument, Office, or Title, of any kind whatever, from any King, Prince, or foreign State.

Offices during good Behaviour, and shall, at stated Times, receive for their Services, a Compensation, which shall not be diminished during their Continuance in Office.

Section 2. The judicial Power shall extend to all Cases, in Law and Equity, arising under this Constitution, the Laws of the United States, and Treaties made, or which shall be made, under their Authority; — to all Cases affecting Ambassadors, other public Ministers and Consuls; — to all Cases of admiralty and maritime Jurisdiction; — to Controversies to which the United States shall be a Party; — to Controversies between two or more States; — between a State and Citizens of another State;[8] — between Citizens of different States; — between Citizens of the same State claiming Lands under Grants of different States, and between a State, or the Citizens thereof, and foreign States, Citizens or Subjects.

In all Cases affecting Ambassadors, other public Ministers and Consuls, and those in which a State shall be Party, the supreme Court shall have original Jurisdiction. In all the other Cases before mentioned, the supreme Court shall have appellate Jurisdiction, both as to Law and Fact, with such Exceptions, and under such Regulations as the Congress shall make.

The Trial of all Crimes, except in Cases of Impeachment, shall be by Jury; and such Trial shall be held in the State where the said Crimes shall have been committed; but when not committed within any State, the Trial shall be at such Place or Places as the Congress may by Law have directed.

Section 3. Treason against the United States, shall consist only in levying War against them, or in adhering to their Enemies, giving them Aid and Comfort. No Person shall be convicted of Treason unless on the Testimony of two Witnesses to the same overt Act, or on Confession in open Court.

The Congress shall have Power to declare the Punishment of Treason, but no Attainder of Treason shall work Corruption of Blood, or Forfeiture except during the Life of the Person attainted.

ARTICLE IV

Section 1. Full Faith and Credit shall be given in each State to the public Acts, Records, and judicial Proceedings of every other State. And the Congress may by general Laws prescribe the Manner in which such Acts, Records and Proceedings shall be proved, and the Effect thereof.

Section 2. The Citizens of each State shall be entitled to all Privileges and Immunities of Citizens in the several States.

A Person charged in any State with Treason, Felony, or other Crime, who shall flee from Justice, and be found in another State, shall on Demand of the executive Authority of the State from which he fled, be delivered up, to be removed to the State having Jurisdiction of the Crime.

[No Person held to Service or Labour in one State, under the Laws thereof, escaping into another, shall, in Consequence of any Law or Regulation therein, be discharged from such Service or Labour, but shall be delivered up on Claim of the Party to whom such Service or Labour may be due.][9]

Section 3. New States may be admitted by the Congress into this Union; but no new State shall be formed or erected within the Jurisdiction of any other State; nor any State be formed by the Junction of two or more States, or Parts of States, without the Consent of the Legislatures of the States concerned as well as of the Congress.

The Congress shall have Power to dispose of and make all needful Rules and Regulations respecting the Territory or other Property belonging to the United States; and nothing in this Constitution shall be so construed as to Prejudice any Claims of the United States, or of any particular State.

Section 4. The United States shall guarantee to every State in this Union a Republican Form of Government, and shall protect each of them against Invasion; and on Application of the Legislature, or of the Executive (when the Legislature cannot be convened) against domestic Violence.

ARTICLE V

The Congress, whenever two thirds of both Houses shall deem it necessary, shall propose Amendments to this Constitution, or, on the Application of the Legislatures of two thirds of the several States, shall call a Convention for proposing Amendments, which, in either Case, shall be valid to all Intents and Purposes, as Part of this Constitution, when ratified by the Legislatures of three fourths of the several States, or by Conventions in three fourths thereof, as the one or the other Mode of Ratification may be proposed by the Congress; Provided [that no Amendment which may be made prior to the Year One thousand eight hundred and eight shall in any Manner affect the first and fourth Clauses in the Ninth Section of the first Article; and][10] that no State, without its Consent, shall be deprived of its equal Suffrage in the Senate.

ARTICLE VI

All Debts contracted and Engagements entered into, before the Adoption of this Constitution, shall be as valid against the United States under this Constitution, as under the Confederation.

This Constitution, and the Laws of the United States which shall be made in Pursuance thereof; and all Treaties made, or which shall be made, under the Authority of the United States, shall be the supreme Law of the Land; and the Judges in every State shall be bound thereby, any Thing in the Constitution or Laws of any State to the Contrary notwithstanding.

The Senators and Representatives before mentioned, and the Members of the several State Legislatures, and all executive and judicial Officers, both of the United States and of the several States, shall be bound by Oath or Affirmation, to support this Constitution; but no religious Test shall ever be required as a Qualification to any Office or public Trust under the United States.

ARTICLE VII

The Ratification of the Conventions of nine States, shall be sufficient for the Establishment of this Constitution between the States so ratifying the Same.

Done in Convention by the Unanimous Consent of the States present the Seventeenth Day of September in the Year of our Lord one thousand seven hundred and Eighty seven and of the Independence of the United States of America the Twelfth. IN WITNESS whereof We have hereunto subscribed our Names,

George Washington,
President and
deputy from Virginia.

New Hampshire:	John Langdon
	Nicholas Gilman.
Massachusetts:	Nathaniel Gorham,
	Rufus King.
Connecticut:	William Samuel Johnson,
	Roger Sherman.

New York:	Alexander Hamilton.
New Jersey:	William Livingston,
	David Brearley,
	William Paterson,
	Jonathan Dayton.
Pennsylvania:	Benjamin Franklin,
	Thomas Mifflin,
	Robert Morris,
	George Clymer,
	Thomas FitzSimons,
	Jared Ingersoll,
	James Wilson,
	Gouverneur Morris.
Delaware:	George Read,
	Gunning Bedford Jr.,
	John Dickinson,
	Richard Bassett,
	Jacob Broom.
Maryland:	James McHenry,
	Daniel of St. Thomas Jenifer,
	Daniel Carroll.
Virginia:	John Blair,
	James Madison Jr.
North Carolina:	William Blount,
	Richard Dobbs Spaight,
	Hugh Williamson.
South Carolina:	John Rutledge,
	Charles Cotesworth Pinckney,
	Charles Pinckney,
	Pierce Butler.
Georgia:	William Few,
	Abraham Baldwin.

[The language of the original Constitution, not including the Amendments, was adopted by a convention of the states on September 17, 1787, and was subsequently ratified by the states on the following dates: Delaware, December 7, 1787; Pennsylvania, December 12, 1787; New Jersey, December 18, 1787; Georgia, January 2, 1788; Connecticut, January 9, 1788; Massachusetts, February 6, 1788; Maryland, April 28, 1788; South Carolina, May 23, 1788; New Hampshire, June 21, 1788.

Ratification was completed on June 21, 1788.

The Constitution subsequently was ratified by Virginia, June 25, 1788; New York, July 26, 1788; North Carolina, November 21, 1789; Rhode Island, May 29, 1790; and Vermont, January 10, 1791.]

Amendments

Amendment I

(First ten amendments ratified December 15, 1791.)

Congress shall make no law respecting an establishment of religion, or prohibiting the free exercise thereof; or abridging the freedom of speech, or of the press; or the right of the people peaceably to assemble, and to petition the Government for a redress of grievances.

Amendment II

A well regulated Militia, being necessary to the security of a free State, the right of the people to keep and bear Arms, shall not be infringed.

Amendment III

No Soldier shall, in time of peace be quartered in any house, without the consent of the Owner, nor in time of war, but in a manner to be prescribed by law.

Amendment IV

The right of the people to be secure in their persons, houses, papers, and effects, against unreasonable searches and seizures, shall not be violated, and no Warrants shall issue, but upon probable cause, supported by Oath or affirmation, and particularly describing the place to be searched, and the persons or things to be seized.

Amendment V

No person shall be held to answer for a capital, or otherwise infamous crime, unless on a presentment or indictment of a Grand Jury, except in cases arising in the land or naval forces, or in the Militia, when in actual service in time of War or public danger; nor shall any person be subject for the same offence to be twice put in jeopardy of life or limb; nor shall be compelled in any criminal case to be a witness against himself, nor be deprived of life, liberty, or property, without due process of law; nor shall private property be taken for public use, without just compensation.

Amendment VI

In all criminal prosecutions, the accused shall enjoy the right to a speedy and public trial, by an impartial jury of the State and district wherein the crime shall have been committed, which district shall have been previously ascertained by law, and to be informed of the nature and cause of the accusation; to be confronted with the witnesses against him; to have compulsory process for obtaining witnesses in his favor, and to have the Assistance of Counsel for his defence.

Amendment VII

In Suits at common law, where the value in controversy shall exceed twenty dollars, the right of trial by jury shall be preserved, and no fact tried by a jury, shall be otherwise re-examined in any Court of the United States, than according to the rules of the common law.

Amendment VIII

Excessive bail shall not be required, nor excessive fines imposed, nor cruel and unusual punishments inflicted.

Amendment IX

The enumeration in the Constitution, of certain rights, shall not be construed to deny or disparage others retained by the people.

Amendment X

The powers not delegated to the United States by the Constitution, nor prohibited by it to the States, are reserved to the States respectively, or to the people.

Amendment XI (Ratified February 7, 1795)

The Judicial power of the United States shall not be construed to extend to any suit in law or equity, commenced or prosecuted against one of the United States by Citizens of another State, or by Citizens or Subjects of any Foreign State.

Amendment XII (Ratified June 15, 1804)

The Electors shall meet in their respective states and vote by ballot for President and Vice-President, one of whom, at least, shall not be an inhabitant of the same state with themselves; they shall name in their ballots the person voted for as President, and in distinct ballots the person voted for as Vice-President, and they shall make distinct lists of all persons voted for as President, and of all persons voted for as Vice-President, and of the number of votes for each, which lists they shall sign and certify, and transmit sealed to the seat of the government of the United States, directed to the President of the Senate; — The President of the Senate shall, in the presence of the Senate and House of Representatives, open all the certificates and the votes shall then be counted; — The person having the greatest number of votes for President, shall be the President, if such number be a majority of the whole number of Electors appointed; and if no person have such majority, then from the persons having the highest numbers not exceeding three on the list of those voted for as President, the House of Representatives shall choose immediately, by ballot, the President. But in choosing the President, the votes shall be taken by states, the representation from each state having one vote; a quorum for this purpose shall consist of a member or members from two-thirds of the states, and a majority of all the states shall be necessary to a choice. [And if the House of Representatives shall not choose a President whenever the right of choice shall devolve upon them, before the fourth day of March next following, then the Vice-President shall act as President, as in the case of the death or other constitutional disability of the President. —][11] The person having the greatest number of votes as Vice-President, shall be the Vice-President, if such number be a majority of the whole number of Electors appointed, and if no person have a majority, then from the two highest numbers on the list, the Senate shall choose the Vice-President; a quorum for the purpose shall consist of two-thirds of the whole number of Senators, and a majority of the whole number shall be necessary to a choice. But no person constitutionally ineligible to the office of President shall be eligible to that of Vice-President of the United States.

Amendment XIII (Ratified December 6, 1865)

Section 1. Neither slavery nor involuntary servitude, except as a punishment for crime whereof the party shall have been duly convicted, shall exist within the United States, or any place subject to their jurisdiction.

Section 2. Congress shall have power to enforce this article by appropriate legislation.

Amendment XIV (Ratified July 9, 1868)

Section 1. All persons born or naturalized in the United States, and subject to the jurisdiction thereof, are citizens of the United States and of the State wherein they reside. No State shall make or enforce any law which shall abridge the privileges or immunities of citizens of the United States; nor shall any State deprive any person of life, liberty, or property, without due process of law; nor deny to any person within its jurisdiction the equal protection of the laws.

Section 2. Representatives shall be apportioned among the several States according to their respective numbers, counting the whole number of persons in each State, excluding Indians not taxed. But when the right to vote at any election for the choice of electors for President and Vice President of the United States, Representatives in Congress, the Executive and Judicial officers of a State, or the members of the Legislature thereof, is denied to any of the male inhabitants of such State, being

twenty-one years of age,[12] and citizens of the United States, or in any way abridged, except for participation in rebellion, or other crime, the basis of representation therein shall be reduced in the proportion which the number of such male citizens shall bear to the whole number of male citizens twenty-one years of age in such State.

Section 3. No person shall be a Senator or Representative in Congress, or elector of President and Vice President, or hold any office, civil or military, under the United States, or under any State, who, having previously taken an oath, as a member of Congress, or as an officer of the United States, or as a member of any State legislature, or as an executive or judicial officer of any State, to support the Constitution of the United States, shall have engaged in insurrection or rebellion against the same, or given aid or comfort to the enemies thereof. But Congress may by a vote of two-thirds of each House, remove such disability.

Section 4. The validity of the public debt of the United States, authorized by law, including debts incurred for payment of pensions and bounties for services in suppressing insurrection or rebellion, shall not be questioned. But neither the United States nor any State shall assume or pay any debt or obligation incurred in aid of insurrection or rebellion against the United States, or any claim for the loss or emancipation of any slave; but all such debts, obligations and claims shall be held illegal and void.

Section 5. The Congress shall have power to enforce, by appropriate legislation, the provisions of this article.

Amendment XV (Ratified February 3, 1870)

Section 1. The right of citizens of the United States to vote shall not be denied or abridged by the United States or by any State on account of race, color, or previous condition of servitude.

Section 2. The Congress shall have power to enforce this article by appropriate legislation.

Amendment XVI (Ratified February 3, 1913)

The Congress shall have power to lay and collect taxes on incomes, from whatever source derived, without apportionment among the several States, and without regard to any census or enumeration.

Amendment XVII (Ratified April 8, 1913)

The Senate of the United States shall be composed of two Senators from each State, elected by the people thereof, for six years; and each Senator shall have one vote. The electors in each State shall have the qualifications requisite for electors of the most numerous branch of the State legislatures.

When vacancies happen in the representation of any State in the Senate, the executive authority of such State shall issue writs of election to fill such vacancies: *Provided,* That the legislature of any State may empower the executive thereof to make temporary appointments until the people fill the vacancies by election as the legislature may direct.

This amendment shall not be so construed as to affect the election or term of any Senator chosen before it becomes valid as part of the Constitution.

Amendment XVIII (Ratified January 16, 1919)[13]

Section 1. After one year from the ratification of this article the manufacture, sale, or transportation of intoxicating liquors within, the importation thereof into, or the exportation thereof from the United States and all territory subject to the jurisdiction thereof for beverage purposes is hereby prohibited.

Section 2. The Congress and the several States shall have concurrent power to enforce this article by appropriate legislation.

Section 3. This article shall be inoperative unless it shall have been ratified as an amendment to the Constitution by the legislatures of the several States, as provided in the Constitution, within seven years from the date of the submission hereof to the States by the Congress.

Amendment XIX (Ratified August 18, 1920)

The right of citizens of the United States to vote shall not be denied or abridged by the United States or by any State on account of sex.

Congress shall have power to enforce this article by appropriate legislation.

Amendment XX (Ratified January 23, 1933)

Section 1. The terms of the President and Vice President shall end at noon on the 20th day of January, and the terms of Senators and Representatives at noon on the 3d day of January, of the years in which such terms would have ended if this article had not been ratified; and the terms of their successors shall then begin.

Section 2. The Congress shall assemble at least once in every year, and such meeting shall begin at noon on the 3d day of January, unless they shall by law appoint a different day.

Section 3.[14] If, at the time fixed for the beginning of the term of the President, the President elect shall have died, the Vice President elect shall become President. If a President shall not have been chosen before the time fixed for the beginning of his term, or if the President elect shall have failed to qualify, then the Vice President elect shall act as President until a President shall have qualified; and the Congress may by law provide for the case wherein neither a President elect nor a Vice President elect shall have qualified, declaring who shall then act as President, or the manner in which one who is to act shall be selected, and such person shall act accordingly until a President or Vice President shall have qualified.

Section 4. The Congress may by law provide for the case of the death of any of the persons from whom the House of Representatives may choose a President whenever the right of choice shall have devolved upon them, and for the case of the death of any of the persons from whom the Senate may choose a Vice President whenever the right of choice shall have devolved upon them.

Section 5. Sections 1 and 2 shall take effect on the 15th day of October following the ratification of this article.

Section 6. This article shall be inoperative unless it shall have been ratified as an amendment to the Constitution by the legislatures of three-fourths of the several States within seven years from the date of its submission.

Amendment XXI (Ratified December 5, 1933)

Section 1. The eighteenth article of amendment to the Constitution of the United States is hereby repealed.

Section 2. The transportation or importation into any State, Territory, or possession of the United States for delivery or use therein of intoxicating liquors, in violation of the laws thereof, is hereby prohibited.

Section 3. This article shall be inoperative unless it shall have been ratified as an amendment to the Constitution by conventions in the several States, as provided in the Constitution, within seven years from the date of the submission hereof to the States by the Congress.

Amendment XXII (Ratified February 27, 1951)

Section 1. No person shall be elected to the office of the President more than twice, and no person who has held the office of President, or acted as President, for more than two years of a term to which some other person was elected President shall be elected to the office of the President more than once. But this Article shall not apply to any person holding the office of President when this Article was proposed by the Congress, and shall not prevent any person who may be holding the office of President, or acting as President, during the term within which this Article become operative from holding the office of President or acting as President during the remainder of such term.

Section 2. This article shall be inoperative unless it shall have been ratified as an amendment to the Constitution by the legislatures of three-fourths of the several States within seven years from the date of its submission to the States by the Congress.

Amendment XXIII (Ratified March 29, 1961)

Section 1. The District constituting the seat of Government of the United States shall appoint in such manner as the Congress may direct:

A number of electors of President and Vice President equal to the whole number of Senators and Representatives in Congress to which the District would be entitled if it were a State, but in no event more than the least populous State; they shall be in addition to those appointed by the States, but they shall be considered, for the purposes of the election of President and Vice President, to be electors appointed by a State; and they shall meet in the District and perform such duties as provided by the twelfth article of amendment.

Section 2. The Congress shall have power to enforce this article by appropriate legislation.

Amendment XXIV (Ratified January 23, 1964)

Section 1. The right of citizens of the United States to vote in any primary or other election for President or Vice President, for electors for President or Vice President, or for Senator or Representative in Congress, shall not be denied or abridged by the United States or any State by reason of failure to pay any poll tax or other tax.

Section 2. The Congress shall have power to enforce this article by appropriate legislation.

Amendment XXV (Ratified February 10, 1967)

Section 1. In case of the removal of the President from office or of his death or resignation, the Vice President shall become President.

Section 2. Whenever there is a vacancy in the office of the Vice President, the President shall nominate a Vice President who shall take office upon confirmation by a majority vote of both Houses of Congress.

Section 3. Whenever the President transmits to the President pro tempore of the Senate and the Speaker of the House of Representatives his written declaration that he is unable to discharge the powers and duties of his office, and until he transmits to them a written declaration to the contrary, such powers and duties shall be discharged by the Vice President as Acting President.

Section 4. Whenever the Vice President and a majority of either the principal officers of the executive departments or of such other body as Congress may by law provide, transmit to the President pro tempore of the Senate and the Speaker of the House of Representatives their written declaration that the President is unable to discharge the powers and duties of his office, the Vice President shall immediately assume the powers and duties of the office as Acting President.

Thereafter, when the President transmits to the President pro tempore of the Senate and the Speaker of the House of Representatives his written declaration that no inability exists, he shall resume the powers and duties of his office unless the Vice President and a majority of either the principal officers of the executive department or of such other body as Congress may by law provide, transmit within four days to the President pro tempore of the Senate and the Speaker of the House of Representatives their written declaration that the President is unable to discharge the powers and duties of his office. Thereupon Congress shall decide the issue, assembling within forty-eight hours for that purpose if not in session. If the Congress, within twenty-one days after receipt of the latter written declaration, or, if Congress is not in session, within twenty-one days after Congress is required to assemble, determines by two-thirds vote of both Houses that the President is unable to discharge the powers and duties of his office, the Vice President shall continue to discharge the same as Acting President; otherwise, the President shall resume the powers and duties of his office.

Amendment XXVI (Ratified July 1, 1971)

Section 1. The right of citizens of the United States, who are eighteen years of age or older, to vote shall not be denied or abridged by the United States or by any State on account of age.

Section 2. The Congress shall have power to enforce this article by appropriate legislation.

Amendment XXVII (Ratified May 7, 1992)

No law varying the compensation for the services of the Senators and Representatives shall take effect, until an election of Representatives shall have intervened.

Notes

1. The part in brackets was changed by section 2 of the Fourteenth Amendment.
2. The part in brackets was changed by the first paragraph of the Seventeenth Amendment.
3. The part in brackets was changed by the second paragraph of the Seventeenth Amendment.
4. The part in brackets was changed by section 2 of the Twentieth Amendment.
5. The Sixteenth Amendment gave Congress the power to tax incomes.
6. The material in brackets has been superseded by the Twelfth Amendment.
7. This provision has been affected by the Twenty-fifth Amendment.
8. These clauses were affected by the Eleventh Amendment.
9. This paragraph has been superseded by the Thirteenth Amendment.
10. Obsolete.
11. The part in brackets has been superseded by section 3 of the Twentieth Amendment.
12. See the Nineteenth and Twenty-sixth Amendments.
13. This Amendment was repealed by section 1 of the Twenty-first Amendment.
14. See the Twenty-fifth Amendment.

SOURCE: U.S. Congress, House, Committee on the Judiciary, *The Constitution of the United States of America, as Amended*, 100th Cong., 1st sess., 1987, H Doc 100-94.

Congressional Information on the Internet

A huge array of congressional information is available for free at Internet sites operated by the federal government, colleges and universities, and commercial firms. The sites offer the full text of bills introduced in the House and Senate, voting records, campaign finance information, transcripts of selected congressional hearings, investigative reports, and much more.

THOMAS

The most important site for congressional information is THOMAS (*http://thomas.loc.gov*), which is named for Thomas Jefferson and operated by the Library of Congress. THOMAS's highlight is its databases containing the full text of all bills introduced in Congress since 1989, the full text of the *Congressional Record* since 1989, and the status and summary information for all bills introduced since 1973.

THOMAS also offers special links to bills that have received or are expected to receive floor action during the current week and newsworthy bills that are pending or that have recently been approved. Finally, THOMAS has selected committee reports, answers to frequently asked questions about accessing congressional information, publications titled *How Our Laws Are Made* and *Enactment of a Law*, and links to lots of other congressional Web sites.

House of Representatives

The U.S. House of Representatives site (*http://www.house. gov*) offers the schedule of bills, resolutions, and other legislative issues the House will consider in the current week. It also has updates about current proceedings on the House floor and a list of the next day's meeting of House committees. Other highlights include a database that helps users identify their representative, a directory of House members and committees, the House ethics manual, links to Web pages maintained by House members and committees, a calendar of congressional primary dates and candidate-filing deadlines for ballot access, the full text of all amendments to the Constitution that have been ratified and those that have been proposed but not ratified, and lots of information about Washington, D.C., for visitors.

Another key House site is The Office of the Clerk On-line Information Center (*http://clerkweb.house.gov*), which has records of all roll-call votes taken since 1990. The votes are recorded by bill, so it is a lengthy process to compile a particular representative's voting record. The site also has lists of committee assignments, a telephone directory for members and committees, mailing label templates for members and committees, rules of the current Congress, election statistics from 1920 to the present, biographies of Speakers of the House, biographies of women who have served since 1917, and a virtual tour of the House Chamber.

One of the more interesting House sites is operated by the Subcommittee on Rules and Organization of the House

Committee on Rules (*http://www.house.gov/rules/crs_reports. htm*). Its highlight is dozens of Congressional Research Service reports about the legislative process. Some of the available titles include *Legislative Research in Congressional Offices: A Primer, How to Follow Current Federal Legislation and Regulations, Investigative Oversight: An Introduction to the Law, Practice, and Procedure of Congressional Inquiry*, and *Presidential Vetoes 1789–1996: A Summary Overview*.

A final House site is the Internet Law Library (*http://law. house.gov*). This site has a searchable version of the U.S. Code, which contains the text of public laws enacted by Congress, and a tutorial for searching the Code. There also is a huge collection of links to other Internet sites that provide state and territorial laws, laws of other nations, and treaties and international laws.

Senate

At least in the Internet world, the Senate is not as active as the House. Its main Web site (*http://www.senate.gov*) has records of all roll-call votes taken since 1989 (arranged by bill), brief descriptions of all bills and joint resolutions introduced in the Senate during the past week, and a calendar of upcoming committee hearings. The site also provides the standing rules of the Senate, a directory of senators and their committee assignments, lists of nominations that the president has submitted to the Senate for approval, links to Web pages operated by senators and committees, and a virtual tour of the Senate.

Information about the membership, jurisdiction, and rules of each congressional committee is available at the U.S. Government Printing Office site (*http://www.access.gpo.gov/congress/ index.html*). It also has transcripts of selected congressional hearings, the full text of selected House and Senate reports, and the House and Senate rules manuals.

General Reference

The U.S. General Accounting Office, the investigative arm of Congress, operates a site (*http://www.gao.gov*) that provides the full text of its reports from 1996 to the present. The reports cover a wide range of topics: aviation safety, combating terrorism, counternarcotics efforts in Mexico, defense contracting, electronic warfare, food assistance programs, Gulf War illness, health insurance, illegal aliens, information technology, long-term care, mass transit, Medicare, military readiness, money laundering, national parks, nuclear waste, organ donation, student loan defaults, and the year 2000 computing crisis, among others.

The GAO Daybook is an excellent current awareness tool. This electronic mailing list distributes a daily list of reports and testimony released by the GAO. Subscriptions are available by sending an E-mail message to *majordomo@www.gao.gov*, and in the message area typing "subscribe daybook" (without the quotation marks).

Current budget and economic projections are provided at the Congressional Budget Office Web site (*http://www.cbo.gov*). The site also has reports about the economic and budget outlook for the next decade, the president's budget proposals, federal civilian employment, Social Security privatization, tax reform, water use conflicts in the West, marriage and the federal income tax, and the role of foreign aid in development, among other topics. Other highlights include monthly budget updates, historical budget data, cost estimates for bills reported by congressional committees, and transcripts of congressional testimony by CBO officials.

Campaign Finance

Several Internet sites provide detailed campaign finance data for congressional elections. The official site is operated by the Federal Election Commission (*http://www.fec.gov*), which regulates political spending. The site's highlight is its database of campaign reports filed from May 1996 to the present by House and presidential candidates, political action committees, and political party committees. Senate reports are not included because they are filed with the Secretary of the Senate. The reports in the FEC's database are scanned images of paper reports filed with the commission.

The FEC site also has summary financial data for House and Senate candidates in the current election cycle, abstracts of court decisions pertaining to federal election law from 1976 to 1997, a graph showing the number of political action committees in existence each year from 1974 to the present, and a directory of national and state agencies that are responsible for releasing information about campaign financing, candidates on the ballot, election results, lobbying, and other issues. Another useful feature is a collection of brochures about federal election law, public funding of presidential elections, the ban on contributions by foreign nationals, independent expenditures supporting or opposing a candidate for federal office, contribution limits, filing a complaint, researching public records at the FEC, and other topics. Finally, the site provides the FEC's legislative

recommendations, its annual report, a report about its first twenty years in existence, the FEC's monthly newsletter, several reports about voter registration, election results for the most recent presidential and congressional elections, and campaign guides for corporations and labor organizations, congressional candidates and committees, political party committees, and nonconnected committees.

The best online source for campaign finance data is FECInfo (*http://www.tray.com/fecinfo*), which is operated by former Federal Election Commission employee Tony Raymond. FECInfo's searchable databases provide extensive itemized information about receipts and expenditures by federal candidates and political action committees from 1980 to the present. The data, which are obtained from the FEC, are quite detailed. For example, for candidates contributions can be searched by Zip Code. The site also has data on soft money contributions, lists of the top political action committees in various categories, lists of the top contributors from each state, and much more.

Another interesting site is Campaign Finance Data on the Internet (*http://www.soc.american.edu/campfin*), which is operated by the American University School of Communication. It provides electronic files from the FEC that have been reformatted in .dbf format so they can be used in database programs such as Paradox, Access, and FoxPro. The files contain data on PAC, committee, and individual contributions to individual congressional candidates.

More campaign finance data is available from the Center for Responsive Politics (*http://www.opensecrets.org*), a public interest organization. The center provides a list of all "soft money" donations to political parties of $100,000 or more in the current election cycle and data about "leadership" political action committees associated with individual politicians. Other databases at the site provide information about travel expenses that House members received from private sources for attending meetings and other events, activities of registered federal lobbyists, and activities of foreign agents who are registered in the United States.

Index

Index